To

_____

From

_____

Date

_____

JOHN BAKER | JOHNNY BAKER
MAC OWEN

Celebrate Recovery®

365 Daily Devotional

HEALING FROM HURTS, HABITS, AND HANG-UPS

JOHN BAKER | JOHNNY BAKER
MAC OWEN

Celebrate Recovery®

365 Daily Devotional

HEALING FROM HURTS, HABITS, AND HANG-UPS

ZONDERVAN®

© 2013 by John Baker, Johnny Baker, and Mac Owens

Requests for information should be addressed to: Zondervan, Grand Rapids, Michigan 49530

Unless otherwise noted, Scripture quotations are taken from the Holy Bible, New International Version®, NIV®. Copyright © 1973, 1978, 1984 by Biblica, Inc.™ Used by permission of Zondervan. All rights reserved worldwide. www.zondervan.com.

Scripture quotations marked NKJV are from the New King James Version. © 1982 by Thomas Nelson. Used by permission. All rights reserved.

Scripture quotations marked GNT are from the Good News Translation in Today's English Version—Second Edition. Copyright 1992 by American Bible Society. Used by permission.

Scripture quotations marked KJV are taken from the King James Version. Public domain.

Scripture quotations marked TLB are from The Living Bible. Copyright © 1971. Used by permission of Tyndale House Publishers, Inc., Carol Stream, Illinois 60188. All rights reserved.

Scripture quotations marked NLT are from the *Holy Bible*, New Living Translation. © 1996, 2004, 2007, 2013 by Tyndale House Foundation. Used by permission of Tyndale House Publishers, Inc., Carol Stream, Illinois 60188. All rights reserved.

Scripture quotations marked CEV are from the Contemporary English Version. Copyright © 1991, 1992, 1995 by American Bible Society. Used by permission.

Scripture quotations marked NCV are from the New Century Version®. © 2005 by Thomas Nelson. Used by permission. All rights reserved.

Scripture quotations marked NRSV are from New Revised Standard Version Bible. Copyright © 1989 National Council of the Churches of Christ in the United States of America. Used by permission. All rights reserved.

Scripture quotations marked THE MESSAGE are from *The Message*. Copyright © by Eugene H. Peterson 1993, 1994, 1995, 1996, 2000, 2001, 2002. Used by permission of Tyndale House Publishers, Inc.

Library of Congress Cataloging-in-Publication Data is available

ISBN 978-0-310-08585-0

Printed in China

19 20 21 22 23 DSC 21 20 19 18 17 16 15 14 13 12 11 10 9 8 7

Dedication

This book is joyfully dedicated to the following:

Our Lord and Savior Jesus Christ. The
one and only true Higher Power!
Our families, especially our wives, for their love and support.
To all the Celebrate Recovery Leaders from all over the world.
And to those just starting their Celebrate Recovery journey.

In His steps,
John, Johnny, and Mac

Acknowledgment

We would like to thank Rodney Holmstrom for his input, ideas, and continued prayer support for the *Celebrate Recovery Daily Devotional*.

Rodney truly loves Jesus, his family, and Celebrate Recovery!

Thank you,
John, Johnny, and Mac

Introduction

"Hi, my name is John Baker. I'm a believer who struggles with alcoholism and food addiction."

Even before God gave me the vision for Celebrate Recovery, reading daily devotionals was a major part of my recovery. However, the recovery devotionals back in the '80s were all missing one very important element—the most important element of our recoveries and lives—Jesus Christ!

I can vividly remember waking up each morning, reaching for my two devotionals, and reading the thoughts for that day. As the days passed, my hunger for growing in my relationship with my Higher Power, the one and only true High Power, Jesus Christ, continued to increase.

It was during that time that God gave me the vision for Celebrate Recovery. For the next six weeks, my wife, Cheryl, and I spent hour after hour putting that vision into words. When we were done, the vision was contained in a thirteen-page, single-spaced letter. I gave that letter to my pastor, Rick Warren. Within a week, he called me into his office and said, "Great, John. You do it!"

Celebrate Recovery was born! The first meeting was held on November 21, 1991. The ministry is now in its third decade. And now we finally have the *Celebrate Recovery Daily Devotional*.

It is my prayer that the *Celebrate Recovery Daily Devotional* will be a very helpful tool in your recovery journey. Each daily devotion contains a Bible verse and an inspirational story. The devotion ends with a short prayer for you to share directly with God to help you live out a new growth opportunity for each day.

If you are a newcomer to Celebrate Recovery, I encourage you to be faithful in using this devotional. It will help you stay connected to your program as it daily encourages you. If you have been in recovery for years, you will be refreshed as you are daily reminded of the progress you have made in your recovery. But, more importantly, you will continue to grow as you focus on each day's new challenges and discover God's ever-present strength and care for you.

I believe that everyone will benefit from hearing from the three different authors of this devotional. You will receive three different perspectives of what we each have learned on our individual roads to recovery. Johnny Baker and Mac Owen are gifted speakers, teachers, and storytellers. The three voices in this devotional all have a different writing style, but our daily messages are all based on what God can do for us through His power and working the Celebrate Recovery program.

The best way to use this devotional is to make it a healthy habit. Use it every day. It doesn't matter if you read it when you wake up or before you go to sleep. Just continue to use it. It is my prayer that as you do, you will daily discover deeper relationships, especially with your Lord and Savior!

To God be the glory!

John Baker

The First Step

*"I know that nothing good lives in me, that is, in my sinful nature. For
I have the desire to do what is good, but I cannot carry it out."*

ROMANS 7:18

No one gets to start in the middle—we're all beginners in one area of
our lives or another. But for many of us, what we need is more like a
new beginning, a fresh start, a walking journey from chaos to wholeness
that is accomplished one step at a time. We call that journey "recovery."
Let's look at that first step:

*Step 1: We admitted we were powerless over our addictions and
compulsive behaviors. That our lives had become unmanageable.*

Our first step is a big one. We are finally ready to admit that we are
powerless to control an addiction or a behavior. The harder we try, the
more unmanageable it becomes. Our lives have descended into chaos.
When we take that first big step—giving up control—we are stepping
away from denial and acknowledging our own need.

There is hope in that first step, for we can't be helped until we admit
that we need help. Until then we are trying to be God in our own lives,
and really we just aren't up to the task. We are powerless to control
much of anything by our own power. Step 1 allows us to find freedom
from ourselves.

PRAYER

*Father God, today I take that first important step toward healing and wholeness. I
admit to you that I'm powerless over the strongholds that have taken over my life. I
desperately need your help. In Jesus' name, Amen.*

DAY 2

A Single Step

Since we are surrounded by such a great cloud of witnesses, let us
throw off everything that hinders and the sin that so easily entangles.
And let us run with perseverance the race marked out for us.

HEBREWS 12:1

I can remember being at a point when I knew my life was spinning out of control. I knew there were a lot of things I needed to change. But I didn't want to alter my current lifestyle too much. So I looked for ways to get some help without having to make drastic changes. I attended some secular meetings, for example, but didn't really commit to their programs. Then when nothing happened, I would say, "Why isn't this working? Maybe God doesn't love me. Maybe I don't deserve to change."

The truth is, I didn't need one more thing to cram into my messed-up life. What I needed was something to *replace* my messed-up life. I needed to let go of my old life and hand it over to God. I finally did that and now, twenty years later, I can't imagine why it took me so long to do something so right and true and amazing.

A race begins with a single step, and so does recovery. The only way to run with perseverance is to hang on to God's hand and let him take the lead. True change comes only when we die to ourselves and allow Christ to set the pace.

PRAYER

Father God, thank you for taking charge of my mess and helping me run my race with confidence. You are responsible for everything I am and ever hope to be. In Jesus' name, Amen.

On a Mission

*Praise be to the God and Father of our Lord Jesus Christ, the
Father of compassion and the God of all comfort, who comforts
us in all our troubles, so that we can comfort those in any
trouble with the comfort we ourselves receive from God.*

2 CORINTHIANS 1:3–4

We had a full house this year for Thanksgiving dinner—kids and grandkids everywhere. Once all our guests had been served, we got our plates and went to find a place to sit. My wife chose to join the ladies, and I sat down with the grandkids. The kids finished quickly, put their dishes in the sink, and hurried outside to play. And I found myself sitting all alone at the table.

I wasn't alone for long, though. In just a minute, our oldest grand-daughter came back in and sat down with me. "I really don't want to go out and play right now. I think I'll just stay here with you, Grandpa," she said sweetly. It touched my heart to know that she was already learning how important it is not to leave people alone. We had a great conversation as I finished my meal. Then she went outside to play.

When we see someone sitting alone, we ought to be the ones who go over and sit down beside them. We don't even have to say much. Just our presence means more than we will ever know. God has promised that he will never desert us or leave us alone. Let's thank him for his faithfulness by being there for others.

--- PRAYER ---

Father, you have promised never to leave us alone. Help us to be that comforting presence to others as we have opportunity. In Jesus' name, Amen.

Best-Laid Plans

Now listen, you who say, "Today or tomorrow we will go to this or
that city, spend a year there, carry on business and make money."
Why, you do not even know what will happen tomorrow.

JAMES 4:13

We all know that our plans don't always go the way we expect them to. For example, recently I was sitting in an airplane, listening to the couple in front of me. They were upset, and with good reason. They had been delayed getting through security and missed their connection, which caused them to lose a day of their vacation in Mexico. Now they were sharing their experience with anyone who would listen. "We have to get a hotel when we land and wait until tomorrow to make our connection." You could tell they were trying to have a good attitude about it, but finding it hard to accept any kind of positive spin.

Such occurrences are just facts of life. We've all made plans and watched them collapse around us. Those are the times we need to leave space for God in our lives. He always has a reason when he disrupts our plans, but he won't necessarily share that reason with us. A traffic tie-up, an unplanned phone call, or a missed connection is very often God's doing, even if it ruins our own carefully laid plans.

I don't know if that couple on my flight will have a God moment as a result of a long TSA line, but I know this: If God decides to mess with our plans, get ready. He will almost surely have something better planned for our day.

— PRAYER —

Heavenly Father, order my day, direct my steps, make my plans conform to yours.
I long to do your will. In Jesus' name, Amen.

What Is Freedom?

"You will know the truth, and the truth will make you free."

JOHN 8:32 NCV

Many years ago when I was in the service, the Fourth of July was approaching. It was the job of my squadron's safety officer to develop a slogan and put up posters discouraging drinking over the holiday weekend.

We had no accidents that year, and it was attributed partly to the slogan this guy came up with: "He who comes forth with a fifth on the fourth may not come forth on the fifth."

What comes to mind when you hear the words *Fourth of July? Independence Day? The Declaration of Independence? World War II?* When I think of the Fourth of July, I think of freedom. But what is true freedom?

Abraham Lincoln said, "Those who deny freedom to others deserve it not for themselves, and, under a just God, cannot long retain it." And we have all heard the great quote from Patrick Henry, "Give me liberty or give me death." But, here again, what is true liberty?

The basic test of freedom is not in what we are free to do but rather in what we are free *not* to do! Today, I am free not to drink! For me that's a very precious freedom.

PRAYER

Heavenly Father, I want to celebrate freedom in my life. Help me to openly and honestly deal with those things that take away my freedom to live in a manner that pleases you. In Jesus' name, Amen.

Anti-Sway

*"I will ask the Father, and he will give you another advocate to
help you and be with you forever—the Spirit of truth. The world
cannot accept him, because it neither sees him nor knows him.
But you know him, for he lives with you and will be in you."*

JOHN 14:16–17

My wife and I were traveling from Louisiana to Colorado, pulling a
trailer behind our truck. We weren't on the road long before the
trailer started swaying almost uncontrollably. Two hours later, after driving well below the speed limit, we pulled into a trailer company to see
what could be done.

One of the employees said he could install an anti-sway bar on the
trailer, and that should solve the problem. One hour and $120 later, we
were back on the road. And lo and behold, the trailer tracked right behind
the truck perfectly. We had stopped, admitted we had a problem, taken
the advice of the technician, and made the application. Now we could
travel on and do it safely.

In Celebrate Recovery we learn that we can't walk the road to recovery alone. Just like the trailer, we can develop a "sway" that will throw
us off track and back into our addictions. So we start by stepping out of
denial and admitting that we do have problems. Then we turn our lives
over to Jesus Christ, the Great Technician. He gives us the Holy Spirit,
who takes up residence within us and serves as an anti-sway Counselor-
Comforter. The Holy Spirit keeps us safe and assures us that we never
have to walk this road alone again.

PRAYER
---

*Heavenly Father, thank you for your Holy Spirit who keeps us safe in this temptation-
filled world. In Jesus' name, Amen.*

Baking Cakes

*"Suppose one of you wants to build a tower. Won't you first sit down and
estimate the cost to see if you have enough money to complete it? For if you
lay the foundation and are not able to finish it, everyone who sees it will
ridicule you, saying, 'This person began to build and wasn't able to finish.' "*

LUKE 14:28–30

Right now my wife and my mother are decorating a birthday cake for
my daughter. It's a pretty princess cake. When I peeked in earlier,
they were getting everything ready, checking to be sure they had everything they needed.

The whole cake business seems pretty simple to me—you bake it,
frost it, eat it. But apparently, to do the job right, there are steps, lots of
steps. For instance, my wife just told me that a cake needs to cool down
before it's decorated. Who knew? They aren't just putting some frost-
ing on the cake and hoping for the best. They're being very methodical,
thinking through each step.

That commitment to doing things right can be applied to all of us.
Whether we're building or baking or rebooting our lives, we need to take
the time to do the job right. It's important to make sure we are set up,
ready to go, at each place in our lives *before* we move on to the next step.

Let's take a moment to stop and think about the process. What is it
God wants to do in our lives next?

— PRAYER —

*Heavenly Father, help me to be wise as I walk through the steps of my life. Show me
how to prepare my heart for each step in its time. In Jesus' name, Amen.*

What's a Nickel Worth?

*"No one can serve two masters. Either you will hate the one
and love the other, or you will be devoted to the one and despise
the other. You cannot serve both God and money."*

MATTHEW 6:24

It's impossible to serve two masters—really, just physically, mentally, and emotionally impossible. Those who foolishly try will find themselves failing at both. Why? The heart that pursues money and possessions will never be satisfied. It will always want more and more—a big house, a new car, a six-foot big-screen TV, trips, and all the other things money can buy.

When those things have been obtained, other things will pop up until finally, they push out everything else in our lives. We find ourselves running around pouring all our time and effort into protecting and maintaining our money and possessions. At that point, what we think we own really owns us!

I know, because this is how I tried to live. All I got for my trouble was an insatiable emptiness on the inside. But that changed when I surrendered my life to Christ! I set my heart in pursuit of God and found all I had been looking for.

I finally understood that the only lasting thing that could fill my emptiness was a personal relationship with the Savior! I began to see that everything I had was a gift from God. Today, I attempt to live my life by using the treasures God entrusts me with to help others. The joy and fullness I experience from living this way is truly indescribable!

PRAYER

*Thank you, Father God, for filling me with your presence. You are all that I
desire, all I could ever want or need. In Jesus' name, Amen.*

Even When I'm Cranky

Shout for joy, you heavens; rejoice, you earth; burst into song, you mountains! For the LORD comforts his people and will have compassion on his afflicted ones.

ISAIAH 49:13

As my wife and I boarded a flight for London to teach at a training seminar, we were told that there would be a delay. The plane was full, and after two hours on the runway, most of us were hot, tired, sweaty, and becoming more and more cranky and agitated. But seated in front of us was a woman who provided a much-needed example of Christlike behavior in uncomfortable circumstances.

This woman was a grandmother, who was juggling a screaming toddler. Though the baby cried for the full two hours, the woman never once lost her composure or let the smile slip from her face. Instead she continued to try to comfort the child. Once the plane finally took off, the baby went to sleep. But the grandmother continued to hold her for the next nine hours. Never once did she complain, set the baby down, or hand her to someone else.

Long after the flight was over, I thought about how our heavenly Father is much like that grandmother. He puts up with us when we are cranky, tired, crying, complaining, and just plain no fun to be around. He never loses his cool or his desire to comfort us. He's right there carrying us, never putting us down or handing us off to someone else. No matter what we're going through, we can trust that he will always be there for us.

--- PRAYER ---

Heavenly Father, I'm thankful for your faithful watch-care over us. You have promised never to leave us no matter what circumstances we encounter. In Jesus' name, Amen.

Hide and Seek

"To him who overcomes, I will give the right to sit with me on my throne,
just as I overcame and sat down with my Father on his throne."

REVELATION 3:21

I was watching my wife play hide-and-seek with our grandkids. All the kids ran off to hide—except one. Our three-year-old grandson ran around a little bit and then put his hands over his eyes. Apparently, he thought that if he couldn't see anyone else, they couldn't see him.

That sounds silly, but when it comes to spiritual things, I sometimes do the same thing. I have been known to reason that if I can't see the devil, maybe he isn't there. Of course, I find out pretty quickly, as did my grandson, the error in that way of thinking. When we cover our eyes, we only make ourselves more vulnerable.

Instead of hiding our eyes, we must stand up and fight—for our recovery, for our relationships, for our lives. Jesus didn't take a seat until he overcame the enemy's most powerful weapon—death! We can't stop fighting either, not until we sit down with our Father in heavenly places.

PRAYER

Lord God, strengthen me as I stand to fight the good fight of faith. I want to take my stand against the enemy until the day you take me home to be with you. In Jesus' name, Amen.

What Makes It Work?

*Praise be to the God and Father of our Lord Jesus Christ, the
Father of compassion and the God of all comfort, who comforts
us in all our troubles, so that we can comfort those in any trouble
with the comfort we ourselves have received from God.*

2 CORINTHIANS 1:3–4

Benjamin Franklin said, "Tell me and I forget. Teach me and I remember. Involve me and I learn." That's a big reason why Celebrate Recovery works. The program acknowledges that just listening—tell me and I forget—isn't enough. Even remembering—teach me and I remember—won't do the trick. The only way to be successful is by doing—involve me and I learn.

We all begin at the same place: acknowledging that we are completely dependent on God's power, surrendered to his will, and committed to working the program's principles and steps. Once we've learned how to break free from our hurts, hang-ups, and habits, we must get involved and start giving back what we have learned by helping others.

As stated in Step 8, we are to yield ourselves to God to be used to bring this Good News to others, both by our example and our words. Step 12 requires that once we have had a spiritual experience as a result of taking the program's steps, we are to carry that message to others and practice those principles in all our affairs.

Healing and wholeness are more than a state of being. They are also a state of doing as we constantly renew our commitment and demonstrate our thankfulness by giving to others.

PRAYER

Heavenly Father, help me once again to acknowledge my dependence on you and confirm that commitment by sharing it with others. In Jesus' name, Amen.

Casting Anxiety

Cast all your anxiety on him because he cares for you.

1 PETER 5:7

Sunday nights in our house have a predictable pattern. Right around bedtime we'll have at least one meltdown. Usually it's our oldest daughter. She worries about school, which is strange because she's really smart. The problem is that she doesn't feel that way.

Every Sunday she worries that there will be something she won't be able to understand. She stresses out about it, cries, begs to stay home. It's sad to watch her struggle so unnecessarily. On Monday afternoons, I usually ask her about her day. Did the things she was worried about happen? Almost always her answer is no.

Many of us carry around a similar weight of anxiety, working ourselves into a ball of tears over things that will never materialize. This is not how God wants us to live. He looks down on us, his precious children, and asks us to turn all those things that are worrying us over to him. He loves us, and he's much more capable of handling those things than we are.

My wife and I have noticed that after our daughter tells us about her worries, she feels better. Nothing has changed, of course, but she no longer feels she is carrying those burdens alone. She knows that we love her and will always be there to help her. We can have that same security by sharing our worries and fears with God. He will always be there for us. He will always help us.

PRAYER

Dear Father, thank you for walking with us and helping us to carry all our burdens, real and imagined. Thank you for loving us. In Jesus' name, Amen.

Nutcracker Ballet

Be devoted to one another in love. Honor one another above yourselves.
Never be lacking in zeal, but keep your spiritual fervor, serving the Lord.

ROMANS 12:10–11

In recovery, we talk a lot about relationships and the importance of rebuilding and repairing the damage that we've done to ourselves and those we love. In order to be devoted to one another and honor one another above ourselves as the Bible instructs, we must change the way we think and operate. Often that means doing things that aren't in our comfort zone. This can be tough, but there is a bonus. Sometimes we find something enjoyable that we never thought we would.

During the holidays, my wife and I attended a production of *The Nutcracker* ballet. A ballet? This is something I never thought I would do. But my granddaughter was a cast member, and that made all the difference. Instead of an event that I would do just about anything to get out of, it was transformed into an event that I wouldn't miss for the world. In fact, it is one of my most enjoyable family memories. And for our granddaughter, our presence made her night complete.

These kinds of events are essential for building meaningful relationships with those we love. They show our devotion and that we are honoring others above ourselves. Sure, it takes some effort to get out of our comfort zone, but the rewards are worth it.

PRAYER

Father, thank you for the uncomfortable choices we make for others that become uncommon blessings for our lives and theirs. In Jesus' name, Amen.

PUSH—(P)ray (U)ntil (S)omething (H)appens

"Be joyful always; pray continually; give thanks in all circumstances, for this is God's will for you in Christ Jesus."

1 THESSALONIANS 5:16–18

Max Lucado once said, "Prayers aren't graded according to style." That is so true. In fact, our prayers aren't graded at all! God hears all our prayers, spoken and unspoken. I saw the PUSH acrostic in a tweet, and I love it. It reminds me to "pray continually" as the Bible tells us.

I've noticed that we sometimes ask God for something, feeling at the moment like it's a very important request. But then we quickly forget about it and move on to something else. We don't follow through. In order to have a successful prayer life, we need to stay focused on sharing our needs with God. Why? Does God forget? Certainly not, but we do. Sometimes we act like children, running through the store begging for everything we see. We must learn to bring our requests to God after careful consideration, fully prepared to wait for his answers.

And he will answer. It may not be in the way we want him to, but he never leaves us hanging. His answers come in one of three ways: yes, no, or not yet. Let us determine today to pray with purpose in mind and follow through until we receive what we have asked of him.

PRAYER

Lord God, forgive me when I am foolish and demanding. Thank you for showing me that you take all my requests seriously, and I must do the same. Thank you for hearing and always answering. In Jesus' name, Amen.

Pulling Out the Weeds

It is by grace you have been saved, through faith—and this is not from
yourselves, it is the gift of God—not by works, so that no one can boast.

EPHESIANS 2:8–9

I woke up one morning to another day of overcast skies at our Louisiana home. It had been pouring rain for two days, and frankly, I wasn't looking forward to more of it. But as I looked over at my garden spot, I was reminded that God uses the rainy, overcast days just like he uses those soaked in sunshine.

During the rains, the soil becomes soft and more pliable. The task of pulling out the weeds becomes much easier. In the same way, God uses the rainy seasons in my life to pull weeds and prepare the soil of my heart to receive his promptings. God confirmed this to me when I ran into a friend who had recently completed his recovery steps.

My friend told me his car had run out of gas one night, some distance from the nearest gas station. It was a big inconvenience, and he was thinking, *Why did this have to happen right now?* Minutes later, an old friend pulled up, someone he hadn't seen since becoming a Christian. As he greeted his friend, he knew exactly why he'd run out of gas at that time and place. He was able to tell his old friend about his new life in Jesus.

—— PRAYER ——

Father, thank you for the rainy weather as well as the sunshiny days. I will savor those days when you are removing the weeds in my life and preparing me to hear your voice. In Jesus' name, Amen.

Celebrate Your Recovery

*You turned my wailing into dancing; you removed my sackcloth
and clothed me with joy, that my heart may sing your praises
and not be silent. LORD my God, I will praise you forever.*

PSALM 30:11–12

Have you ever wondered why Celebrate Recovery is called *Celebrate Recovery*? Well . . . people usually seek help when things are bad. Which means none of us has much to celebrate when we first enter the program. That isn't always the case, of course, but usually people begin coming to Celebrate Recovery when things are far from ideal.

But soon, God begins to change things. He takes our pain and gives us purpose. He takes our crying and turns it into praise. He gives us joy and peace and freedom from our hurts, hang-ups, and habits. He gives us reason to celebrate.

Of course, it doesn't happen all at once. There will still be days when we hurt, feel stuck, or don't believe there is much to celebrate. There are sure to be hard times in recovery—pain we have to face, amends we have to make, forgiveness we must offer. But for those who hold on, there is hope and healing. There is reason to celebrate!

The important thing to remember is that we must hold fast to our commitment. We must refuse to quit. Each day we actively work toward our recovery, we will be able to thank God and share our testimony with someone who needs to hear it. Each day, we come one step closer to complete healing for our lives.

PRAYER

Father, I feel stuck right now. Please give me the resolve to continue to seek recovery. In Jesus' name, Amen.

Change Is Possible

*Outwardly we are wasting away, yet inwardly
we are being renewed day by day.*

2 CORINTHIANS 4:16

Some words are like oxygen to my soul: "I was struggling in hopelessness but now have hope." "God is changing me." "I could not have made it through this storm without Christ." "I have a new family for life now." "I have learned so much about myself, and for the first time I like what I see." "I am now the spouse I know I was called to be." "My relationship with my kids is growing healthier!"

There is nothing sweeter than seeing life change up close and personal. None of us is "fixed" but one thing is for sure: growth and change are becoming daily realities in so many lives. God has lifted me up and taught me some incredible lessons, even through times of hurt and pain. It has been said, "You can forgive what hurt you in the past. Just never forget what it taught you."

When we get to that place of surrender where we can say to God, "I'm tired of doing this on my own," then we can begin the process of allowing him to change us. No matter what we find ourselves in the middle of, no matter what poor choices we've made, no matter what struggles and hurts we've experienced, God still loves us and desires to comfort, protect, and guide us out of our mess and pain. In the process, he teaches us how to live more fruitfully.

PRAYER

Lord in heaven, thank you for teaching me even through the hurt and pain in my life. In Jesus' name, Amen.

Small Changes

*You were taught, with regard to your former way of life, to put off
your old self, which is being corrupted by its deceitful desires; to
be made new in the attitude of your minds; and to put on the new
self, created to be like God in true righteousness and holiness.*

EPHESIANS 4:22–24

Sometimes big changes come in the smallest ways. When I first entered recovery and began my new life in Christ, my sponsor told me change was essential to my sobriety. This is how he instructed me: "It's best to start small. If you shave the left side of your face first, then tomorrow morning, start on your right side. If you put your right shoe on first, put your left shoe on first. If you step into your left pants leg first, then step into the right leg first." You get the point. Making small changes, he assured me, would make it much easier to make big changes when I needed to.

Change is still not easy for me, but I've seen the positive results it brings. I've seen how it has helped me to get rid of negative thoughts and mind-sets. So today I'm open for any change God wants to make in my life. It will be hard work, because my mind still fights change. But today I will choose to hear and implement God's direction and will.

Remember, too, that God often sends the message of change in the form of another human being. If our ears and hearts are open, though, we will be ready to hear God's voice in their words.

─── PRAYER ───

*Holy Father, soften me, make me more flexible, more easily able to bend to your
will and your purpose. In Jesus' name, Amen.*

Hitting Bottom

"Come to me, all you who are weary and burdened, and I will give you rest."

MATTHEW 11:28

A few months ago, someone told me, "I'm ready to hit bottom. When will I get there?" This is how I answered: "When you stop digging!" It's simple, really. We hit bottom when we finally get tired of being beat up by ourselves and others. Then and only then, at the point of complete surrender, do we find rest. This isn't the sitting and doing nothing kind of rest—it's peace of mind.

Peace of mind is the greatest rest of all. But before we can get there, we have to wave the white flag and say, "I give up!" It's not easy, but there are a few things that can help you. First, surround yourself with people who are having victories and making progress in their recovery and in their lives. Second, stop digging your hole deeper by flooding your thoughts with the bad thinking that has gotten you where you are. Third, fill your mind with good things by memorizing Scripture and reading encouraging books.

Peace of mind is attainable, but it requires a new lifestyle, new habits, new behaviors, and relationships that are strong and upright. With God's help, we can all find our way, but nothing less than complete commitment will get us there.

--- PRAYER ---

Father, I want peace of mind. I have been a captive to my painful, troubling, disobedient thoughts for far too long. As I surrender to you, surround myself with good people, and flood my mind with your Word, I pray that you will bring me the gift of peace. In Jesus' name, Amen.

The Power of Forgiveness

"Do to others as you would have them do to you."

LUKE 6:31

A guy once told me, "John, you won't catch me getting ulcers. I just take things as they come. I don't ever hold a grudge, not even against people who have done things to me that I'll never forgive." Right! Forgiveness is a beautiful idea until we have to practice it.

There are a lot of jokes about forgiveness, but forgiveness is not something that those of us in recovery can take lightly, because forgiveness is clearly God's prescription for the broken. No matter how great the offense or abuse, forgiveness lies along the path to healing.

We all know that one of the roots of compulsive behavior is buried pain. So facing our past and forgiving ourselves and those who have hurt us, as well as making amends for the pain that we have caused others, is the only lasting solution. Forgiveness breaks the cycle! It doesn't settle all the questions of blame, justice, or fairness, but it does allow relationships to heal and possibly start over.

In order to be completely free from our resentments, anger, fears, shame, and guilt, we need to give and accept *forgiveness* in all areas of our lives. If we do not, our recovery will remain incomplete. God wants much more than that for us. He wants us to walk in wholeness, ready to follow the path he planned for us before the beginning of time.

--- PRAYER ---

Father, what a gift I've found in forgiving and receiving forgiveness. Thank you for your goodness to me. In Jesus' name, Amen.

Getting Rid of the Stains

*If we claim to be without sin, we deceive ourselves and the truth
is not in us. If we confess our sins, he is faithful and just and will
forgive us our sins and purify us from all unrighteousness.*

1 JOHN 1:8–9

When we moved to our new home in Colorado, we had to have the water tested. This house had not been lived in for quite a while, so we wanted to make sure the well water was safe. The test results told us that the water was safe to drink, but we would have to watch the iron and manganese levels.

Unless water has extremely high concentrations of these minerals, they are not hazardous to one's health. But they can be a real nuisance because they stain everything orange or black. Upon further investigation, we found out that with the proper filter, both these minerals could be eliminated. So we installed the filter, and immediately our water was pure. It took some work to get rid of the stains, but in time they began to fade.

This reminded me that when we turn our lives over to Christ, forgiveness is immediate and complete, just as the filter immediately purified our water. But it will take some work to get rid of those stains that sin has left in our lives. The good news is that God is there to help us as we work to clean up our lives and relationships. He will help us break the silence and give up the secrets. And he will wash us white as snow.

—————————— PRAYER ——————————

*Father God, thank you for purifying my heart and helping me get rid of the stains
that sin has left on my life and relationships. In Jesus' name, Amen.*

Changes

*Give praise to the LORD, proclaim his name; make
known among the nations what he has done.*

1 CHRONICLES 16:8

Whenever we spend time in recovery and turn our lives over to Jesus, whenever we determine to trust him daily, we are bound to see changes. Those changes might be big, and they might be small. They might be the kind that happen only on the inside, or they might be the kind that no one can miss. Regardless of what form they take, they are reason to give thanks to God.

It could be that we notice we are patient, when before we would have lashed out. It could be that we celebrated a holiday sober, when before we might have used the occasion for an excuse to drink or use. Maybe we were able to set a boundary in a relationship instead of allowing ourselves to be manipulated. Whatever the change may be, big or small, it is a reason to thank God and praise him for what he is doing in our lives.

Thanking God for the changes in our lives reminds us that he is the reason for our change, not us. Thanking God also shows other people that he is ready and able to give us the power we need to put the past behind us and win in life.

So, let's lift our voices and thank him for all he's done for us. Then let's tell those around us that God can help them change their lives as well.

PRAYER

Father God, you are good and merciful and kind. Your grace has given me a second chance to win in life. I thank you for all you have done and all you will do. In Jesus' name, Amen.

Seven Billion People

They took offense at him. But Jesus said to them, "Only in his hometown and in his own house is a prophet without honor."

MATTHEW 13:57

It's human nature to want to be liked by everyone. But that is not a realistic or healthy expectation. Jesus understood this. He knew that people who had known him throughout his life had a preset idea of who he was that could not be easily changed. He also understood that his message was controversial. As he spoke to the crowds, he was sure to make enemies.

Like Jesus, we will all be judged wrongly by some, criticized by others. We will all have enemies if we are proclaiming the kingdom of God. There will also be people who simply don't like us. So how should we respond?

In his Sermon on the Mount recorded in Matthew 5, Jesus encouraged us to be peacemakers and to rejoice and be glad when people insult us, persecute us, and say evil things about us, for our reward in heaven will be great. He doesn't say "if" these things happen; he says "when."

The message here is that we can't make people like us. Just like Jesus, we can't please everyone. We are to be peacemakers whenever we can, while accepting that some will dislike—even despise—us no matter what we do. Their disapproval must never keep us from pleasing God!

PRAYER

Father, I will not run after the approval of others. Instead I surrender my heart to you. I will bask in your great love for me and work to please you in all I do. In Jesus' name, Amen.

Walk This Way

*Whether you turn to the right or to the left, your ears will hear
a voice behind you, saying, "This is the way; walk in it."*

ISAIAH 30:21

As usual, we arrived at the airport with plenty of time to check our bags, get our boarding passes, and make it through security before our flight was scheduled to leave. We were ready to go, but our flight wasn't. A delay left us cooling our heels for the next two hours.

As we waited, sitting in front of those huge airport windows, watching the planes arrive and depart, I saw something that made me think. A huge plane, one of the biggest I'd ever seen, was being towed by a small cart attached to its front wheels.

Since I've turned my life over to Jesus Christ, I no longer move under my own power. Just as that jumbo jet had to turn off its big engine and be led, I too must relinquish control of my life to the Holy Spirit and let him move me wherever God wants me to go. He doesn't bully me with his great power but directs my life with small nudges and gentle whispers.

I have learned in Celebrate Recovery to pay attention to those seemingly small nudges, which often come through other people. They keep me grounded and moving in the right direction.

—————————— PRAYER ——————————

Father in heaven, thank you for leading me gently through my life, keeping me focused on fulfilling your purpose for me. In Jesus' name, Amen.

One Day at a Time

*I urge you, brothers and sisters, in view of God's mercy, to
offer your bodies as a living sacrifice, holy and pleasing
to God—this is your true and proper worship.*

ROMANS 12:1

Most of us don't seek help until we realize that something is out of
control in our lives. Sometimes another person realizes it for us,
but either way, we come looking for help in an area that obviously needs
attention. After we've been in recovery for a while, however, it becomes
clear that flaws in our character may have been what got us into big trouble in the first place. If we don't deal with them, they will keep us from
living a life fully committed to Christ.

The bad news is that we all have these character flaws. No one is perfect. Maybe we are people pleasers, or we have anger issues. We might
feel we have to spend money to feel good about ourselves, or we use food
to stuff our emotions. We may have control issues. Whatever the case,
these character flaws are always at the root of our big problems.

It's important to acknowledge these character flaws and offer them
to God. We start with the big issue, the one causing us the most pain, and
then we begin working on all the smaller areas God reveals to us. The
process works because God is in it. All we need to do is acknowledge
the need for change, offer ourselves to him, and then work alongside him
while he works those things out in our lives.

PRAYER

*Thank you, Lord, for helping me to see the flaws behind my failings. With your
help, I will face them one day at a time. In Jesus' name, Amen.*

Conscious Contact

Let the word of Christ dwell in you richly.

COLOSSIANS 3:16

We have all been given one great choice: how we will live our lives. We can live them "our way," as Frank Sinatra sang. Trouble is, on our own, we lack the resources and understanding we need to avoid disaster. Most of us find that out the hard way. Or we can live our lives according to society's norms and expectations. That sounds good, but aligning ourselves with the naturally evil hearts of men is also fraught with danger and disaster.

There is another option, however. One that is sure to work in our favor. We can choose to align ourselves with God and live our lives his way.

God instituted a plan for each of us long before we were born, and he has given us the gifts and insights we need to follow that plan successfully. He has guaranteed our success before we even start.

To find God's will for our lives, we must spend time alone with him. Even Jesus spent much time praying and listening for his Father's voice so he could carry out the mission for which he was sent. He made conscious contact with God, and we must do the same. God must be more than a concept to us.

Conscious contact with God begins in his Word—his love letter to us. In its pages, we find his will for us and learn how to make right choices.

PRAYER

Father, thank you for the care you took in giving me all I need to live a successful life. I want to be all you created me to be. In Jesus' name, Amen.

Can We Help?

*Each of you should use whatever gift you have received to serve
others, as faithful stewards of God's grace in its various forms.*

1 PETER 4:10

My wife passed me with her cleaning supplies, headed for the sliding glass door. A couple of "little ones" had left handprints all over it. Just then our two grand-boys—the ones responsible for the handprints—noticed what she was about to do. "Can we help?" they asked with pleading eyes. My wife smiled, knowing full well that the job would now take much longer with two pint-sized helpers involved.

My wife is a wise grandmother, though. She could see that there were valuable lessons to be learned, so she said, "Sure!" I watched from my recliner as the three of them chose a spot and got to work. The boys felt important and needed. They got to be part of the solution.

When people come into our churches and recovery groups, their hearts are longing for a place where they can feel at home. They want to feel useful and needed. They want to be part of the solution. The best thing we can do is put them to work serving others. And for those times when we are struggling to feel like we belong, the answer is the same— get busy serving others. Serving others always puts us right in the thick of things, where God can heal and encourage us.

PRAYER

Father, make us sensitive to those who need to feel needed, and give us the wisdom to ask for their help, even when we could do it faster without them. In Jesus' name, Amen.

Engine Light

They did not listen or pay attention; instead, they followed the stubborn inclinations of their evil hearts. They went backward and not forward.

JEREMIAH 7:24

A few days ago, the check engine light came on in my car. I dread this because it's never good news. I had just spent a considerable amount of money fixing up my wife's car, and I was in no mood to let things get out of hand, so I drove straight to the shop. Turns out it was time for an oil change. No big deal.

This made me think, though. Sometimes a warning light goes on in our lives, and we don't pay attention to it because we're afraid of what we'll find. Maybe the warning light is a phone call from a loved one who is hurt by something we said or another night spent acting out in a behavior we abhor. Maybe the warning light is an "insufficient funds" message at the ATM. Whatever it is, when that light goes on, it can be tempting to ignore it.

But that's never the right move. In fact, that's denial. God may be sending you a warning light to help you avoid trouble—something that, if left unchecked, can lead to a bigger issue. An oil change is no big deal, but without it, my car's engine could have been destroyed.

We should always be watching for God's warning lights. If we don't pay attention, we are apt to fall backward into old hurts, hang-ups, and habits. Our loving God wants to spare us more pain and shower us instead with his blessings.

PRAYER

Heavenly Father, thank you for the warning lights you place in my life. I know they are there to help me rather than harm me. In Jesus' name, Amen.

A Front Is Moving In

*It is dangerous to be concerned with what others think
of you, but if you trust the LORD, you are safe.*

PROVERBS 29:25 GNB

I just saw today's forecast. A front is moving in. That means the weather is about to change. One air mass is about to push another air mass out of the way. And you know, that got me to thinking about the different "fronts" I used to put on around people. I could be whatever someone wanted me to be. All I wanted to do was make people happy. I was what we call a "people pleaser." Trouble was, it brought storms rather than sunshine. None of us can be all things to all people.

In my case, I told myself I was doing the right thing, holding everything together for the sake of others, but the more I tried, the more hopeless and dissatisfied I felt. And the thing was, my fronts weren't working for anyone else either. I finally learned through Celebrate Recovery that it isn't my job to please everyone, and I couldn't do it even if it were. I am learning that when Christ said "love others as yourself," he didn't mean at the expense of myself.

As a result of this change in my thinking, God is slowly calming the self-initiated storms in my life. He has instructed me to strive to please him and let him take care of the rest. That brings the sunshine back into my life.

PRAYER

Father, thank you for freeing me of the notion that I have to put on a front to please everyone. And thank you for teaching me that being who I was created to be is what pleases you. In Jesus' name, Amen.

The Second Step

It is God who works in you to will and to act according to his good purpose.

PHILIPPIANS 2:13

The admission that we are powerless over an addiction or compulsive behavior in our lives opens us up to reach out to God. We begin to understand that he wants to fill our lives with his love, his joy, his hope, and his presence. That first step turned our eyes away from ourselves as the source of healing, and the second step turns our eyes toward God.

Step 2: We came to believe that a power greater than ourselves could restore us to sanity.

If we can't heal ourselves, then who can we turn to for help? God is the only one who has the power to exchange our chaos for freedom. Of course, he knew long before we did what would be needed. He sent Jesus to save us from sin and sickness. He sent his power player to earth, someone who was tempted as we are in all ways but without sin. He is not just a higher power. He is the highest power, because he has conquered all life can dish out. He did that for us so we could imagine freedom from sin in our own lives.

What freedom it brings to know that when we are powerless, we have an ally to help us through the hard times—and all the times are hard, aren't they?

—————————— PRAYER ——————————

Heavenly Father, I've made such a mess of things. I'm so grateful that you care for me and came to show me the way out of chaos and into freedom. In Jesus' name, Amen.

I Surrender!

Prepare your minds for action; be self-controlled; set your hope fully on the grace to be given you when Jesus Christ is revealed. As obedient children, do not conform to the evil desires you had when you lived in ignorance.

1 PETER 1:13 – 14

Recently I was working on a roof over a small porch. It was a very sunny day, so I was wearing sunglasses. Trouble is, I don't see as well as I used to. I had to put on my reading glasses, while still wearing my sunglasses, in order to cut the boards with a skill saw—a little dangerous, to say the least. Of course, I could buy a pair of prescription sunglasses, but I would rather take chances than make an effort to do that.

Early in my recovery I tried to manage my problems, hurts, hang-ups, and habits by myself, instead of asking for advice from those who have already experienced what I was going through. And sure enough, I often found myself in dangerous situations. I still tend to be a little hard-headed—like wearing two pair of glasses at the same time. But today I know I can't afford to try to manage my struggles by myself. I must surrender my pride and ask for help.

Sooner or later we all learn that true freedom comes when we turn our problems over to God and open ourselves to the hard-learned wisdom that others can provide. Asking for help doesn't make us weak, but refusing to ask sure does.

PRAYER

Father, when I feel pride and independence rising up in me, remind me that surrender to you and the wisdom of others is the only way to be truly free. In Jesus' name, Amen.

My Truck Takes Diesel

*In your anger do not sin; Do not let the sun go down while
you are still angry, and do not give the devil a foothold.*

EPHESIANS 4:26–27

I know my wife thought she was helping me when she filled my truck with gas. The problem is that my truck is a diesel. Now she was phoning me to come rescue her because the truck wouldn't start! I told her I was on my way, but all I could think about was what my wife's actions were going to cost me—anything from draining the tank to replacing the engine.

I wish I could say I was just a little frustrated, but the truth is I was angry. I prayed and asked Jesus to help me respond in the right way. Then, because I need to be accountable, I called one of my brothers in recovery and told him what had happened and how angry I was.

When I saw my wife, the first words out of my mouth were, "I am so sorry this happened to you. I know this wasn't in your plans today." It felt good talking to my brother later and telling him that God had helped me with my anger and given me a good response when I saw my wife. I had acted on, rather than reacted to, a bad situation. It turned out the truck was fine. I drained the tank, put diesel in, and started it right up. The best part is that because I made a good choice, I won't have to make amends.

PRAYER

Father, thank you for helping me choose to be kind and forgiving rather than rude and judgmental. Things always go better when I surrender to you. In Jesus' name, Amen.

A Picture of Redemption

*"If you do what is right, will not you be accepted? But if
you do not do what is right, sin is crouching at your door;
it desires to have you, but you must master it."*

GENESIS 4:7

Every once in a while God gives us the chance to witness a miracle!
Recently, a leader in Celebrate Recovery shared this miracle with me:
"A year ago a man walked into my office, broken, at his wit's end,
with a heart full of despair. He was angry and trying to cope with a host
of substances and other unhealthy habits that were destroying his mind
and hardening his heart. He was ready to abandon his wife and family.
Last night I saw this man again at a Celebrate Recovery graduation service. Now, eleven months sober, he is a completely different man.

"With tears in his eyes, he accepted his 12-Step chip and then
expressed his love for his wife who was sitting close by. I was humbled as
I heard him talk about the restoration that had come to his marriage and
how his kids are rejoicing and talking about God. He then quoted the
following Bible passage, changing *you* to *I*: 'If I do what is right, will I not
be accepted? But if I do not do what is right, sin is crouching at my door;
it desires to have me, but I must master it.'

"The man I met a year ago is no more. In his place, a new leader has
been born. That's what I call a true miracle—the transformation of a
human life."

PRAYER

---

*Dear God of miracles, I stand in awe of what you have done in so many lives. My
words cannot express your greatness. In Jesus' name, Amen.*

I Won!

You also were included in Christ when you heard the message of truth, the gospel of your salvation. When you believed, you were marked in him with a seal, the promised Holy Spirit, who is a deposit guaranteeing our inheritance until the redemption of those who are God's possession—to the praise of his glory.

EPHESIANS 1:13–14

I really enjoy bowling with my two youngest grandsons—ages three and four. In their already very independent way, they pick up the ball, march up to the line, and hurl the ball with all their strength. Many times the ball moves so slowly that it barely makes it to the pins. But the lane we use has bumper pads instead of gutters, so eventually, some pins go down. It really doesn't matter to the boys how many. They watch intently as the ball rolls down the lane. Then they jump for joy with hands raised in the air and shout, "I won!"

I can't help but wonder how much better my life would be if I were to follow the technique my little grandsons have chosen. After all, my heavenly Father has said that I've already won. I've been crowned with salvation because of Jesus. He has given me bumpers—his Holy Spirit— to keep me out of the gutter. He isn't concerned about how many pins I knock over; he just wants me to keep doing the things he has asked me to do.

Throughout the day and especially at the end of each day, I should be jumping for joy, raising my hands, and shouting, "I won!"

PRAYER

Father, you are so good to me, so merciful and gracious. Thank you for the promise of an unqualified win! In Jesus' name, Amen.

The Checkout Line

Better a patient person than a warrior, one with self-control than one who takes a city.

PROVERBS 16:32

I have a gift that no one wants. It's kind of like my superpower. I can find the slowest line in a grocery store. It's uncanny. Give me the choice of twenty-five checkout lines in a superstore, and I'll find the one moving at a snail's pace. My line will be the one with a trainee behind the register, a person with twenty-two items in the fifteen or less express line, a person with a double coupon for each item, or someone who needs to write a check. (Do people really write checks anymore?) I've noticed that even when I find a line that seems to be moving briskly, things change as soon as I step into it.

I do not handle this gift well. I shift my weight from foot to foot, check my watch, crane my neck to see if a new line has opened, and huff audibly to show my disdain. Those things don't make the line move faster, but they do make me more miserable.

I have considered the possibility that God allows me to wait in line a lot because I need to practice the virtue of patience. I've certainly known him to use adverse circumstances as a teaching aid in my life before. And patience is a pretty important commodity. It's listed as one of the fruits of the Spirit! So maybe if I weren't so thickheaded, I'd get through the checkout line a lot faster.

—————— PRAYER ——————

Father, open my heart and mind to all the lessons you want to teach me. Give me a desire to walk in godliness. In Jesus' name, Amen.

Alone Time with God

After he had dismissed them, he went up on a mountainside by himself to pray. When evening came, he was there alone.

MATTHEW 14:23

Our lives are full to overflowing these days. It's not easy to set aside a daily quiet time with God. But, we insist, we're in constant communication with him throughout the day. That's good. We should have God in mind at all times. But there are just some important things we can't do on the run.

For example, daily self-examination is essential for a strong recovery. Where better to do that than away from all the noise and distractions? There, alone and silent in God's presence, we can take a good, hard look at ourselves and deal with what we find. We also need time apart to read God's Word—our instruction manual—allowing it to prepare our hearts for the battles ahead. We also need time for prayer, not just the chatter about daily life, but a full-on conversation with our loving Father.

The Bible tells us that Jesus made a habit of getting away from the crowds and spending time with his Father. If the perfect Son of God needed that time, how much more do we need it to steady our shaking hands and feet? Time apart with God keeps us strong, courageous, and focused. It keeps us tuned in to him.

PRAYER

Lord, help me today and every day to set aside time alone with you. I desire more from you than just fellowship in passing. I want the joy that comes with hearing your voice and knowing that you've heard mine. In Jesus' name, Amen.

I'm Sorry, Really?

*It is for freedom that Christ has set us free. Stand firm, then, and
do not let yourselves be burdened again by a yoke of slavery.*

GALATIANS 5:1

Several years ago, my son-in-law asked me to teach him cabinetmaking. He had never done this kind of work before, so I agreed. We immediately ran into a problem. My son-in-law was eager to learn, but he didn't understand the value of wood. He would often make mistakes and then say, "I'm sorry." The next day he would repeat the same mistake and make the same response.

After a while, I realized I would have to confront him. I called him into my office and said to him, "These mistakes are costing me money. I don't want to hear you apologize again until you're ready to start doing things differently."

I noticed a change that very day. My son-in-law started paying more attention to what he was doing, and his mistakes were reduced dramatically. He understood that his mistakes were costing someone—me. He doesn't have to say, "I'm sorry," much anymore, and he has become a fine cabinetmaker!

When I fail to understand the price that was paid for me, I repeatedly make poor choices. Grace is not free. The price that was paid for me is greater than my human mind can comprehend. That's why I pay attention to what God has instructed me to do and carefully consider my choices before I jump into something. My mistakes cost me nothing, but they cost God his Son.

---- PRAYER ----

Oh my Father, forgive my careless mistakes and help me to consider my ways carefully. In Jesus' name, Amen.

It's Just Coffee

*Since, then, you have been raised with Christ, set your hearts on
things above, where Christ is, seated at the right hand of God.
Set your minds on things above, not on earthly things.*

COLOSSIANS 3:1–2

I'm a big coffee drinker. I drink coffee in the morning, afternoon,
and—although I often regret it when I can't sleep—night. Part of the
fun of making coffee is the ritual. I weigh the beans, get the water the
right temperature, and use the right apparatus for the right kind of coffee.
I admit, I'm a bit of a fanatic about it.

But the thing is, it's just coffee. It doesn't really matter. If I make a bad
cup of coffee, so what? I can just throw it out and make a new one. Okay,
I can just drink it and then make a new one. In the big picture, it doesn't
really mean anything. So why do I spend so much time thinking about it,
obsessing over it? It's coffee; it's temporary.

I'm not suggesting we shouldn't have hobbies or interests, but, like
coffee, they are temporary rather than eternal. How much of our time
and attention should be spent on pursuits that have no lasting meaning?
And if we wanted to take this up a notch, what about when we obsess
over what people think of us or what will happen tomorrow? These are
all temporary as well.

What if we were to stop obsessing about those things that don't
really matter and focus our attention on things with eternal significance?
How would that change our lives, our tomorrows?

———— PRAYER ————

*Father in heaven, help me to focus on those things with lasting importance—
eternal importance. In Jesus' name, Amen.*

The Alpha and Omega

*"I am the Alpha and the Omega," says the Lord God, "who
is, and who was, and who is to come, the Almighty."*

REVELATION 1:8

The third step of the secular version of the 12 Steps says, "We made
a decision to turn our wills and our lives over to the care of God, as
we understood him." I don't know about you, but when I got into recovery, I wasn't looking for a God I could understand. I needed a God who
was *beyond* my understanding, far beyond my limited, finite comprehension. I needed the one and only God—the Alpha and Omega, who is and
was and is to come!

As we make this difficult journey to recovery, we need a present-tense God *who is* to guide us in our everyday lives, giving us what we
need to be victorious one day at a time. We also need a past-tense God
who was there from the very beginning and who created us in his own
image and likeness. We must have a future-tense God as well. Our God
who is to come is able to make good on his promises to us. This is why
Celebrate Recovery's third step reads a little differently. It says, "We
made a decision to turn our lives and our wills over to the care of God."

Our God is so much more than enough; he is incomprehensible. He
helps us deal with our past, stay grounded in the present, and be filled
with hope for the future.

─────────── PRAYER ───────────

*Lord God, you are my everything. Thank you for touching my life from one end to
the other. In Jesus' name, Amen.*

Is It Now, Father?

Listen to my instruction and be wise; do not ignore it. Blessed is the man
who listens to me, watching daily at my doors, waiting at my doorway.
For whoever finds me finds life and receives favor from the LORD.

PROVERBS 8:33–35

I've been a builder all my life, so when my grandson asked me to help him build something with a new toy that resembles an erector set, I was all in. Unfortunately, I was right in the middle of something important, so I told my grandson I would help him as soon as I had finished my other work.

Of course my grandson faithfully reminded me every five minutes that he was ready to begin. "Is it now, Papa?" he would say. Each time I would tell him, "Not yet, but in a few minutes." Finally, after an hour, which I'm sure seemed like an eternity to him, I stopped what I was doing and said, "Let's build it!"

Sometimes it seems like an eternity as I wait for God to do certain things that I've been asking of him. While in recovery, though, I've learned that practicing patience and waiting on God's timing is part of the Holy Spirit's work in my life. When these virtues are coupled with self-control (meaning under God's control), I am better able to wait. Quite honestly, in my perspective, it seems like he comes through at the very last moment—but the fact is that he always comes through.

It's never easy to wait, but things always work out better when we do.

PRAYER

My loving Papa God, thank you for helping me learn patience and self-control as I
wait for your perfect timing. In Jesus' name, Amen.

How Bad Was It?

*Be careful that you do not forget the LORD, who brought
you out of Egypt, out of the land of slavery.*

DEUTERONOMY 6:12

Randall looked terrible. His face was so swollen his eyes were almost shut.

"What happened to you?" I asked.

Randall told me he had been stung by a wasp right in the middle of his forehead. He knew he was allergic to bee and wasp stings, but he didn't seek medical help because it had been a long time since he'd been stung, and he'd forgotten how bad it was. Later, when his throat started to swell and he couldn't breathe, he had to be rushed by ambulance to the hospital.

Sometimes we start doing better, living normal lives, and we forget what brought us to recovery. The memory of how bad it was starts to dim. We forget what our lives were like before God brought us out of slavery, and we think we can pick up that old habit again. We tell ourselves that it wasn't that bad, and after all, we're stronger now. We can handle it. Then, before we know it, we're back in critical care, fighting for our lives once again. We can't afford to forget who we were before Jesus came into our lives.

God has taken our filthy rags and given us lives, real lives. Thanking him every day will keep us from becoming careless and forgetful.

PRAYER

My Father God, thank you for all you've done for me, for all you've given me, for taking the ruins of my life and replacing them with goodness and purpose. Help me to always remember who I was before you rescued me. In Jesus' name, Amen.

Am I Grateful Enough?

If I'm sleepless at midnight, I spend the hours in grateful reflection.

PSALM 63:6 MSG

It was a beautiful day in Southern California. But I didn't notice until I got out of my car and the warm winter's sun shone down on my face! Until then, I had taken it all for granted.

After years in recovery, we have a tendency to take God's love, grace, healing, gifts, and forgiveness for granted. Sure, I try to be faithful with my "Gratitude List." But even that sometimes becomes going through the motions, without true feeling.

I've learned that I need to recommit myself to start and end each day with a grateful heart! Otherwise, there will be days when I get busy and distracted by other things, taking my eyes off the Cross and what Jesus did for me there.

I once heard it said, "What if tomorrow you received from God only those things you were grateful for today?" Of course that is *not* how God works. He does not withhold from us. Instead he heaps blessing upon blessing, but it's a good thing to pause and think about. Are we living our lives in the center of gratitude? When we awaken in the night, are our thoughts filled with gratitude to our wonderful God? If not, we need to ask him to refresh and renew us.

Our heavenly Father has given us so much—more than we could ever adequately thank him for. Let's be sure we don't take it all for granted.

—————————— PRAYER ——————————

Father, thank you for your watchfulness over me both day and night. May my voice constantly be lifted in praise to you. In Jesus' name, Amen.

Shark-Infested Water?

*I urge you, brothers, in view of God's mercy, to offer your bodies as
living sacrifices, holy and pleasing to God—this is your spiritual act of
worship. Do not conform any longer to the pattern of this world, but be
transformed by the renewing of your mind. Then you will be able to test
and approve what God's will is—his good, pleasing and perfect will.*

ROMANS 12:1–2

I was with my ten-year-old nephew the first time he went swimming
in a lake, and he had a few questions for me before he slipped into
the dark water. First, he wanted to know if the lake was shark infested! I
assured him that there were no sharks in the lake. He reflected on that for
a moment and then asked, "Are there any carnivores in this lake?" Once
again I assured him that the waters were safe, and he finally decided to
plunge in.

After I'd had a few chuckles, it occurred to me that it might be a
good idea to ask a few questions before I jump into new situations—
like, *Is there something in this situation that can harm me?* If I realize there
is, then I can wisely take another course. If the answer is "I don't know,"
I can get input from a sponsor or accountability partner before taking
the plunge.

After all, I've been in shark-infested waters before and barely made
it out with my life. I think next time I'll stop and check the water before
I dive in.

PRAYER

*Lord God, you are so faithful to keep me from harm and to rescue me when I fool-
ishly go where I shouldn't. I promise to check with you before I dive into unfamiliar
waters. In Jesus' name, Amen.*

Course Correction

We take captive every thought to make it obedient to Christ.

2 CORINTHIANS 10:5

Most of us tend to think that we have a lot of control over our lives. But the reality is that what we truly have control over is a pretty short list. Take just a moment to think about it—the only things we can control are our choices and our reactions. In so many ways we are powerless, but we do have the ability to make course corrections in our choices and reactions along the way. We need to ask ourselves these probing questions:

- Do I see myself heading down a road that won't end well for me? Course correction.
- Am I tempted to do something I know is wrong? Course correction.
- Have I seen myself react in an inappropriate way? Course correction.
- Am I aware of certain relationships that aren't good for me? Course correction.
- Am I involved in a situation that I know could lead to disaster? Course correction.

It's true that we don't have much control over our lives. It's better just to acknowledge that. But we do have the power to correct our course and change the situation we're in. We have the power to call someone for support, pray over the situation, make adjustments when necessary. When we hear ourselves say, "I don't have a choice," we should think twice. We always have a choice. We may not make the right one or react the right way every time, but we have the ability, with God's power, to change things in our lives.

PRAYER

Father, help me to make good choices for my life—choices that will keep me headed toward all you have for me. In Jesus' name, Amen.

Satisfying a Hunger

*"Blessed are those who hunger and thirst for
righteousness, for they will be filled."*

MATTHEW 5:6

D ad, I'm still hungry!" How many times have I heard those words?
When my son was going through a growth spurt as a kid, it was
unbelievable how much he could eat. He would literally get up from the
dinner table, rinse his plate, walk into the living room, and say, "Dad, can
I get something to eat? I'm still hungry." Our grocery bill was through
the roof.

These memories bring a smile to my face, and they also make me
think. Our heavenly Father has designed us, his children, to hunger and
thirst for more and more of him. He built that into us so we would seek
him out to help us soothe the deep ache inside us that nothing else can
satisfy. I kind of think that's a really big deal—the Creator of the universe has gone to such lengths to draw me to him and keep me there in
his presence.

Someone once said, "You cannot tell a hungry child that you gave
him food yesterday." In the same way, I am learning that I cannot tell
my hungry spirit that I ate yesterday. I have to go to the Father daily so
that he can feed me. He wants us to be filled with the food that only he
can provide.

--- PRAYER ---

*Father God, I can't imagine why you love me so much, but I'm glad you do. Thank
you for providing food for my soul. In Jesus' name, Amen.*

It's All Your Fault

[God] will yet fill your mouth with laughter and your lips with shouts of joy.

JOB 8:21

Flight delays due to weather kept my wife and me from arriving at our destination until after dark. It had been a long, tiring day, and we were both bushed. We use a GPS everywhere we go. We call it the "Marriage Saver" because if we get lost, we can blame it on the GPS rather than on each other. Good idea, right?

We ran into a problem, though. About a year ago, the piece that fastens the GPS to the windshield went missing. I searched on the Internet and found a replacement piece. All would have ended well if my wife hadn't dropped the GPS on our way to the rental car. She picked it up, but neither of us noticed the new fastener was gone until I went to attach it to the windshield as we pulled out of the rental lot. I circled back around, and we saw it reflected in the headlights. Someone had run over it.

At that moment, I had a decision to make—a test. My natural response would be to blame my wife. Fortunately, the Lord reminded me about one of my favorite recovery tools—laughter. We both started laughing at our frustrating situation, and the tension melted away. We all face situations that test the limits of our patience. Usually it's the smaller ones that get to us the most. But we can overcome them by stopping long enough to choose to act appropriately.

─────────── PRAYER ───────────

Heavenly Father, thank you for saving me even from myself and teaching me ways to manage frustration and anger. In Jesus' name, Amen.

The Right Thing

He guides the humble in what is right and teaches them his way.

PSALM 25:9

I'm feeling a little overwhelmed today. In the last few days I have had to make some tough decisions. They were the right choices to make, but they have not been popular. As a people pleaser, this is hard for me. A part of me would rather make everyone happy than make the right choice.

But there are times, and we all face them, when we have to make decisions that won't please everyone. In fact, the decision to trust Jesus and change the way we live probably didn't sit well with everyone who knows us. But it was the right thing to do.

So whenever we're faced with a tough decision and we know the right thing to do, that's what we must do. It might be to stop enabling someone or to get help for a behavior that has grown out of control. It could be choosing to speak the truth in love rather than pretending everything is just fine. It could be getting out of a hurtful situation.

There will be times when the path is a little muddy and we don't know what to do. But if we pray and ask God to show us, he will. He'll make the choice clear if we ask him—and then when we've done the right thing, he'll honor it.

PRAYER

Father God, you are all wise and all knowing. Help me to see things clearly and always strive to do the right thing. In Jesus' name, Amen.

Battle Lines

"He who stands firm to the end will be saved."

MATTHEW 24:13

Last night I heard an interview with the quarterback of the winning Super Bowl team. He said that what made the win so special was knowing and reflecting on what he and his team had overcome throughout the year.

I was thinking about how true this is in my life, especially my marriage. My wife and I have been through some pretty tough times. We even suffered through a 13-month separation at one point. I am grateful that God not only saw us through that painful period but also actually made our marriage stronger.

Neither one of us would want to relive those days, but we now look back and take heart from what God has done in our lives. Our marriage is stronger because my wife and I are stronger in faith and character. We are now fighting on the same side, holding each other up, encouraging each other. Don't get me wrong, we slip back into old patterns at times. But now that we've learned those hard lessons, we are quick to remember who we are and ask forgiveness.

We all have battle lines in our lives. But when God is fighting alongside us, we come out knowing that we are stronger, better people because of what we've overcome.

PRAYER

My Father, thank you for the wife you have given me and for using even my suffering to mold me into a better, stronger person. In Jesus' name, Amen.

Reach Out and Reach Up

*The God of all grace, who called you to his eternal glory
in Christ, after you have suffered a little while, will himself
restore you and make you strong, firm and steadfast.*

1 PETER 5:10

A friend confided in me that because of a bad choice he'd made, his marriage was over, and he had to step down as senior pastor. He was at the point of despair and considering ending his life. He was at a store looking at pistols when he got a call from a friend who knew about his circumstances and asked if they could meet. The pastor agreed.

The pastor's friend invited him to attend a Celebrate Recovery meeting. He reluctantly agreed. At an "open share group," he thought, *I'll never share like these guys! This isn't for me.* But God kept drawing him back, and finally the walls of his heart started to come down. He began to share his personal struggles and experience healing.

Today that pastor is whole again because someone cared enough to invite him to a meeting he didn't want to attend. He is now the ministry leader for a Celebrate Recovery group in a church that has opened its doors wide to embrace the hurting. It took an act of courage on the part of both men, but the result was a cycle of healing and wholeness. Sometimes God asks us to reach out, and sometimes he asks us to reach up. When we do, he always meets us with his redeeming grace and power.

PRAYER

Father, I was lost but you sent someone to show me the way. Give me the courage to reach out to others who are hurting. In Jesus' name, Amen.

Your Path

The path of the righteous is level; you, the Upright One,
you make the way of the righteous smooth.

ISAIAH 26:7

While in Colorado, my wife and I drove to the top of Mt. Evans, the highest paved road in the United States. The road did not have a shoulder or a middle line. What it did have were many narrow, hairpin curves. I was flooded with many emotions as we made our way to the top.

I felt a rush of nervousness each time I passed a car coming the other direction on the narrow road. The altitude made it difficult to breathe. The drop-offs were just plain scary. Then, at the summit, I experienced an overwhelming response to sheer beauty. All the other emotions were swallowed up in appreciation for what God had created.

Recovery can bring these same emotions to bear in our lives. We are often anxious about being able to stay away from those things that have proven to be bad for us. Sometimes all the change makes us feel like it's hard to breathe. It's scary knowing that one little slip can cause us to crash and burn. But when we reach that summit, that place where we can say, "Thank you, Father, for bringing healing and wholeness to my life," all the rest is quickly swallowed up in praise and thankfulness.

PRAYER

Oh Father, how my heart praises you for all you've done in my life. You've seen me through the anxious moments, the places where I had trouble getting my breath, and those times when I was really scared. Thank you. In Jesus' name, Amen.

Are You Listening?

*My dear brothers and sisters, take note of this: Everyone should
be quick to listen, slow to speak and slow to become angry.*

JAMES 1:19

You might be surprised to know that the average person speaks more
than 16,000 words per day! That's a lot of talking. No wonder it's
difficult for some of us to keep from monopolizing every conversation.

I have no idea how long it would take to verbalize 16,000 words, but I
can't help but think how different things would be if each of us spent half
that much time listening. Most of us are way more likely to be quick to
speak and slow to listen. Think about how much we must miss when we
are listening to our own voices most of the time.

I've often found myself, especially in recovery small groups, thinking about what I'm going to say as soon as I get a chance rather than
listening to what someone else has to say. Reflecting on those times, I
realize that I wasn't showing much love or respect to the person who was
talking. It may have even slowed my recovery.

We all need to practice the art of listening. I can think of three good
reasons: (1) We might learn something. (2) It's the polite and respectful
thing to do. (3) God's Word instructs us to do so.

Let's all make listening a priority by consciously turning on our listening ears and then testing ourselves by asking after each conversation,
"What did I learn from that person?"

PRAYER

*Father, help me to learn to listen to those around me, showing that I value each
person by valuing what that person has to say. In Jesus' name, Amen.*

Just Do It!

This day I call heaven and earth as witnesses against you that I have set before you life and death, blessings and curses. Now choose life, so that you and your children may live and that you may love the LORD your God, listen to his voice, and hold fast to him.

DEUTERONOMY 30:19–20

I love Deuteronomy 30. It's what I call the Nike text because it is where God says, "Just Do It." Essentially, he says this: "What I am telling you to do is not too hard when you stop and think about it. It's not in outer space, and it's not across the ocean. No, it's right here before you. You will have to make a choice, though, and I won't do that for you. But when you make the choice to follow me, you and your children will live, and I mean really live!"

God says, "When I set before you the opportunity to make the right choice, *just do it!* When you see the next right thing to do, *just do it!* What I'm offering you is a choice between life and death—now choose life!"

There will be opportunities to do both good and evil today, good which leads to life, evil which leads to death. It's a choice each of us will make. It's a lot easier to decide what we will do before we are faced with the actual choice.

PRAYER

Father, help me as I make critical choices today that will affect my life and the lives of those I love. I know you want only the best for me. In Jesus' name, Amen.

Doubting Thomas

He [Jesus] said to Thomas, "Put your finger here; see my hands. Reach out your hand and put it into my side. Stop doubting and believe."

JOHN 20:27

I feel bad for Thomas having to wear the label of "doubter" wherever he goes. All he wanted was some solid proof that Jesus had risen from the grave. He had heard the reports, but he wanted to see for himself.

Jesus answered his doubts by giving him the proof he needed. He held out his hands for Thomas, invited him to examine them carefully, to note the nail prints. Then he told Thomas to put his hand into the hole in his side where the Roman sword released the last of his lifeblood. He wasn't insulted; he didn't hide. Jesus allowed Thomas to face his doubts straight on and settle them once and for all.

Most of us have doubts from time to time, even those of us who have been believers for a while. Jesus isn't afraid to confront those doubts. He doesn't judge us for having them. Instead, he asks us to remember—just as he asked Thomas to remember the rusty nails and the sword—what God has done for us, how he has changed our lives. Remembering what God has done in our lives will chase away all doubt.

PRAYER

Thank you, Father, for making my life living proof that you are who you say you are. I am a witness to your power to rescue us from darkness and fill us with new life. In Jesus' name, Amen.

Living in the ER

"LORD, help!" they cried in their trouble, and he saved
them from their distress. He led them from the darkness
and deepest gloom; he snapped their chains.

PSALM 107:13–14 NLT

The other day I heard a friend teach on being powerless. As he spoke he placed on the stage three big cardboard boxes, each with a syllable of the word *powerless* written on it, forming an acrostic .

As I was looking at these boxes, I noticed how the letters break down. Think about this:

POW—when we try to live under our own power, we are in essence a *prisoner of war* and a slave to our junk.

ER—when we don't allow God to lead us in our lives, we live in a constant state of emergency, remaining in an emotional and dysfunctional *emergency room.*

LESS—I now know that when I recognize that I am not God and rely *less* on me and more on him, the foundation for my life change begins to take shape.

He not only has the *power* to help us recover, but he also cares, he is willing, he is more than able, and the best part—we matter to him. We don't have to live like *POWs*, in and out of the *er*, hoping each time that our wounds will be healed. We can all rely *less* on ourselves and more on him. We are *powerless* in our weakness, but with God's *power*, we can be made *strong*!

PRAYER

Lord God, I no longer want to live a powerless life. Help me to lock into your power
and receive the healing and wholeness you want for me. In Jesus' name, Amen.

Let It Out

Always be prepared to give an answer to everyone who asks you to give the reason for the hope that you have. But do this with gentleness and respect.

1 PETER 3:15

One Sunday morning, our Sunday school teacher asked who would like to quote a favorite Bible verse. My hand shot up immediately, and I said, "Hebrews 8:12—God forgives my wickedness and remembers my sins no more."

I was new to the class, but I was so excited that God had chosen to forgive and forget my past that I couldn't contain myself. When the teacher called on me, I quickly replied, "I just have to say it. I can't hold it in!"

Sometime later, one of the men who had been in the class that Sunday told me he had made the following remark to the person sitting next to him: "Wow, he sounds pretty fired up. But I bet that will be gone in a few years." Then he said, "But I can see I was wrong. You're *still* fired up!" And now, more than twenty-five years later, I'm fired up even more because I now know God has not only rescued me from my old destructive path, but he has also been faithful throughout the years to keep me on the right path, one that leads to hope and joy. I can't possibly keep it to myself.

No matter how good or bad we are, we are never good enough. God has to rescue every one of us. We should never keep that to ourselves.

PRAYER

Father, thank you for rescuing me and giving me a new start. I will be grateful for as long as I live and also for eternity. In Jesus' name, Amen.

Be Prepared

Fix these words of mine in your hearts and minds; tie them as symbols on your hands and bind them on your foreheads. Teach them to your children, talking about them when you sit at home and when you walk along the road, when you lie down and when you get up.

DEUTERONOMY 11:18−19

Every time my wife and I see some kind of disaster reported on the news, we go through the house to verify that we have all the supplies we need in case of a disaster in our area. We check to be sure that the flashlights have batteries, there's an adequate supply of food and water, and the first aid kit is stocked up and ready to go. We want to be sure that we're ready for any emergency.

Memorizing Scripture is like preparing for an emergency. Especially when we are in recovery, each one of us is going to go through tough times that will test our faith. Maybe we'll be faced with some big temptation or the consequences of someone else's bad choice. By fixing God's Word in our hearts and minds, we are ensuring that we are spiritually and mentally ready to come through victoriously.

Some people say that memorizing Scripture is too hard. They don't have a good memory. But God's Word has a force all its own that supersedes our natural ability to remember. If we apply ourselves, the Holy Spirit will help us to put God's words down deep in our spirits.

PRAYER

Lord God, as I apply myself to memorizing your Word, I pray that you would quicken my mind to take hold of and remember each verse. In Jesus' name, Amen.

Remembering Bag Phones

Jesus Christ is the same yesterday and today and forever.

HEBREWS 13:8

I remember when cell phones first came out. I was so excited to get one. It was one of those big old bulky phones—nothing like the cute little numbers we have today. Talk about heavy! It was a pain to lug around. My phone bill was huge due to roaming charges. Since then I've watched as phones have gotten smaller and smaller. Now some are no bigger than the palm of my hand.

But wait . . . phones are starting to get bigger again to accommodate bigger screens. Big to small, small to big. Change, change, change.

Through the years, we've watched many things change—our tastes, surroundings, cars, houses, hairstyles, and so on. But I'm glad there is one thing that will always stay the same. God says that he stays the same yesterday, today, and forever. He was, is, and will always be the great I AM. No, God does not change, but I do. I'm grateful for the change he has made in me.

Today, I acknowledge him as the great I AM. I am eager to praise his name for all the years I have left on this earth and for eternity as well. Let us thank him together for what he has done in each of our lives.

PRAYER

Father, I'm grateful for two things: that you do not change and that I am constantly changing as I become, by your power, more and more like you. In Jesus' name, Amen.

Let It Snow

Though we live in the world, we do not wage war as the world does.
The weapons we fight with are not the weapons of the world. On
the contrary, they have divine power to demolish strongholds.

2 CORINTHIANS 10:3–4

Where we live in Colorado, we get lots of snow, and we love it. Our grandkids come over to go sledding, have snowball fights, make snowmen, and eat snow ice cream. A few days ago, we all went over to our favorite sledding hill. We had more kids than sleds, so while some were sledding, the rest of us built a snowman.

We rolled and stacked our three giant snowballs, and then we gathered sticks for arms, grass for hair, and rocks for eyes. When we were finished, we stood back and admired our work—an awesome snowman more than four feet tall.

A week later I went back to the sledding hill. The warm sun had been shining, so all the snow was melted except for the snowman. He was still standing but was much smaller and much less awesome. A couple more days and he disappeared completely.

That snowman made me think about the strongholds that once controlled my life. Even after I came to Jesus, there were areas of my life that needed attention. Like the snowman, they stood strong and proud until exposure to the sun (or in this case, the Son!) brought them down to size. Once I started attending church and recovery meetings regularly, they melted away to nothing. It was the Son who did it!

PRAYER

Father, thank you for bringing down the strongholds I had built in my life. The light of your person keeps me free to worship you. In Jesus' name, Amen.

Encourage Others

Finally, brothers and sisters, rejoice! Strive for full restoration,
encourage one another, be of one mind, live in peace.
And the God of love and peace will be with you.

2 CORINTHIANS 13:11

My middle daughter, Chloe, is a fashion girl, and at all of six years old, she loves shoes, fancy dresses, and earrings. Yes, this could mean trouble. The other day Chloe and I went shopping. The idea was to have some "Daddy and daughter" time. We talked, laughed, and enjoyed being together. She told me about something that was happening at school with a friend and how she was handling it. I told her that I was proud of her and that I loved being her daddy.

I wish you could have seen her reaction. She sat up straight, her chin poked out, and she had a look in her eyes that I will not soon forget. I could see that my words meant a lot to her, more than any of the things we had purchased on our shopping trip.

This isn't something only children respond to. Everyone likes to hear encouraging words. They warm our hearts and help us to sort out the good images we have of ourselves from the bad. God has filled his Word, the Bible, with encouraging words that strengthen us and bring us life. We should all open it each day and read what our heavenly Father wants to say to us.

PRAYER

Lord, thank you for your encouraging words. I can't wait to hear that you love me and always will. In Jesus' name, Amen.

The Third Step

Therefore, I urge you, brothers, in view of God's mercy,
to offer your bodies as living sacrifices, holy and pleasing
to God—this is your spiritual act of worship.

ROMANS 12:1

One step at a time—that's how it's done! In the first step, we acknowledged that we were powerless over our addictions and compulsive behaviors. In Step 2, we came to believe that there is a power greater than ourselves who loves us and wants to restore us to wholeness. Those first two steps were so important they established a cause for action. Step 3 is our first action step.

Step 3: We made a decision to turn our lives and our wills over to the
care of God.

God has given each of us a precious gift: the freedom to choose. It was a risky proposition for him. He wanted us to choose good but knew we might choose evil. He wanted us to choose life, but what if we chose death? He wanted us to choose freedom but knew we might choose addiction. Still, it was a risk he was willing to take so that he would know this: when we ask him into our lives, it is because we have freely chosen to have him there.

The third step offers us the opportunity to choose to surrender our lives to God, an opportunity to choose freedom over our self-will, which always falls short of God's mark for us.

PRAYER

Lord God, thank you for giving me the power to choose. I see that it is a wonderful
gift. Help me use it in a way that is pleasing to you. In Jesus' name, Amen.

The Yellow Streak

The LORD said to Samuel, "Do not consider his appearance or his height,
for I have rejected him. The LORD does not look at the things people look at.
People look at the outward appearance, but the LORD looks at the heart."

1 SAMUEL 16:7

Last week I was driving down the interstate when I saw a bright yellow streak coming up behind me. As it passed me, I saw an emblem on the back that told me it was a Ferrari. I would have loved to have checked it out a little better, but it was traveling so fast that all I saw was a blur.

Ten miles down the road, I saw that Ferrari again. Only this time it didn't look so good. It had tangled with the guardrail. The driver was standing beside it, shaking his head. Fortunately, there were no passengers, and he didn't seem to be hurt.

As I rambled on down the road, I was reminded that no matter how good we look to others, we are all subject to a crash when we get reckless and don't keep our focus on God and the principles of his Word. It's always when we think nothing can stop us that suddenly something does, with painful consequences. We can seriously damage this beautiful new life God has given us if we fail to pay attention to the rules of the road.

PRAYER

Lord God, thank you for the amazing life you've given me. I will guard and protect it by living my life your way! In Jesus' name, Amen.

First Things First

I cry to you for help, Lord; in the morning my prayer comes before you.

PSALM 88:13

We all have trouble at times deciding what is important and what isn't. I look at my calendar and to-do list, and a lot of times I just freeze. Should I try to keep every appointment, make every meeting, complete every project? And what about being a good husband and father? When do I put my family first? And if I do all that, will my recovery suffer? Or should my recovery be the most important thing of all?

Weighing these choices and keeping them in place is stressful. They are all important, and there just aren't any general rules to help me sort it all out. When I can't decide, I put the choice in God's hands; I let him tell me where to start.

Spending the first early minutes of the morning with God, asking him to help us navigate through the known and the unknown in the hours ahead, will do more to get our priorities in place than hours of soul-searching and weighing our options.

God sees everything from start to finish, and his perspective is perfect in every way. He also knows all the facts about everything we might encounter on any given day. He knows us and our situation, our loved ones, our hopes and dreams, trials and temptations. When we add to that the fact that God wants us to succeed, we have everything to gain from those early sunrise moments with him.

PRAYER

Father, take charge of my schedule today. Help me to stay focused on you so that I can be the person you created me to be. In Jesus' name, Amen.

He Loves You Too Much

*"I will give you a new heart and put a new spirit in you; I will remove
from you your heart of stone and give you a heart of flesh."*

EZEKIEL 36:26

Our neighbor's dog was a sweetheart and everyone in the neighborhood loved her. But she had a talent for getting out of the yard. One
day, she managed to escape and was hit by a car, leaving her badly injured
and lying in a ditch. We rushed to help her, but as so often happens with
injured animals, she lashed out at us, growling, barking, and snapping.
The dog's owner wouldn't take no for an answer though. He pushed past
his dog's hostile response and took care of her—because he loved her.

I have had times in my life when I was the one lying in the gutter,
broken and hurting. God came to me there and pushed past my angry
and hostile reactions—because he loves me. In spite of my restless
behavior and my foolish protests, he stuck with me, healing, restoring,
and changing me.

God has big plans for me, too big to leave me lying in the gutter, lick-
ing my own wounds. He had a plan to get me back on my feet and make
me productive for his kingdom. He's given me a new heart and a new
spirit, and he'll never give up on me—because he loves me.

PRAYER

*Father, thank you for picking me up and putting me back on my feet. Thank you
for loving me so much that you helped me even when I fought against your loving
care. In Jesus' name, Amen.*

I'm Making Myself Sick

It is God who works in you to will and to act according to his good purpose. Do everything without complaining or arguing, so that you may become blameless and pure, children of God without fault in a crooked and depraved generation, in which you shine like stars in the universe.

PHILIPPIANS 2:13–15

Years ago I met a man who was in the late stages of alcoholism. I shared the simple story of Jesus and assured him that he could be forgiven of anything and everything he had ever done. The man responded quickly by asking Jesus to come into his life, forgive his sins, and become his Lord and Savior. Soon after he was baptized.

That man became a good friend, and the two of us spent a lot of time together. It was a privilege to watch him grow. But there was one thing, one stronghold in his life, that he continued to struggle with. He had a negative streak, and it made him unpleasant to be around.

Then one day he came to me and said, "I complain so much I make my own self sick." I was impressed. From that day on, my friend worked hard to establish an attitude of gratitude. He performed every task to the best of his ability without questioning or complaining. Soon he became a joy to be with.

Negativity is just one of the strongholds that can cause us to be isolated from others, just one of the issues that can impede our spiritual growth. But God is willing to reveal our flaws to us and help us to overcome them.

—— PRAYER ——

Father, show me those remaining strongholds in my life and help me to overcome them. In Jesus' name, Amen.

Forgiving Others

*Be kind and compassionate to one another, forgiving
each other, just as in Christ God forgave you.*

EPHESIANS 4:32

It isn't easy to forgive those who have hurt us. It feels wrong somehow, like we're perverting justice, letting those off the hook who deserve to pay for their actions. Looking at it another way, though, don't we want others to forgive us quickly when we do the wrong thing and harm someone in the process?

Jesus Christ is the greatest of all forgivers. He went to the cross and paid the debt for our sins, so that now we have been declared "not guilty." The Bible says that remembering how much we've been forgiven will always make the forgiveness process easier. Christ did not pervert justice, but satisfied it in its purest and most perfect state.

Like he always does, God teaches us, his children, by example. He knew we would struggle to forgive because our human nature is primarily self-serving. He knew the only way for us to free ourselves and others from the burden of unforgiveness would be to demonstrate it in a most spectacular way. When we remind ourselves what Jesus did, we can better accept what we must do.

PRAYER

Father, thank you for the forgiveness you have poured out on me. It is unearned in every way. Thank you for not giving me the pure justice I once thought I wanted. In Jesus' name, Amen.

Bobbing for Apples

*The wages of sin is death, but the gift of God is
eternal life in Christ Jesus our Lord.*

ROMANS 6:23

There are some things in life that I question. Like, why did God create asparagus? It's a vile weed that smells just as bad as it tastes. Or how about the game "bobbing for apples"? Really? I can remember as a little kid being grossed out by seeing kids open their mouths and plunge into a pool of bacteria. When my turn came around, I'd say, "Uh ... no thanks. I believe I'll pass."

Something else that baffles me is how much I listen to the enemy. I mean really, nothing he has to say is productive. "C'mon, doesn't that apple look juicy lying in that clear water?" Liar!

Adam and Eve learned how convincing Satan is, and it didn't turn out too well for them—or the rest of us for that matter! I like to remember that if I bob for apples with the devil, it won't end well. I won't change him, but he sure might change me. I understand how important it is for me to saturate myself in God's Word daily.

Staying in God's Word and being accountable and invested in healthy relationships allow Christ to help me discern a pool full of bacteria from God's life-giving water. The enemy can sure make that "apple" look good and enticing, but for me, it's not worth all the bacteria that comes with it. I choose God.

―――――――――― PRAYER ――――――――――

Father, help me to stay in your Word and keep my life free of sin. Fill me up with your life-giving water. In Jesus' name, Amen.

Cranberry Bagels

"I say to you: Ask and it will be given to you; seek and you will find; knock and the door will be opened to you. For everyone who asks receives; he who seeks finds; and to him who knocks, the door will be opened."

LUKE 11:9–10

Once we enter into relationship with God, the Bible tells us that he becomes our heavenly Father, and he invites us to come to him any time with our requests. But sometimes because of our past mistakes, we feel we should not ask him for anything—at least nothing too small or insignificant—until we've proven ourselves.

Of course, God answers our prayers in accordance with his own goodness, not ours, and he loves us despite our mistakes. I saw this principle at work a few weeks ago. On visits to see our kids, I have made it my habit to go out early in the morning, while everyone else is asleep, and pick up cranberry bagels. But on a recent visit, I had not yet done that. On the evening of the fourth day, I was saying good-night prayers with my two-year-old grandson. "Please help Papa get some bagels," he prayed. I hadn't realize how important this tradition had become to him.

Guess what was waiting for him the next morning? That's right, warm fresh bagels. It didn't matter how my grandson had acted since we'd arrived. He asked, and I responded. Our Father God is waiting to hear from us—from the biggest request to the smallest. When we reach out to him, he is always listening.

PRAYER

Father, thank you for always hearing my prayers. I'm so grateful for your love and your care. In Jesus' name, Amen.

Four Friends

When Jesus saw their faith, he said to the paralyzed
man, "Son, your sins are forgiven."

MARK 2:5

In chapter two of the gospel according to Mark, we read about an incident that happened when Jesus was teaching in someone's home. It was very crowded. Everyone wanted to see Jesus and touch him since they had heard news of his miracles. People not only filled the house but the yard as well. Four men heard that Jesus, the healer, would be there and had the idea to take a friend who was paralyzed. They felt certain that if they could get their friend in front of Jesus, something could be done for him.

Seeing that the doors and windows were blocked, they decided that they might be able to drop their friend down through the roof on a mat. And guess what, their crazy scheme worked! They peeled back the roofing and made a hole large enough to lower their friend down. Jesus, seeing their faith, immediately responded. He both forgave the man's sins and healed him.

That man was certainly fortunate to have four friends ready not only to take him to Jesus but also to fight to get him in front of the one person who could heal him. We all need to be that kind of friend because there are people all around us who need miracles. Let's keep our eyes open for opportunities to use our faith on behalf of others.

————— PRAYER —————

Thank you, Father, for showing me who it is that needs my help finding a miracle.
Show me how to bring that person to you. In Jesus' name, Amen.

Can You Help Me Fix This?

I trust in you, LORD; I say, "You are my God." My times are in your hands.

PSALM 31:14–15

So what's the problem?" the tow truck driver asked when he picked me up on the side of the road. "I don't have a clue," I told him. "Cars aren't exactly my *thing*." Fortunately the repair shop knew exactly what was wrong—the water pump—and they knew how to fix it too.

God has shown me that it's okay if I don't have all the answers. When I don't know what to do, he's teaching me to reach out to others who have the wisdom and understanding I need. This is one of those disciplines that can be difficult, especially when we are new in our recovery. Our pride tells us people will think we're weak and don't have it together. But once we get past that lie of the devil, we can see that reaching out for wisdom and counsel can help us avoid a world of additional messiness. Can you imagine me trying to fix my car on my own? I would create far more problems than I fixed.

Yes, I plan to keep on learning all the lessons God has for me. I admit it—I'm weak at times, I often don't have it all together. I know I need the Lord and all the friends he has given me. Those godly men and women in our lives are true treasures.

PRAYER

Thank you, Father, for those you have placed in my life to help me find answers when I need them. I know they are your gift to me. In Jesus' name, Amen.

Minor Surgery

We do not lose heart. Though outwardly we are wasting away, yet
inwardly we are being renewed day by day. For our light and momentary
troubles are achieving for us an eternal glory that far outweighs them
all. So we fix our eyes not on what is seen, but on what is unseen.
For what is seen is temporary, but what is unseen is eternal.

2 CORINTHIANS 4:16–18

It's only *minor* surgery when it's happening to someone else!" I don't know where I heard that, but it sure rings true with me. Our struggles may look small and insignificant to someone else, but when we're going through them, they always feel big and sometimes even overwhelming.

My sponsor used to say, "This too shall pass." I always disliked that statement because it made me feel like my struggle wasn't worth feeling bad about. I felt I had the right to complain when things weren't going well. Of course that was not all my wise sponsor and friend would say. He'd follow those words with "What are we going to do to work through this problem together?" That was his way of telling me that I had the right tools to find a solution, that he would be right there with me, and finally—he was right—that my problem really wouldn't be around forever; it would pass.

We all face struggles, and many of them are tough. But God has not left us to face them alone or unprepared. He's given us what we need to solve each problem and move on with our lives.

PRAYER

Lord God, when I'm facing a difficult situation, remind me to call on those people and principles you've placed in my life to help me come through victoriously. In Jesus' name, Amen.

I Got Money

*"His master replied, 'Well done, good and faithful servant! You
have been faithful with a few things; I will put you in charge of
many things. Come and share your master's happiness!'"*

MATTHEW 25:21

The other day my four year-old grandson came with my iPad in hand
and said, "Papa, we need to buy this new game."

"Those games cost money," I told him, "and besides, we have more
than enough games." He left with no argument, but I thought he might be
back. A few minutes later, he came with a coin purse filled with pennies.

"It's okay, Papa. I got the money!" he exclaimed.

That's when I realized I wasn't going to get off so easy. I explained
that it's not that I don't have the money but that it's not the best game for
him. And really we already have a lot of games. And we need to be good
stewards of what we already have.

We're all a little bit like that, aren't we? We see something we want,
and we ask for it. When we don't get it right away, we start thinking,
"Never mind. I can get it myself!" In fact, our Father hears every request.
The difference is that he's looking at the big picture, and we're seeing only
the here and now. He sees all the angles, and he knows what's best for us.

—————— PRAYER ——————

*I know it's true, Lord: You know what I need and what I don't need. Thank you
for always seeing what's best for me. In Jesus' name, Amen.*

Catch Me, Daddy

The eternal God is your refuge, and underneath are the everlasting arms.

DEUTERONOMY 33:27

When my kids were small, one of our favorite games was "Catch Me, Daddy." I would stand them on the sofa and say, "It's okay, son. I'll catch you." Then I'd step back and tell them to jump into my arms. The first few times they were always a little worried that I wouldn't catch them. But soon they became confident that I would be there as promised to swoop them up. "Catch me, Daddy," they would say. As a dad, it was a joy for me to hold them in my arms after their step of faith and trust in me.

Remembering this sweet game reminds me that God is always there to catch me when things get tough in my life. I am confident that my heavenly Father has mighty arms willing and ready to catch me at a moment's notice. All I have to do is call out to him, "Catch me, Daddy," and he will be there.

God is delighted when his children demonstrate their faith and trust in his loving-kindness, in his faithfulness, in his unfailing promise to be there when we need him. There is nothing sweeter than his mighty and protective arms around us. The first few times might take some courage as we learn to trust him. But soon we gain confidence in his promise: he will always be there.

PRAYER

Thank you, Lord, for catching me in your mighty and protective arms whenever I take a leap of faith. In Jesus' name, Amen.

My Mind Told Me

*Since, then, you have been raised with Christ, set your hearts on
things above, where Christ is seated at the right hand of God. Set
your minds on things above, not on earthly things. For you died, and
your life is now hidden with Christ in God. When Christ, who is
your life, appears, then you also will appear with him in glory.*

COLOSSIANS 3:1–4

O ur daughter came over with one of our grandsons in tow and asked
to borrow a pair of tweezers. She needed to remove a piece of paper
our grandson had rolled up and stuck in his ear! When asked why he
did such a thing, he answered, "My mind told me to." Wow! At six years
of age his mind is already suggesting things that are definitely *not* in his
best interest.

Frankly, that's why most of us are in recovery. We are losing the battle that goes on between our ears. We haven't learned to make the right
choice when our minds are in conflict with our hearts. We learn that
lesson only by listening to God, reading his Word, and filling our minds
with things that are good, positive, and beneficial.

Of course it's *still* a battle. It will *always* be a battle! But it's a battle
we are sure to win if we've trained our minds to know when something
doesn't line up with God's principles.

I can't lie, my mind still tells me to do stuff—it's just that now I know
when to listen and when to just say no.

PRAYER

*Father, you are always looking out for me, always showing me the right way to go.
Thank you for loving me with such a great and amazing love. In Jesus' name, Amen.*

Four Questions

*See what great love the Father has lavished on us, that we should
be called children of God! And that is what we are! The reason
the world does not know us is that it did not know him.*

1 JOHN 3:1

Every night, when I tuck my kids into bed, I ask them the same four questions. It goes like this:

"How big do I love you?"

"Huge!"

"How long will I love you?"

"Forever and ever."

"Well, what could make me stop?"

"Nothing!"

"Why not?"

"Because you're our daddy, and nothing could make you stop."

They are right, of course. I don't love them because they are good, and I don't stop loving them because they are sometimes bad. I don't love them because of anything they have done, but simply because they are my children.

God feels that way about all of us who have surrendered to him and call him Father. He loves us just because we are his children. We can't earn his love, and we can't lose it either. It's in his heart to love us, just as it's in my heart to love my children.

— PRAYER —

*Father in heaven, thank you for making me your child and loving me with a love so
big that I cannot describe it or comprehend it. In Jesus' name, Amen.*

Clear Mind, Clean Heart

Do not conform to the pattern of this world, but be transformed
by the renewing of your mind. Then you will be able to test and
approve what God's will is—his good, pleasing and perfect will.

ROMANS 12:2

Once we've made progress, how can we keep from slipping back into old habits? Are there things we can do to preserve the work we've put into changing our lives for the better? I believe these three things will help us remain strong on our journey:

Maintain a clear mind. To do this, we must empty the trash in our minds and fill the empty places with good things from God's Word. "Those who live according to the flesh have their minds set on what the flesh desires; but those who live in accordance with the Spirit have their minds set on what the Spirit desires" (Rom. 8:5).

Maintain a clean heart. This means no more secrets. We strive to live openly before God and others. "Wisdom will enter your heart, and knowledge will be pleasant to your soul" (Prov. 2:10).

Maintain an awareness of God's love. This is the most important thing of all. There is no hope of spiritual growth or lasting wholeness without an understanding of God's great power and love for us. "The thief comes only to steal and kill and destroy; I have come that they may have life, and have it to the full" (John 10:10).

If we have a clear mind, a clean heart, and an awareness of God's love, we can't lose!

PRAYER

Father, help me maintain a clear mind and a clean heart. I would be nothing with-
out your love, but with it, I am a winner! In Jesus' name, Amen.

What God Can Do

Carry each other's burdens, and in this way you will fulfill the law of Christ.

GALATIANS 6:2

I led a friend of mine to Jesus and then became his sponsor for more than ten years. I was heartbroken when he went back to his old lifestyle. He lost everything—his leadership position, relationships, business, possessions, everything. I hadn't heard from him in a year, and I was concerned that he might not make it back. Yesterday I told my wife I wished my friend would call and let me know if he's okay.

That very morning, I received this phone message: "Just wanted to call to tell you how sorry I am and ask for your forgiveness. Some phone numbers can never be forgotten and yours will always be close to my heart. My wife and I are rebuilding our marriage, and I am going to a Celebrate Recovery group and just listening."

God is so good, isn't he? Of course, I let my friend know right away that I would love to hear from him, and as for the forgiveness—it's done!

My sponsor told me years ago to never give up on anyone as long as they are still breathing. What wise advice! We never know what God is going to do in someone's life. The situation might seem altogether hopeless, but our God is a God of miracles, a God of restoration, a God of new beginnings.

PRAYER

Thank you, Father, for restoring and rebuilding so many lives. Some are precious to me, but all are precious to you. In Jesus' name, Amen.

Fruit of the Spirit

*The fruit of the Spirit is love, joy, peace, forbearance, kindness,
goodness, faithfulness, gentleness and self-control.*

GALATIANS 5:22–23

In recovery and in life, how do we know we are making progress? The best way is to check ourselves daily to see if the fruit of the Spirit can be seen in our lives. At the end of each day, we should ask ourselves these questions:

Was I loving toward anyone today? Did anyone see God's love in my life? If so, how? If not, why not? Was I joyful today? How did I respond in situations that tested my joy? How is my serenity? Did I allow anything to steal my peace? Was I patient with others today? Did anything cause me to lose my patience? How kind was I today? Did I act in an unkind way toward anyone? Could I describe this day as "good"? Have I demonstrated God's goodness to others? How was my faith today? Did I act unfaithfully? How was my gentleness? If I needed to have a confrontation, was I gentle? How was my self-control? Did I give in to something instead of standing firm?

Answering these questions might take some time at first, but soon they will become second nature to us, inspiring godly behavior and healthy habits.

PRAYER

Father, more than anything, I want your Holy Spirit to rule in my life, helping me to produce godly fruit that is pleasing to you. In Jesus' name, Amen.

Daddy, I'm Scared

*Let him have all your worries and cares, for he is always thinking
about you and watching everything that concerns you.*

I PETER 5:7 TLB

A few years ago, my young daughter insisted on riding a gigantic roller coaster at Sea World. She had never ridden a roller coaster of any size before, so I tried to talk her out of it. But she was determined that she was ready.

She was all smiles as we stepped into the seats, buckled up, and waited for the upward climb. But the higher we got, the more concerned she looked. She began to lose a little color in her face as we began the climb, and her nervousness spiked as we neared the top. Just before we began the descent, I saw fear in her eyes, so I leaned into her, held her hand, and said as calmly as I could, "Daddy has you, sweetie. You don't need to be afraid. I'm here." I will never forget the rest of the ride—she did not enjoy a single moment of it! Afterward, she felt sick for the rest of the day.

When we face life's trials and scary roller coaster moments, we can feel confident that our Daddy, the Abba Father, is leaning into us, holding our hand, and saying, "Daddy has you; don't be afraid. I am here." Even when we find ourselves in situations of our own choosing, circumstances we weren't quite ready for, he is there taking the ride right along with us because of his great love for us.

PRAYER

Heavenly Father, thank you for holding my hand as I face the challenges in my life. Thank you for loving me constantly and unconditionally. In Jesus' name, Amen.

Never Too Old

By dying to what once bound us, we have been released
from the law so that we serve in the new way of the Spirit,
and not in the old way of the written code.

ROMANS 7:6

A couple in their seventies started coming to our Celebrate Recovery. One night I asked what brought them to the program. This is what the husband told me: "The people my wife and I see coming into the church because of Celebrate Recovery are the people we tried to run out of the church for years. But one day it hit me: these are the very people Jesus spent time with! We've decided to make these meetings a regular part of our week. If these are the people Jesus chose to fellowship with, then they ought to be the people we fellowship with too!"

Not long after he shared this revelation with me, this man passed away. But until the day he went home to be with Jesus, I don't believe he ever missed a meeting. Several months after his passing, the man's wife called me to say she was selling their home and moving in with her kids. She wondered if our recovery house could use their dishes, pots, and pans, since she would no longer be needing them. Of course I told her that would be great.

I was touched to realize that even in her time of grief, she was serving others instead of running them off. God is more than able to change our hearts—at any age!

PRAYER

Thank you, Father, for those who learn your ways and remain faithful. In Jesus' name, Amen.

Stored Away

Let us examine our ways and test them, and let us return to the LORD.

LAMENTATIONS 3:40

My garage is a mess. Old boxes, broken toys, tools that haven't been put away. You name it. Our Christmas decorations are mixed in with our Fourth of July stuff, which is mixed in with the things we put out for fall. We have dusty guitars, spare tires, books, photographs, and things we brought from our last move almost a decade ago, still in packing boxes. I'm tempted at times to call one of those services to come and haul all that junk away. But if I did that, we would lose all the good stuff along with the worthless and obsolete.

Lots of times when we begin taking a spiritual inventory, we are tempted to call our whole lives junk, just dismiss it all. But none of us is made up of only bad, or only good, character traits. We all have things we like about ourselves and things we aren't at all proud of.

A spiritual inventory should take note of everything—the good and the bad. There is reason to be encouraged by the qualities we like in ourselves. If we can't really think of anything good, we can ask our friends to point them out for us. The important thing is that we recognize that in every life, there are some jewels buried in there with all the junk.

PRAYER

Lord God, thank you for helping me to rightly appraise myself and rejoice in what is good. In Jesus' name, Amen.

Do You Feel Defeated?

My enemy will say, "I have overcome him," and my foes will rejoice
when I fall. But I trust in your unfailing love; my heart rejoices in your
salvation. I will sing to the LORD, for he has been good to me.

PSALM 13:4–6

There will be days on our journey to recovery when we will feel lost, abandoned, even defeated. There are three primary reasons why this happens.

1. Recovery isn't easy! No one ever said it would be. We may have been living with our hurts, hang-ups, or habits for years. We can't expect all that to change overnight!
2. The enemy does not want us to change. Our free will and Satan's lies are what got us into trouble in the first place!
3. We may be neglecting to work the program, missing meetings, flirting with temptation, failing to reach out to our sponsors and accountability teams. The program works only when we work it.

When we feel defeated. When we feel like giving up. When we feel like running back to those hurts, hang-ups, or habits. That's when we need to run to our Higher Power instead. Only God can give us the strength to battle on until we've overcome. I love what our great former President Ronald Reagan said: "We are never defeated, unless we give up on God."

PRAYER

Heavenly Father, you are my Higher Power, the only one who can change my destiny from defeat to victory. Thank you for never giving up on me. I promise never to give up on you or the work you're doing in my life. In Jesus' name, Amen.

New Habits

Since through God's mercy we have this ministry, we do not lose heart.
Rather, we have renounced secret and shameful ways; we do not use deception,
nor do we distort the word of God. On the contrary, by setting forth the truth
plainly we commend ourselves to every man's conscience in the sight of God.

2 CORINTHIANS 4:1–2

When I hear the word *habits*, the first thing that comes to mind is "bad" habits, such as those things we do in secret, things that bring shame to our lives and the lives of those we love. In fact, though, habits can also be good. In recovery, one of the most important things we do is learn new habits, good habits. We learn to pray, study our Bibles, faithfully attend meetings, keep our word, and show kindness to our church family.

Establishing good habits is a process that begins with a decision. Our thoughts—which are made known through our words—move us to action, which brings about and forms new habits.

We can start the process at any time. We decide on something like reading the Bible every day. We've already thought it; now we can put it into words by telling someone else what we're doing. Then we set a time to take action. It takes only about 21 days to turn that action into a habit. So what are we waiting for?

— PRAYER —

Father, help me as I resolve today to add a good habit to my life. In Jesus' name, Amen.

Work in Progress

*Being confident of this, that he who began a good work in you
will carry it on to completion until the day of Christ Jesus.*

PHILIPPIANS 1:6

We all have days when we don't feel well, we're tired, we're frustrated. We wonder if we're making progress in our lives, if change is coming fast enough. Sometimes we're just plain in a slump, feeling like throwing in the towel and giving up.

When we feel like this, when we are wondering if we will ever be free from our hurts, hang-ups, and habits, we need to be reminded that God is in charge of the good work that is taking place in us. He's the contractor. When we give in to negative thoughts and feelings, we are saying that God isn't doing his job well enough or fast enough.

So since the work in us is God's doing, we can best find out what he thinks by reading his Word, the Bible. As his words bless and encourage us, the negative thoughts and feelings are sure to flee. Feelings, thoughts, they aren't reliable anyway. But God's words certainly are. If we want to know what's really going on, where we are in the process of recovery, we can get those answers only from God.

PRAYER

Father, when I'm tempted to think negatively and wallow in self-pity, help me to remember that you are the one who is at work in my life and you aren't finished with me yet. In Jesus' name, Amen.

The Stains

"Come now, let us reason together," says the LORD. "Though
your sins are like scarlet, they shall be as white as snow;
though they are red as crimson, they shall be like wool."

ISAIAH 1:18

Mr. Grant owned several rental properties. As a teenager, I would get jobs from him: yard work, painting, or cleaning. I was grateful, but I despised the painting. Sometimes Mr. Grant would come through to check my work and notice that it hadn't been completed correctly. He was always gracious about it. "Do you see the old stains showing through there?" he would ask. I'd act surprised for a few moments, pretending I hadn't seen them. But eventually I would give in and finish the job right.

In some ways our lives can be compared to those painted walls. We know the old stains are there, but when God points them out to us in his gracious way, we act surprised, pretending that we don't see them.

God isn't fooled. He knows we must admit that the stains are there before we can get rid of them. I can almost see him smiling and saying, "Okay, now let's get to work. I want to help you get rid of those stains so that one day you can help others get rid of theirs."

God can and will cleanse our stains. Our part is to acknowledge them and work to be made whole.

PRAYER

Heavenly Father, I offer the stains of my past to you. Cleanse me, and help me to help others get rid of their stains as well. In Jesus' name, Amen.

No One Walks Alone

I thank my God every time I remember you. In all my
prayers for all of you, I always pray with joy because of your
partnership in the gospel from the first day until now.

PHILIPPIANS 1:3–5

Last week, I took two of my grandsons to an indoor playground at the local recreation center. Very exciting! I noticed something interesting, though. Even though they didn't know a single kid there and would probably never see these kids again, they started right away to make friends by being friendly in a number of little ways.

They would suggest a race to the slide but look back to make sure they weren't getting too far ahead of their new friend. If they were, they'd slow down and allow the other kid to catch up. If one of the kids got hurt, they would stop what they were doing and gather round to show their support. In other words, they did what friends do, and they did it instinctively.

We will all meet people this week—at church, meetings, school functions, sporting events, etc. All around us there are people who are hurting to one degree or another and are looking for hope. Maybe they just need a kind word or a smiling face or a show of concern—those little signs of friendliness. Sometimes we even have a chance to share what God has done in our lives. Let's be ready to reach out to everyone God places on our path. All it takes is a little friendliness.

—— PRAYER ——

Father, friendship is one of the things you offer us when we come into relationship
with you. Show us how to be friendly to those around us. In Jesus' name, Amen.

Breaking the Silence

*Trust in the LORD with all your heart and lean not on
your own understanding; in all your ways submit to
him, and he will make your paths straight.*

PROVERBS 3:5–6

I just don't see how sitting around talking about my problems without anyone saying anything back is going to help." That's what one of the frustrated members of our step group said last week. I completely understood what he meant. One of the things that seems strange about Celebrate Recovery at first is that we don't offer advice or what we call "cross talk," that is, feedback on the sharing that happens in group. We're used to people responding and giving advice, but soon we realize that there are two very important things going on: We are breaking the silence first by sharing, then by relating to others through listening.

Breaking the silence is so important, because the things we can't talk about own us. When we share openly, the power of those secrets over our lives is broken. Because no one can reply, we don't have to worry about being corrected or judged. We get to express what is in our hearts without fear.

As we listen without speaking, we realize how many things we all have in common. We are able to relate to people we might have shied away from before. We begin to see how God is working in other lives, giving us hope that he can work in ours as well. We are not alone.

—— PRAYER ——

Lord, thank you for the wisdom that allows me to open up and gain strength from others. In Jesus' name, Amen.

Dry Sponges

*Dear children, let us not love with words or
tongue but with actions and in truth.*

1 JOHN 3:18

One way to think about the recovery process is to imagine what
water does to a dry sponge. We come into the process dried up and
thirsting for life. We've tried other things, but so far nothing has helped.
We have come to the realization that no one but our Creator is going to
be able to provide what we so desperately need.

In the same way a dry sponge soaks up all the water it is exposed to,
the Celebrate Recovery process allows us to soak up God's peace, love,
grace, and forgiveness. Oh, how good that feels when our dry spirits soak
up all that life-giving water! Eventually, though, we reach our saturation
point. We can't hold any more until we allow ourselves to be wrung out
on those around us through our service. Then we can soak up more. This
is a healthy process, because—as we all know—a waterlogged sponge
left on the counter for a few days will begin to stink.

The old saying "You can't keep it unless you give it away" is right.
This is why service is so important. If we come into the process, soak
up God's goodness, then fail to give back, we'll soon be like that waterlogged sponge: we become rancid and begin to smell. God's way is to fill
us, wring us out, and fill us again.

PRAYER

*Holy Father, I love to feel your life-giving Spirit flowing within me. Remind me
to stay fresh and healthy by sharing with others what you've given to me. In Jesus'
name, Amen.*

No Stone Unturned

*Jesus replied, "No one who puts a hand to the plow and
looks back is fit for service in the kingdom of God."*

LUKE 9:62

My four-year-old grandson is an avid bug catcher! He spends hours in the rock garden turning over every stone, looking for roly-polies or other tiny, buglike creatures. He's extremely focused, and should one of us wander into the yard while he's bug hunting, he's happy to enlist our help with his mission.

As I noted my grandson's devotion to bug catching, I realized an important truth: If we're not willing to turn over every stone in our search for wholeness, we may miss some of the treasures God has waiting for us. He loves to reward our hard work with unexpected blessings, but we won't find them unless we are searching diligently.

In recovery, it's not enough to just get by. To find true peace, healing, forgiveness, courage, and all the rest that wholeness provides, we must stay focused and dedicated at all times. We have to be willing to use all the resources God has provided and call on every person we know to help us. We have to be all-in. Like my grandson, we have to turn over every stone.

PRAYER

*Heavenly Father, put a passion and fire in my heart to fully commit to my recovery
and find every unexpected blessing you have for me. In Jesus' name, Amen.*

Growing Up

When I was a child, I talked like a child, I thought like a child, I reasoned like a child. When I became a man, I put childish ways behind me.

1 CORINTHIANS 13:11

Our middle daughter is having a birthday today. She's seven going on seventeen. We're celebrating the event by playing hooky and heading to an amusement park. I love days like this. Now I realize there have been six birthdays before this one, but it seems like I blinked and my tiny little daughter became a first grader. Where does the time go?

Like lots of parents, I've spent a lot of time lately looking at my daughter's baby pictures and remembering some of the special moments. It might seem like all those days went by in a blur, but we actually lived each one. And some of them, like when we were seriously sleep-deprived, seemed to last an eternity.

It can feel like that in recovery at times. We finish our steps and wonder where the time went, but then we remember back to days, even weeks, when we felt like we were making no progress at all. We felt stuck. Now, though, we can see that we have become more like Jesus in how we react to adversity, love people who are unlovely, and see things from a better perspective.

PRAYER

Father, thank you for seeing me through and reminding me that you have been here with me all the way. In Jesus' name, Amen.

The Fourth Step

Let us examine our ways and test them, and let us return to the LORD.

LAMENTATIONS 3:40

Now that our feet are moving, we're ready to get to work. The fourth step begins the cleanup process. In Steps 2 and 3, we assessed our condition, made changes in our thinking, and decided to surrender our lives to God, our Higher Power. To use a simple analogy, we have discovered and acknowledged that we have tooth decay. We have decided to do something about it, and now we are ready to start chipping away at the decay brought on by our past mistakes. This decay has built up over the years and kept us from seeing the truth about our past and present situations.

Step 4: We made a searching and fearless moral inventory of ourselves.

The fourth step requires us to free ourselves from denial and face our secrets. As we chip away at the decay, we are faced with the truth about ourselves and others. It can be frightening, unsettling, uncomfortable, but God doesn't expect us to go through it alone. Because we've invited him, he is there with us, whispering words of comfort and encouragement.

We've come a long way already, and we've learned that every step is a victory in and of itself. Recovery is tough because it requires us to face harsh truths, but the truth always sets us free.

PRAYER

Father, I want to be free to serve you with all my heart and soul and mind, but I'm afraid of what lies ahead on the path. Thank you for your promise never to leave me. In Jesus' name, Amen.

The Whole Truth

*Do not lie to each other, since you have taken off your old self
with its practices and have put on the new self, which is being
renewed in knowledge in the image of its Creator.*

COLOSSIANS 3:9–10

I recently heard an ad on the radio in which a certain company was talking about their high level of success making predictions in the financial world. Their first five predictions had come true, and for that reason, we were being urged to act quickly on their next prediction. If we wanted to make money and not lose what we had, all we had to do was buy into their pitch and act on the truth—as they had presented it.

I think we all do that sometimes: we want people to buy into the truth as we present it. Trouble is, like the radio ad, what we present is often just a half-truth. And make no mistake, a half-truth is—and always will be—a whole lie. Isn't that what we learn in Celebrate Recovery? Aren't we challenged to change our lives to fit the truth rather than changing the truth to fit our lives?

In fact, there is no such thing as a half-truth or a little white lie or even stretching the truth. We either speak the truth, live by the truth, believe the truth—or we don't. It's that simple. That might be the most important lesson of all, because until we learn to live by the truth, we will never be completely whole.

PRAYER

*Lord, I understand that my new life must be built on truth, the whole truth. Show
me how to reject the half-truths and live wholly for you. In Jesus' name, Amen.*

The Trouble with Grudges

*"Forgive us our debts, as we also have forgiven our debtors. And
lead us not into temptation, but deliver us from the evil one."*

MATTHEW 6:12–13

The only possible way we could avoid being hurt by others would be to live completely alone. As long as there is more than one person, hurts will happen. They are the cutting edge of every relationship. We can't keep ourselves from getting hurt from time to time, but we can control our reactions. And that is seriously important.

One of the ways we often react to hurt is by bottling up the resentment until it becomes a grudge. We reason that as long as we hold on to that hurt, the person who hurt us isn't getting away with it. Unfortunately, those who hurt us are often unaware, and we end up harboring a grudge that only keeps us from healing.

Revenge is another way we might react to being hurt. We feel sure that getting even, hurting back as much as we've been hurt, will relieve the pain and satisfy our longing for justice. Instead, revenge just poisons our souls and keeps us focused on the past.

The only sure way to get rid of a hurt is to forgive the one who hurt us. By forgiving, we call the debt settled, and it no longer has power over our lives. No wonder God asks us to forgive. He knows it will always be for our good.

PRAYER

Thank you for helping me to forgive those who have hurt me. I can see that holding grudges and seeking revenge only keep me anchored to the past. In Jesus' name, Amen.

Drying Out the Mold

*Whoever lives by the truth comes into the light, so that it may be
seen plainly that what he has done has been done through God.*

JOHN 3:21

Mold thrives in dark places. Expose it to the light, and it dries up. Sin is like that too. I remember those days when I used to hide. I hid my addictions, my emotions, my pain, and my struggles. It's exhausting to always be in hiding. The enemy likes it because he wants sin to thrive in our lives. He knows that if sin is brought out into the light, it will soon dry up.

The tools we learned to use during recovery can help us keep our sin exposed and dealt with. Two principles are especially important.

1. Reserve a daily time with God for self-examination, Bible reading, and prayer. That is how we know God and his will for our lives, as well as gain the power to follow his will.
2. Yield to God to be used to bring this Good News to others, both by example and by words.

We must never try to hide our sin. Adam and Eve tried that, and it cost them everything: the Garden they called home and, especially, their sweet fellowship with their Creator. It's simple really. Mold thrives in the darkness but dries when exposed to the light. In the same way, we must not allow sin to thrive in our lives, but instead, expose it and deal with it.

--- PRAYER ---

*Lord, I know it is human nature to think that I can hide my sin from you, but you
see all, even the darkest places in my life. Expose all that I am to your healing light.
In Jesus' name, Amen.*

One at a Time

No temptation has seized you except what is common to man.
And God is faithful; he will not let you be tempted beyond
what you can bear. But when you are tempted, he will also
provide a way out so that you can stand up under it.

1 CORINTHIANS 10:13

My grandson came into the kitchen and asked for his vitamins. He loves them because they taste like candy. He is allowed to have two, and we let him reach in the bottle and get them himself, one at a time. On that day, however, he decided to get a whole handful. Guess what? He couldn't get his fist out of the jar, creating a dilemma. He could hold onto the handful and get nothing, or let go and get the two he is allowed to have, one at a time. After a little convincing, he made the right choice.

In recovery, balance is key. Even trying to do too many *good* things can end in disaster. If we get so busy doing good things that we neglect our families or cut back on our fellowship time with God, we have done harm to ourselves and those we love. Of course God has things for all of us to do, good acts of service for his kingdom, but we can't just grab them up all at once. Doing that might cause us to get sidetracked, bringing the work of recovery, spiritual growth, and caring for family to a stop.

I know it's hard to say no when people ask us to get involved. Just remember, we don't have to say no to everything. Balance is the key.

PRAYER

Father, thank you for your wisdom that keeps my life balanced and moving forward. In Jesus' name, Amen.

Guard My Words

Set a guard over my mouth, O Lord; keep watch over the door of my lips.

PSALM 141:3

I have to confess, I don't always react well to certain situations. I speak before I think things all the way through, and I often say things I don't mean, wishing I could take them back. Unfortunately, I often do this with my children. When one of them disobeys, I'm likely to say something like, "Okay. Fine. You don't want to share with your sister? I'll just take away all of your toys." I know I'm not going to do that, and so do they. It's an empty threat.

When we admit our powerlessness, we see that our powerlessness doesn't apply just to our hurts, hang-ups, and habits, but to pretty much every area of our lives, even our tongues. We like to think we are in control of our words, but let something surprise us and the truth soon comes out.

That doesn't mean that we should say anything we want and then just say, "Hey, don't get mad at me—I'm powerless!" Instead we should ask God to help us with our words, just as we surrender other areas of our lives to him. We can ask him, like the psalmist did, to guard our mouths—helping us not to make promises we can't keep, or say things that are untrue or hurtful. If God is truly in charge of our lives, he should certainly be in charge of what we say as much as what we do.

PRAYER

Heavenly Father, thank you for helping me take control over my words. I know that they can be used as weapons to hurt others. Use mine instead to bless others. In Jesus' name, Amen.

Empty Promises

"Happy are those whose greatest desire is to do what God requires."

MATTHEW 5:6 GNT

Have you noticed those photos on Facebook that ask you to do something? I saw one depicting sharks in a lobby. It said, "Click on photo, hit 'Like,' type the number 2, then watch what happens." Guess what? Nothing happened. What is remarkable is that several thousand people did the same thing.

Isn't that so much like what the enemy does in our lives? We are given empty promises of hope and satisfaction only to be disappointed with nothing but emptiness.

In the past, I was always looking for happiness. I'd happen on some new thing and declare, "This is it!" A new car, new clothes, new house, etc. But soon I'd be searching frantically for something else.

I love how Pastor Rick Warren puts it: "What happens outwardly in your life is not as important as what happens inside you." In Celebrate Recovery, we learn that true happiness comes only from God. The Beatitudes in the book of Matthew tell us that we are happy and blessed when we commit our lives to him. This is a new kind of happiness, the kind that has nothing to do with external circumstances.

We're too smart to keep getting duped by empty promises. I've given my heart to the only true source of happiness—the God who loves me.

PRAYER

Father, I'm through following empty promises. Instead, I will rejoice in your constant goodness and grace. In Jesus' name, Amen.

One Corner at a Time

*Whatever you do, work at it with all your heart, as working for the
Lord, not for men, since you know that you will receive an inheritance
from the Lord as a reward. It is the Lord Christ you are serving.*

COLOSSIANS 3:23–24

Our family cabinet shop can get pretty messy, especially when big
orders come in. After one particularly big job, the shop was in a
horrendous mess. I told one of our new employees to start cleaning up in
preparation for the next job. He looked at me, then he looked back at the
shop and said, "That will take forever!"

Everybody who works in our shop is in recovery. And since he was
new to the shop and new to recovery, I thought this would be a good
teaching moment. I replied, "I'll tell you what. Start in that corner and
clean up a 30-by-30-foot area, and when you finish that, start on the next
one." After two hours, he came into the office with a big grin on his face
and exclaimed, "All done, Boss!"

I told him that the shop is like our lives. We come in with a bunch of
problems, too many to tackle all at once. We get the job done by working
on one problem at a time and doing it to the best of our ability.

PRAYER

*Lord, help me not to be overwhelmed by what it will take to clean up my life,
but to take one thing at a time and do it in a way that is pleasing to you. In Jesus'
name, Amen.*

Guilt and Shame

*Godly sorrow brings repentance that leads to salvation and
leaves no regret, but worldly sorrow brings death.*

2 CORINTHIANS 7:10

Most people think that the words *guilt* and *shame* mean the same thing. But in fact, they are very different, and they bring different outcomes in our lives. Guilt is what Paul called "godly sorrow" because it's the feeling we get when we've done something wrong. God uses guilt to bring about repentance in our lives. Repentance means that we agree with God and have come clean about our mistakes. When we repent, we are telling God we don't want to continue doing something unpleasing to him and are asking him to help us stop. It doesn't mean we are perfect, but it does mean we have taken action to be right with God.

Shame, on the other hand, is worldly sorrow. Shame says there is something wrong with us. Sometimes we heap it on ourselves; other times it's put on us by others. Shame is unlike guilt in that it doesn't lead us to repentance. Instead of drawing us closer to God, it causes us to walk away from him. Shame says, "You're not good enough."

When we do the wrong thing, God's Spirit will convict us of our wrongdoing. He will lovingly guide us back to a relationship with him. Once we repent of our sin, he forgives us and the guilt goes away. Christ died for that sin. He covered it. We don't have to hold on to it anymore and feel ashamed.

PRAYER

Lord God, thank you for showing me how to deal with the guilt in my life. And thank you for showing me that shame has no place in my relationship with you. In Jesus' name, Amen.

Establishing a Beachhead

Freedom is what we have—Christ has set us free! Stand, then, as free people.

GALATIANS 5:1 GNT

In Celebrate Recovery, we are taught this principle: "I consciously choose to commit all my life and will to Christ's care and control." In other words, we are asked to make a choice, followed by a decision, which initiates a process.

Phase 1 of that process is for God to soften up our pride, fears, worries, and doubts by helping us consistently look to someone beyond ourselves. After that, he helps us establish a beachhead, a fortified position on a beach from which an attack on the mainland can be launched. In this way, God establishes a presence in our lives, a beachhead from which he can liberate us from our hurts, hang-ups, and habits.

The enemy works in a similar manner. He comes in and slowly softens us up with seemingly minor things: an inappropriate thought or a temptation to go back and visit unhealthy friends. Then he attempts to establish a beachhead, an active presence in our lives.

We choose who will control our minds and hearts. If it isn't God, it will be the enemy, who is committed to destroying us. That's the way it is in battle. Foolish choices can cost us our lives. Let's wise up and keep our eyes focused on healing and wholeness.

PRAYER

Father God, thank you for reminding me that I'm in a battle with the enemy of my soul. I choose to establish your presence in my life. In Jesus' name, Amen.

Ongoing Inventory

If you think you are standing firm, be careful that you don't fall!

1 CORINTHIANS 10:12

My wife was asleep in the car as we were returning from a trip. The cars in front of me suddenly slowed down, but I wasn't paying attention. Overcompensating for my late reaction, I put on the brakes a lot more aggressively than I should have. My wife was jerked awake, catapulted forward, and suddenly stopped by her seatbelt. She responded by shouting in fear, "What in the world are you doing?" I snapped right back at her, "Go back to sleep. I've got this under control!"

As soon as I said the words, I knew I had a choice to make:

1. I could admit that I was wrong. I should have been paying attention to my driving, and I should not have snapped at my wife.
2. I could make amends. I could say I was sorry for speaking so sharply and not paying better attention.
3. I could do nothing. I could wait until later and risk rationalizing the incident away, creating resentment between us. After all, she should have known I had it under control. We've never been in a wreck, have we?

I chose numbers one and two. In the past, I might have been tempted to choose number three. It's often easier to rationalize our way out of something than to admit we are wrong. That's why it's so important to let God help us keep a constant inner inventory.

PRAYER

Lord, thank you for helping me make the right choices, those that are pleasing to you. In Jesus' name, Amen.

Handmade

You created my inmost being; you knit me together in my mother's womb.

PSALM 139:13

There is something special about a handmade gift. My wife loves to sew, and one Christmas she made me a wonderful quilt. She found fabrics that she knew I would love and carefully cut them into shapes to make an intricate design. When she gave it to me, I couldn't believe my eyes. It made me feel so loved and special.

When we read the Genesis account of the creation of the world, we see that God spoke things such as light, water, plants, and animals into existence. But he used a different process to create us. When he created humankind, he used his hands. He knit us together. Like the quilt my wife made for me, the process was painstaking and amazingly detailed. He created each one of us, slowly and carefully, in his own image. No two of us are exactly alike.

At times, we feel as if God is far off and uninterested in what we are going through. It can feel as though we are on our own. When those times come, we must remember that we were handmade by God. That makes us very special indeed.

PRAYER

Father, I can almost see you creating me, adding your loving touches here and there, knitting me together slowly and carefully. Thank you for showing me how special I am. In Jesus' name, Amen.

Safe Boundaries

Brothers, if someone is caught in a sin, you who are spiritual should restore him gently. But watch yourself, or you also may be tempted.

GALATIANS 6:1 GNT

We've all had friends who have relapsed. It's heartbreaking. It feels like a piece of us goes with them, doesn't it? One of the hardest things for me early on was establishing a balance between being *involved* in someone's recovery as opposed to *living* their recovery. Although we love one another, pray for one another, and share with one another, we must always remember that recovery is a personal choice—one that each person has to make. Forget that, and we run the risk of falling off the cliff with them.

I have learned that when love and concern and fellowship fail, all I can do is make myself available to welcome my friends home if and when they are ready to deal with the consequences of their poor choices. We are not to become so consumed with someone else's recovery that we jeopardize our own. We need to establish a boundary line.

Along the rim of the Grand Canyon are barriers meant to safeguard the lives of the many tourists who visit there. To venture past those boundaries can be deadly. We can continue to love, encourage, and warn those who insist on ignoring the warnings and stepping into harm's way. But we must not allow ourselves to endanger ourselves as well.

PRAYER

Father, thank you for giving me boundaries to keep me safe from falling. In Jesus' name, Amen.

Open the Lock

Always be prepared to give an answer to everyone who asks
you to give the reason for the hope that you have.

1 PETER 3:15

When we purchased our new home, I was given a handful of keys. Some were to the house, and others were to a couple of sheds located on the property. I went to check them out and found that one of the sheds was locked with a padlock that had obviously been around for a long time. I looked through the keys and found one that was pretty old looking, thinking that one best matched the lock. But it wouldn't open. I then tried the other keys with no success. I began to think that nothing would open that old lock. Finally, there was just one key left—a bright, shiny new key that I was sure wouldn't open that ancient lock. But I tried it anyway, and that old, beat-up lock popped right open.

After I'd had a chance to think about it, I realized that the old lock is a lot like me. Nobody thought I would amount to anything, but all I needed was the right key to unlock my heart—and that key was Jesus. We didn't look like much of a match, me with all my sin and him so pure and holy. But when he came into my life, I opened right up.

All that business about never amounting to anything is just a pack of lies. God is saying to each of us, "You're worth everything to me. Let me unlock your heart."

PRAYER

You gave everything for me, Father. I can't comprehend that, but I'm so glad you
sent Jesus to unlock my rusty old heart. In Jesus' name, Amen.

Dark Days

"With man this is impossible, but with God all things are possible."

MATTHEW 19:26

Don't let anyone fool you—recovery is tough. There are days when we feel like giving up, throwing in the towel. Days when it seems like the deck is stacked against us, and nothing is ever going to change.

To be honest, I have these days a lot. I wake up in the morning just knowing the day isn't going to go well. Old hurts, hang-ups, and habits keep pressing on my mind, and I wonder if it wouldn't be easier to just give up. That's when I have to purposefully stop and remember that I'm a child of God. I love the way that sounds. In fact, it's the most wonderful thing anyone has ever called me. We don't have to give in to our old habits. All things are possible with God, and we are his children.

God changes everything! Things that were once impossible are now well within our reach. We've already seen that this is true. So let's kick those bad feelings and negative thoughts out of the picture. Let's reclaim our dark days by bringing God's light into them. Let's thank God for making everything possible by making us his children.

PRAYER

Thank you, Father, for making me your own blessed child. I know that those things that were once impossible are now the best part of my life. In Jesus' name, Amen.

Excuses

I will lift up mine eyes unto the hills, from whence cometh my help.
My help cometh from the LORD, which made heaven and earth.

PSALM 121:1–2 KJV

I don't have time for this! I really think I'm fine! I have a lot going on right now! I just couldn't commit to something so big! I'm not as bad as those other guys! I'm too tired! I work a lot of hours!

These are just a few of the excuses I've heard from people who aren't yet ready to start changing their lives. George Washington Carver said, "Ninety-nine percent of the failures come from people who have the habit of making excuses."

Excuses keep us stuck where we are—and we can become very good at using them. I am, for example, a pro at filling up my schedule. It makes me feel better about not doing some of the things I know I should do, such as spending more time with God or praying for my wife and family, serving more in my ministry, going to my meetings, exercising, etc.

In my old life I never had trouble finding the time I needed to deny my character defects—bitterness, resentments, worry, anxiety, fears, and addictive behaviors. However, I quickly realized I wasn't nearly as good at making time for my recovery.

That's why a sponsor or an accountability partner is so important. We all need someone who can see through our stalling techniques and help us find the courage to live honestly.

PRAYER

Father, thank you for placing true friends in my life who will see through my excuses that stall my recovery and keep me from becoming all you created me to be. In Jesus' name, Amen.

Parting the Sea

Humble yourselves, therefore, under God's mighty hand, that he may lift you up in due time. Cast all your anxiety on him because he cares for you.

I PETER 5:6-7

I've read the verse in 1 Peter about humbling ourselves hundreds of times. But this morning in our quiet time, my wife read this verse again and it struck me head-on. I quickly realized that it wasn't because I was going through some great trial and needed the reassurance. It was because my Father's words had penetrated my heart with the message that if I would humble myself and acknowledge my need, he would take care of everything I faced that day—and every day—no matter how great or small.

My wife brought it into perspective for me when she said, "Can you believe the same God who parted the sea for Moses wants to help us today?" Think about it. When Moses was faced with the greatest obstacle in his life, his enemy hot on his heels and a sea before him, God said, "I want you to go right through it. Not around it, under it, or over it but right through it."

God wants us to cast all our cares on him—*all our cares*, great and small. Once he's in the lead, he will take us straight through to the other side and give us peace.

PRAYER

Father, I need your help today and every day. I give all my worries to you. Thank you for giving me peace as we go through the waters together. In Jesus' name, Amen.

A Call for Accountability

A friend loves at all times, and a brother is born for a time of adversity.

PROVERBS 17:17

There are 365 days in a year, in the course of which we go through good times and bad times. There may be crises—big and small—and days when we just feel stressed out or blue. That's why it's essential for each of us to form an accountability team. We all need other people to hold us up when we're hurting, people who will love us through hard times.

So . . . what is an accountability team? These are just other followers of Christ who agree to spend time with us. They are people who will be there for us and call us on our junk when we need a voice of reason. Those on our accountability team should be the same gender. We exchange contact information with these important people so we can text or talk on the phone or meet for coffee. When the chips are down, these are important relationships designed to keep us safe and tightly bonded to God and his people.

Satan would like nothing more than to isolate us and then begin to mess with our heads. It's important to have someone to call, someone who can deliver a word of encouragement, pray with us, and most of all, remind us that we are not alone, that there is power in numbers.

PRAYER

Heavenly Father, show me the people I should approach about becoming members of my accountability team. I look forward to growing strong in the midst of those important relationships. In Jesus' name, Amen.

Pass It On

Jesus said to him, "Today salvation has come to this house, because this man, too, is a son of Abraham. For the Son of Man came to seek and to save the lost."

LUKE 19:9–10

I was in the drive-thru line at Starbucks thinking about the great cup of coffee I had just ordered—a triple shot of espresso, caramel macchiato, venti, skinny, at 180 degrees. Actually, I was thinking that just learning how to place my Starbucks order was quite an accomplishment!

As I pulled up to the window, money in hand, the friendly cashier said, "The car in front of you paid for yours." I was taken aback by this unsolicited act of kindness and wrestled with what to do. Just thanking the cashier didn't seem like enough. Should I try to find my benefactors so I could thank them and ask why they did it? That's when it hit me: I needed to accept the gift and pass it on.

Through Celebrate Recovery, God has given me a great second chance. I don't know why, because in my eyes I'm not worthy. But before I spend a lot of time and energy trying to figure out why, I think I'll accept the fact that Jesus thought I am worth the ultimate price! I can't wait to tell someone else God thinks they are worthy too.

Jesus said he came to "seek and save the lost." He also says we are his ambassadors, so our mission is his mission. Let's be on the lookout.

PRAYER

Lord God, thank you for your great act of kindness. I will tell everyone I see what you have done for me. In Jesus' name, Amen.

Falling Trees

He is like a tree planted by streams of water, which yields its fruit in season and whose leaf does not wither. Whatever he does prospers.

PSALM 1:3

A friend of mine shared this insight with me: "When I was a young boy, I would help my stepfather cut wood for the stove that heated our house. We always looked for dead trees to cut down. Once we found the tree we wanted, we would start sawing the trunk. It was slow going at first. But eventually we would saw all the way through, and the tree would fall with great force. The interesting thing was that in the forest, it always hit other trees as it was coming down. Limbs on other trees would be knocked off as it fell."

This story reminds me that one of the most devastating things to watch is a man or woman falling. Almost always others—wives, parents, children, friends—are hurt and damaged as well. I'm grateful that God has given us tools to mend not only our own broken limbs but also those caused by someone else's fall.

If we are not willing to stick with our recovery for our own sake, then we should do it for those around us, those who love us, those whose limbs are intertwined with ours. It's so rewarding to see them thriving as they watch us stand strong with God's help.

--- PRAYER ---

Dear Father, thank you for helping me stand strong for the sake of those who love me and are watching my life. In Jesus' name, Amen.

Pick a Place and Start

Lazy hands make a man poor, but diligent hands bring wealth. He who gathers crops in summer is a wise son, but he who sleeps during harvest is a disgraceful son.

PROVERBS 10:4–5

Our daughter and her family live in another state. Her husband is going to school, and she has her hands full with three active toddlers underfoot. So when we arrived for a visit, we found the sink full of dishes. We helped our daughter put the kids down for a nap and then suggested she catch one also. While they were resting, we tackled some of the chores.

As I stood in front of the sink, I thought, *Wow, this is going to take forever, but it won't get done unless I get started.* I surveyed the mess closely and chose a big pot that was taking up a lot of room. I washed it, dried it, and put it away. When I got back to the sink, things looked more manageable. I took care of another item, and then another, and before I realized it, the sink was empty and the kitchen was clean.

Starting our relationship with Jesus is a lot like that, especially for those of us in recovery. Our lives are such a mess that we often feel overwhelmed. But with the help of God and our sponsors, we pick the most glaring problem and tackle that first. Then we move on to the next and the next. As long as we remain diligent, relief is certain.

--- PRAYER ---

Father, thank you for helping me work through my problems one at a time. In Jesus' name, Amen.

Hiding from God

When I kept silent, my bones wasted away through my groaning all
day long. For day and night your hand was heavy on me; my strength
was sapped as in the heat of summer. Then I acknowledged my sin
to you and did not cover up my iniquity. I said, 'I will confess my
transgressions to the LORD.*' And you forgave the guilt of my sin.*

PSALM 32:3−5

In the Garden of Eden, after Adam and Eve disobeyed God and committed the first sin, their response was to hide from God. Of course
they couldn't, but they tried. There have been times in my life when I
have tried to hide my sins and mistakes from God and others. I have to
say, it's exhausting.

Many of us have a picture of God as someone who wants to punish
us for our mistakes, so we hide from him. We act like children who are
afraid of being spanked. But the fact is, we have a God who wants to forgive our sins. There may be consequences associated with our actions,
but we don't have to carry around the shame and fear of punishment.

Instead, we can confess what we have done, the mistakes we've
made, the bad choices we've made, the sins that separate us from God.
When we seek him, he promises that we will find him. When we ask to
be forgiven, he forgives us. It's as simple as that. Any time we are ready to
freely surrender our sins, he is ready to love us, forgive us, and show us a
better way.

PRAYER

Yes, Lord, I don't ever again want to have to hide from you. Thank you for inviting
me to come before you, sins and all, and ask for forgiveness. In Jesus' name, Amen.

False Advertising

Submit to God. Resist the devil, and he will flee from you.
Draw near to God and he will draw near to you.

JAMES 4:7–8

We're all familiar with those advertisements in which a medication is described in glowing terms by people with bright smiles, followed by a daunting list of possible side effects. "Do you have acne problems? Try our medicine: Warning! May cause constipation, dizziness, increased sweating, light-headedness, damage to your heart, loss of appetite, vomiting, weakness, bleeding in your ears, loss of your fingernails, and more."

These ads make me think about our choices in life. There are things that look great on the surface, but they come with a long list of side effects. Each time, the Holy Spirit is warning us, "Don't do it! I know how this will end."

At that point, we have a choice: Prepare to live with the consequences, or ask God for strength to resist. Let's be honest; sin often looks like fun. If it didn't it would be far less difficult to resist. What isn't fun is the consequences, made worse by the fact that we ignored the warning and did it anyway.

Yes, some things in life look so good, so enticing, but the real consequences to ourselves and those we love are reason enough to heed the warning and stay away.

PRAYER

Father, make me wise to the false claims made by the enemy of my soul. I renew my commitment to listen when your Holy Spirit warns me to stay away. In Jesus' name, Amen.

Pomp and Circumstance

*"His master replied, 'Well done, good and faithful servant! You
have been faithful with a few things; I will put you in charge of
many things. Come and share your master's happiness!'"*

MATTHEW 25:21

I was as proud as a grandfather could be as I watched our twin grandsons walk across the stage to receive their kindergarten graduation diplomas. The energetic group of five- and six-year-olds had marched proudly into the room and given a captivating performance, which was topped off by the presentation of diplomas and the official moving of the tassel to the opposite side of the cap.

I thought about our Father, as he watches us march across the stage of this life. How he must smile as he watches every moment of our growth. We are not all growing at the same pace. We are not all achieving the same goals in life, but we are moving toward spiritual maturity. What matters is progress, not perfection.

Getting better one day at a time is what the Bible calls sanctification. Becoming more like Jesus one moment at a time, one step at a time, one day at a time is what we call recovery. At the end of our race, we have a diploma waiting for us, and right at the top are the words, "Well done, good and faithful servant." At the bottom, it's already been signed by Jesus, the one and only perfect person.

PRAYER

Lord God, thank you for helping me clean up my life one moment at a time. In Jesus' name, Amen.

In the Morning

In the morning, LORD, you hear my voice; in the morning
I lay my requests before you and wait expectantly.

PSALM 5:3

The best time to fellowship with God is anytime. He's always waiting, always inviting. But if we want to receive the most from our time with him, there is one thing we should consider: we should choose a time when we are at our best, fresh and awake, ready to receive from him. For some, that is first thing in the morning; others might find that evening is better. Still others might prefer midafternoon or right before lunch. All that matters is that we choose a part of the day that feels best to us and stick with it.

So what does fellowship with God consist of? Prayer? Bible meditation? Yes. It also means being quiet and listening to what God has to say to us. The most important thing to remember is that this fellowship shouldn't feel forced. Think of it as sitting down with a close friend or loved one. In such cases, we talk about lots of things—our needs, our wants, our circumstances, our burdens, and more. Conversation takes place, along with smiles, humor, encouragement, and words of loving affection.

Fellowship with God shouldn't be a chore. It should be a time we look forward to every day, an oasis of peace and devotion in our busy days. How wonderful is it that God wants to be with us?

PRAYER

Thank you, Lord, for inviting me to spend time with you every day, for time to talk through challenges, be refreshed, and cast off my burdens. In Jesus' name, Amen.

Feeling Alone

[He] will never leave nor forsake you.

HEBREWS 13:5 GNT

As we all know, it's possible to be in a room full of people and still feel overwhelmed by loneliness. There were times in my own life when a room full of people seemed like the loneliest place in the world. The enemy is clever that way. He takes advantage of our unresolved hurt and convinces us to pull away from those we were designed to be in relationship with.

God did not intend for us to be alone. When I find myself feeling lonely, I remind myself that my Father God is always with me. He has promised never to leave me. I am not alone. Once I've reconnected with that truth, I feel I have the strength to reach out to others with honesty and transparency.

We've all been hurt at one time or another. Most of us have been hurt many times by those we loved and trusted. Human beings are capable of inflicting a lot of pain on themselves and others. But this does not mean we should stop reaching out. We need community. We need each other too much to stay away, too much to draw back, too much to isolate ourselves from our brothers and sisters in Christ.

PRAYER

Lord God, you know I've been hurt, but loneliness hurts as well. Give me the courage I need to reach out to others again. In Jesus' name, Amen.

Put Me In, Coach

We are therefore Christ's ambassadors, as though God were
making his appeal through us. We implore you on Christ's behalf:
Be reconciled to God. God made him who had no sin to be sin for
us, so that in him we might become the righteousness of God.

2 CORINTHIANS 5:20–21

Our six-year-old twin grandsons are playing T-ball this year. One plays shortstop, and he knows there is almost always a force out at second base. When he gets the ball, which is often, he runs right to second base. Sometimes he gets there first, and the runner is out. Other times the runner gets there first and is safe. The interesting thing is that no matter who gets there first, my grandson's reaction is always the same—sheer joy! With hands raised in the air, he jumps up and down, as proud as he can be just to be in the game.

What a lesson for me! Why can't I be joyful even when things don't go the way I want them to? James, the brother of Jesus, said that we should consider it all joy when we face trials and tribulations. James acknowledges that there will be stumbles, setbacks, and some lack of success in every race. But the important thing is that God has chosen us to be in the game!

No one but Jesus plays a perfect game. But because he did, we are all winners. That's a lot to be joyful about.

PRAYER

Father God, thank you for choosing me to play on your team. It is the greatest thrill of my life. In Jesus' name, Amen.

In the Weeds

We are hard pressed on every side, but not crushed; perplexed, but not in despair; persecuted, but not abandoned; struck down, but not destroyed.

2 CORINTHIANS 4:8–9

I worked in a restaurant for five years. When we were buried, slammed, as busy as we could be, we would say we were "in the weeds." When everyone is in the weeds at the same time, chaos ensues! But here's what I've learned:

When we're in the weeds, we have two choices. We can panic or get to work. Panicking is easy, but all it does is waste time and energy, both of which are in short supply. And even worse, we only end up right back where we started.

Getting to work is a much better option. But it's a step-by-step process. First, we have to determine what is the biggest need and meet that need first. Then we do the next thing, then the next thing, until the shift is over. If you try to do it all at once, you'll be as bad off as if you had panicked.

Many of us are "in the weeds" when it comes to our lives and our recovery. It just seems like we are running as fast as we can and getting nowhere. We're behind in everything, and we feel like we're out of control. When we find ourselves in that situation, we have to take one step at a time, determining the greatest need and taking care of that. Then the next, and the next. We will make it if we keep our heads and refuse to panic.

PRAYER

Father, thank you for helping me to get my life in order. Show me each new day what I need to do first. In Jesus' name, Amen.

Frozen in the Starting Block

Forget the former things; do not dwell on the past.

ISAIAH 43:18

A runner jogs in place, warming up for the big race. He places his feet in the blocks, poised to shoot forward. He shakes one hand and then the other, getting loose before positioning his fingers on the track before him. He listens for the announcer's words—*Ready! Set!*—and then the starting gun fires! The other competitors shoot forward, but he is frozen in his spot and can't move. He never even starts the race. What a tragedy that would be!

When we allow ourselves to be consumed with the past, it's like we're frozen in the blocks, unable to run our race in the present. I spent many years wishing my past had been different, going over it and over it in my mind. That rearview perspective kept me from living out my present and investing in my future.

The problem facing the frozen runner is pride. It's the reason many people never start the race and many others never finish. They are too proud to admit they need help. Instead, they rehearse the past, hoping to find a way to blame someone or something else for their trouble.

Letting pride keep us in denial is a costly exercise that shuts us out of the race. But God tells us that if we humbly bring our past to him, he will take our past and forgive it, renew it, and restore it. Then we can run our race to win!

PRAYER

Thank you, Father, for providing all that I need to move forward with my life. Poised with my feet in the blocks, I'll focus on you rather than my past. In Jesus' name, Amen.

Walk and Talk

As water reflects the face, so one's life reflects the heart.

PROVERBS 27:19

I'm going to get in shape! This time, I'm serious." I found myself making this sweeping statement to my wife one night. For years physical fitness had been important to me, but as work and life got busier, I allowed it to slip into the background. Working out, which I once saw as an enjoyable way to unwind and release tension, now felt like a chore. My once pristine diet was now full of unhealthy foods.

It was a great idea, but somehow I never quite got there. I planned to wake at 5 a.m. to work out. I said I would eat healthy. But I still haven't started. I meant to—really I did—but I haven't followed through. My good intentions were no more than empty talk.

When something is truly important to us, we can see it in the way we live. It's more than just words; there is corresponding action. That's why we all have to ask ourselves how important recovery is in our lives. Are we just saying we want to change? Or do we mean it enough to follow through with our actions? If we really want freedom, healing, and wholeness, we have to put in the effort. We have to go to our meetings, attend church regularly, read God's Word, and apply the principles we learn. We have to work to be transparent. Our walk has to back up our talk.

PRAYER

Lord God, help me to put feet to my good intentions, so that I can live the life you planned for me, one filled with hope and joy. In Jesus' name, Amen.

The Fifth Step

Therefore confess your sins to each other and pray
for each other so that you may be healed.

JAMES 5:16

As soon as we confess our sins to God, we experience his forgiveness. Being free from the penalty of our sins and living in fellowship with God is true freedom and more than we could have ever thought or imagined. But our loving, generous God has given us more—the love and support of our brothers and sisters in Christ.

Step 5: We admitted to God, to ourselves, and to another human
being the exact nature of our wrongs.

In recovery we hear, time and time again, that we are only as sick as our secrets. In Step 5, we discover we are free to share those secrets in a safe place, with safe people. We learn that this is not a journey to be taken alone—that we need others in our recovery to support us, pray for us, and encourage us.

Of course, we should choose wisely before confessing our past sins to others. But I'm confident that God has placed people in each of our lives who are willing to respect our confidences and support us as we move toward healing. Celebrate Recovery was formed to provide that kind of confidentiality and support. God knows exactly what we need to complete our journey to wholeness.

PRAYER

Thank you, Lord, for understanding my need for brothers and sisters in the faith who can strengthen and support me as I share my secrets and walk toward wholeness. In Jesus' name, Amen.

Put on the Old Clothes?

*In Christ Jesus you are all children of God through faith, for all of you
who were baptized into Christ have clothed yourselves with Christ.*

GALATIANS 3:26–27

My wife and I have developed a system for doing our laundry. We start by gathering up all the dirty clothes and placing them in stacks in the laundry room. Whites go with whites, darks go with darks, some need to be washed in cold water, some need hot water, and so on. But one thing we don't do is put on any of that dirty laundry before it goes through the cleaning process. Why would we, when we can wear clean, fresh items right out of the dryer?

That got me to thinking about how we have been washed white as snow (see Isaiah 1:18). Why would I consider clothing myself in any of those old, filthy habits and behaviors I used to wear when I can wear those that God has washed clean and spotless? I can't imagine how uncomfortable it would be to wear a stained, sweat-soaked shirt, when I have plenty of clean ones hanging in the closet. And I can't imagine wearing old, dirty behaviors and ways of thinking when God has helped me replace them with fresh, clean behaviors and plenty of wonderful thoughts.

That's it for me. No putting on dirty clothes, not for me, not ever!

PRAYER

*Lord God, thank you for clean, spotless garments, every one of them washed in your
perfect cleansing blood. In Jesus' name, Amen.*

Time to Celebrate

A cheerful heart is good medicine, but a crushed spirit dries up the bones.

PROVERBS 17:22

One of the traps we need to avoid is getting caught up in the tough-ness or hard work of recovery. Yes there are things that are uncomfortable, and it isn't easy learning new habits or breaking old ones. Going through things like taking inventory and making amends can be tough. But there is great joy in recovery as well. Each day is one day closer to the life of freedom that you and God desire.

As we begin to experience change and growth, as we see that the hurts, hang-ups, and habits we have carried around all our lives are beginning to lose their grip on us, there comes a time to enjoy what God is doing. He is giving us lives full of joy. It may be difficult to believe, but the pain won't last forever. As we choose to move past the pain, God's healing power begins to work in our lives, bringing us to wholeness.

This is more than a one-time-does-it-all choice. It must be a day-by-day decision that takes hold more and more as time passes. If we are patient and persistent, there will be a time of celebration in our future. In anticipation of that sure-to-come victory, we can break through the sadness and allow ourselves times of laughter and fun. A good place to begin is by singing a song of praise and thanksgiving to our merciful and loving God.

PRAYER

Father, even in this difficult time, dealing with the pain that leads to healing and wholeness, I celebrate your presence in my life. In Jesus' name, Amen.

Full of Life

He frees the prisoners.... He lifts the burdens from
those bent down beneath their loads.

PSALM 146:7–8 TLB

What is your life like today? Does it reflect a person full of life and hope, or does it reflect someone who is hopeless and lifeless?

Last year a close friend of mine visited the country of Jordan. While there he took a short side trip to the Dead Sea. "It was quite an experience," he told me later. "The water is so salty that nothing can survive in it. It's literally dead—just like it says. A couple of times I got the water in my eyes, and the salt was so strong that it burned. And it's true what they say: you can't sink in the Dead Sea. I jumped into the water and immediately floated to the top. It was a most bizarre feeling."

The book of Revelation mentions a river that will flow from the throne of God. The Bible calls it "the river of the water of life." In the book of Ezekiel, we learn that this river expands as it flows eastward, nourishing everything in its path, until finally it empties into the Dead Sea, making the salty water fresh and able to support life.

If God can give life to the lifeless Dead Sea, he most definitely can bring us life. No matter how vile and polluted our lives have been, his living water flowing through us will let us experience life to the fullest.

PRAYER

Lord God, you are the Giver of living water. Flow through my sin-polluted heart and make it fresh and clean once again. In Jesus' name, Amen.

Whoever Comes

*This righteousness is given through faith in Jesus Christ to all who
believe. There is no difference between Jew and Gentile, for all have
sinned and fall short of the glory of God, and all are justified freely
by his grace through the redemption that came by Christ Jesus.*

ROMANS 3:22–24

The number-one question people asked Jesus about himself was,
"Why do you eat and drink with sinners? Why do you hang out
with people like that?" One group even called him "a friend of sinners."
And they didn't mean it as a compliment.

As a Christian and follower of Jesus Christ, I believe that faith in him
has the power to bring us into an intimate relationship with God. That
means anyone and everyone, whoever comes—the sick, wounded, and
hurt included. As God's church, we must open up the doors, invite them
in, and let them know, "You are welcome here!" It might get a little messy,
but God can handle that—and so can we.

Jesus knew that, in God's eyes, one sin is no worse than any other. All
sin, great and small, separates us from God. When we come to him with
open hearts, he won't turn us away. He will love us, forgive us, and help us
find the healing we need.

PRAYER

*Thank you, Father, for receiving me when I was unworthy of your attention. In
Jesus' name, Amen.*

Introduce Yourself

They promise them freedom, while they themselves are slaves of
depravity—for a man is a slave to whatever has mastered him.

2 PETER 2:19

A t Celebrate Recovery, we have a special way of introducing ourselves. We say, "Hi, my name is [Name], and I'm a believer in Jesus
Christ who struggles with [area of struggle]." We introduce ourselves in
this way for two reasons. First, we are making it clear that our identity
rests in our faith in Jesus Christ, not in our struggle with alcohol or code-
pendency or inappropriate images or spending money or any other hurt,
hang-up, or habit. Once that has been established, we state our area of
recovery because we want to be honest about the things that are out of
control in our lives.

For newcomers, this can be challenging, even intimidating, the
first few times we do it. It isn't easy to tell strangers about our areas of
struggle. It's tough, but it's also freeing because it's the first big step out
of denial and into an honest appraisal of our problem. Some might say
that revealing our struggles makes us appear weak, but instead it demonstrates courage and determination. It shows that we care more about
others than we do ourselves.

Hiding our problems behind a wall of silence locks us into a lifetime
of dysfunction, sadness, and broken relationships. There is no recovery,
no wholeness, no healing until we are willing to take the first step and put
it all on the line.

PRAYER

Father, thank you for helping me reveal my struggle so that you can make me
whole. In Jesus' name, Amen.

Faith and Hope

*"If you have faith as small as a mustard seed, you can
say to this mountain, 'Move from here to there,' and it
will move. Nothing will be impossible for you."*

MATTHEW 17:20

It's reassuring to know that we don't need a large amount of faith to begin the recovery process. We need only a small amount, "as small as a mustard seed," to bring change and begin to move our mountains of hurts, hang-ups, and habits. If we will put the faith that we have in Jesus, our lives will be changed! We will find hope in the only Higher Power, Jesus Christ.

Hope gives us the courage to reach out and hold Christ's hand, while facing the present with confidence and the future with realistic expectancy. Simply put, my life without Christ is a hopeless end; with him it is an endless hope. Let's look at what the word **HOPE** means.

H stands for "Higher Power." The only true Higher Power is Jesus
Christ.
O stands for "open to change."
P stands for "power to change."
E stands for "expect to change."

If this is our definition of hope, the changes we have longed for are just steps away. We must not give up until we receive our miracle from God. Our faith assures us that he exists and that he has the power to help us overcome the hurts, hang-ups, and habits that have ruled our lives.

―――――――――――― PRAYER ――――――――――――

*Father, I place my faith in you and your mighty power to free me. I will not give
up. I will hope in your goodness. In Jesus' name, Amen.*

Going the Extra Mile

Do not withhold good from those to whom it is
due, when it is in your power to act.

PROVERBS 3:27

My grandson was having a birthday, and it was my job to get two five-foot-long balloons—one shaped like a clown fish and the other like a shark—filled with helium. The clerk in the party store assured me they could fill them, but every store worker who came to the counter took one look and said, "Sorry. I'll have to get someone else to do that." This task was turning out to be tougher than I had expected, but it was for my grandson, so I didn't mind.

Finally, a woman came to the counter and told me she could fill the balloons, but it would cost six dollars each. "No problem," I told her. "These are for my grandson." After fifteen minutes, she came back with the filled balloons and a warning: "Don't let these get away from you, or you'll never get them back." The only problem was she had tied them together with a faulty knot. One balloon came loose immediately and floated up to the twenty-foot ceiling. Thirty minutes later, we were finally able to retrieve it. I took the balloons out to the car, wrestled them in, and finally made it home, where I presented them to my happy grandson.

Why would I go to all that trouble? Because I love my grandson. Love is the only thing we take with us when we die. Nothing else really matters. That makes the things we do for love the most important of all.

PRAYER

Thank you, Father, for loving me and healing me so that I can love others. In Jesus'
name, Amen.

Inviting Others

*"You will receive power when the Holy Spirit comes on
you; and you will be my witnesses in Jerusalem, and in all
Judea and Samaria, and to the ends of the earth."*

ACTS 1:8

When our lives have been changed by Jesus Christ and the power of the Holy Spirit now resides within us, we need to tell others about what has happened to us. When we see that Celebrate Recovery is working in our lives to help us overcome our hurts, hang-ups, and habits, we need to tell others about it. If we've found answers for our lives, why wouldn't we want to share them with other hurting people.

We all know why, don't we? We don't want to be labeled a religious fanatic or be asked questions we aren't sure we can answer. But being labeled a fanatic is a small price to pay for a real, living relationship with God. And answers? No one has all the answers. And no one expects us to do more than just telling others the simple truth about what Jesus has done in our lives. We can all do that.

Let's think about the people we know who need Jesus. Then let's pray for those people, asking God to provide an opening for us to share what has happened to us and invite them to experience true freedom as we have. While we're at it, let's ask God to relieve any fears we may have and give us the words that others so desperately need to hear.

PRAYER

Lord God, I'm no salesman. I don't have the gift of persuasion, but I ask that you would give me the words to tell others about the wonderful things you have brought to my life. In Jesus' name, Amen.

Who Needs Pain?

You can't heal a wound by saying it's not there!

JEREMIAH 6:14 TLB

Wouldn't it be great if we could snap our fingers and suddenly there were no more pain in the world? Well, yes and no. While no one wants to experience pain, it does serve a number of important purposes in our lives. C. S. Lewis said, "God whispers to us in our pleasures, speaks in our conscience, but shouts in our pain. Pain is God's megaphone to rouse a deaf world."

Pain is God's way of letting us know something is wrong. If, for example, my appendix were about to burst and I felt no pain, how would I know to get help before the deadly infection spread throughout my body?

Pain is also God's fire alarm. If an alarm goes off, we don't say, "Oh, there goes that stupid fire alarm again!" We call the fire department. But when our "pain alarm" goes off, instead of dealing with the source of the pain, we often try to mute the noise with people, work, food, alcohol, sex, and many other things.

An important point needs to be made here: just because God *allows* pain to enter our lives doesn't mean he *causes* the pain, and it certainly doesn't mean he enjoys seeing us in pain. God often allows the natural consequences of our poor choices to play out. The miracle is that he brings *good* out of our pain by using it to demonstrate his goodness and grace.

PRAYER

Father, I am hurting. I pray you use my pain for good. During these days of suffering, I ask you to help me to feel your presence. In Jesus' name, Amen.

Active Gratitude

*Let the word of Christ dwell in you richly as you teach and admonish
one another with all wisdom, and as you sing psalms, hymns
and spiritual songs with gratitude in your hearts to God.*

COLOSSIANS 3:16

The Gratitude Experience" was the title of the sermon one Sunday morning. I was pulled in right away because I know gratitude is the only appropriate response to the work God has done to rescue me and make me his own. During that sermon, I also realized that gratitude must be more than a mental acknowledgment. I had to *demonstrate* my gratitude because of the great price paid for me!

For the rest of that Sunday, I looked for opportunities to demonstrate my gratitude. And that turned out to be a liberating and joyous experience. I began by thanking God for redeeming me and showed it by inviting someone to our recovery group. When a new attendee sees all the transformed lives, they realize there is hope for them as well.

I also thanked God for my godly wife, who saw the good in me when others didn't and never gave up on me. Then I gave her a hug and a kiss and told her how much I appreciate her. The day went on from there with my demonstrating gratitude for all the aspects of the redeemed life God has given me.

We truly express gratitude when we demonstrate it actively rather than passively feel grateful. There are countless ways to do that. It's an experience we won't forget.

PRAYER

Heavenly Father, I'm so grateful for all you've done for me. Help me to demonstrate my gratitude in all I say and do. In Jesus' name, Amen.

Jesus Wept

When Jesus saw her weeping, and the Jews who had come along with her
also weeping, he was deeply moved in spirit and troubled, "Where have
you laid him?" he asked. "Come and see, Lord," they replied. Jesus wept.

JOHN 11:33–35

When we enter recovery, surrendering to God and admitting that our lives are out of control, we find that we begin to come out of a condition known as denial. Denial is a common coping mechanism that we employ in an effort to keep ourselves safe emotionally. If we can pretend a problem doesn't exist, we don't have to deal with it and it can't harm us. Of course, the opposite is true. Denial can hurt us badly by numbing our emotions and keeping us from dealing with problems until they become critical.

Denial manifests itself in many ways. Some people turn to shopping, sex, drugs, overeating, inappropriate images, risky relationships—anything that can keep us from facing reality. These problems are then added to the underlying problem, and we are in even more trouble than we were before.

In the book of John, we read that Jesus had lost a friend, a man named Lazarus. This man and his two sisters frequently invited Jesus to stay in their home when he was in the area. When Jesus arrived, the two women were crying. He didn't ask them to deny their grief and pretend they weren't grieving. Just the opposite. He wept along with them. It's always better to face things squarely than to sweep them under the rug.

PRAYER

Father, it's natural to want to sweep the bad stuff under the rug, but that's not how
you taught me to deal with unwelcome circumstances. Thank you for teaching me
to deal with things squarely. In Jesus' name, Amen.

Green Bay Wins

In the same way, faith by itself, if it is not accompanied by action, is dead.

JAMES 2:17

I'm a big Green Bay Packers fan. Every year I follow their games enthusiastically, hoping they will make it to the Super Bowl and win big! But this morning I got to thinking, *What if the sports announcer started the season by saying, "Let's hear it for the Green Bay Packers, our new Super Bowl champions!"* Sure, I'd be excited for about three seconds, and then I'd say, "But wait . . . they didn't do anything!"

Holding the trophy without playing the game or taking the journey wouldn't mean as much, would it? In fact, the victory is not at the end of the journey, but in the midst of the journey. God wants us to experience the joy of carrying that ball into the end zone.

As those who have pledged our faith in God, we already know how the "season" will end. We know we have already been given the gift of salvation, and we have been assured that victory is already ours. However, God has entrusted us with talents, time, and treasures, and he has asked us to go the distance to prove to ourselves what he already knows—we are winners. He also wants us to help those who are still struggling on the field.

PRAYER

Thank you, Father, for letting me peek into the future and see the final score! Thank you as well for giving me the privilege of playing the game and being part of the big win! In Jesus' name, Amen.

Shelter from the Storm

The LORD is my rock, my fortress and my deliverer; my God is my rock, in whom I take refuge, my shield and the horn of my salvation, my stronghold.

PSALM 18:2

Our daughter and grandkids had spent the summer with us, and we were traveling through Kansas, taking them back to Colorado. We were about two hours from their house when we saw a storm ahead of us. Lightning lit up the sky every few seconds, and the radio blasted a warning to take shelter from a quickly approaching line of severe thunderstorms with damaging winds.

As we left the interstate, we saw a Walmart store nearby. The winds were coming fast and hard from the west, so we pulled in as close as we could get along the east side of the building. The storm raged all around us, rain sweeping horizontally. All manner of debris flew past and over us, but we were safe in the shadow of that large building.

In the same way, the storms of life can flatten us and sweep us away. That's why God urges us to take shelter in his presence. The Bible says he is our refuge and hiding place from the storm. We are safe in his shadow.

—————————————— PRAYER ——————————————

Father, thank you for shielding me from the storms of life. Though they are raging around me, I am safe in your shadow. In Jesus' name, Amen.

Staying Focused

Since, then, you have been raised with Christ, set your hearts on things above, where Christ is, seated at the right hand of God. Set your minds on things above, not on earthly things.

COLOSSIANS 3:1–2

I get distracted easily. There is just so much to think about, so many responsibilities. We all have bills to pay, meetings to attend, people to deal with, families to care for. No wonder we can't keep our minds quiet during our prayer time with God. Many times our minds get pulled away from where they should be and focused on what they shouldn't be, putting us at risk of relapsing into old hurts, hang-ups, and habits.

It happens to all of us from time to time. It's not easy to stay focused on heavenly things when the earthly things are making so much more noise. The best and maybe the only way to stay focused on the right things is to always keep Jesus front and center. That means we understand that he is with us throughout the day, as close as our breath. He's always there to help us at a moment's notice, encourage us, instruct us, strengthen us, and protect us.

God knows who we are. He understands what we're made of. That's why he sent his Holy Spirit to dwell in us. He doesn't have to come from some faraway place to hear us and help us. When we focus on his presence within us, everything else will fall into place.

--- PRAYER ---

Father, thank you for your Holy Spirit that dwells within me, ready to help me stay focused on those things that are most important. In Jesus' name, Amen.

Grieving with Hope

The Spirit of the Sovereign LORD is on me, because the LORD
has anointed me to proclaim good news to the poor. He has
sent me to bind up the brokenhearted, to proclaim freedom for
the captives and release from darkness for the prisoners.

ISAIAH 61:1

A close friend told me that he heard a certain song on his way home the other day. It was the same song he had been listening to the last time he talked to his mother. "The tears began to flow, and my heart was aching," he told me. "I was missing my mom so much." Then he said this: "The old me would have stuffed all that emotion down inside and told no one about it. But because of what God has shown me in my recovery, I was able to share what I was feeling with my wife and bring all that pain into the light. I was able to run to the Father for strength."

What a wonderful testimony! I love how God not only brings comfort for our grieving hearts but also opens us up to receive it. My friend went on to say that God was with him as he grieved, reminding him that no matter what we go through, as God's children, we always have hope.

God is constantly planting hope in us as we seek him, rebuilding the ruins in our lives that may have come from generations of messiness, restoring places long devastated. The times of pain are inevitable, but hope is both constant and eternal.

—— PRAYER ——

Father, I know you are with me in all the difficult places in my life. Thank you
for the hope you are constantly using to brighten my path. In Jesus' name, Amen.

Someone's Watching

"You are the light of the world. A city on a hill cannot be hidden.
Neither do people light a lamp and put it under a bowl. Instead
they put it on its stand, and it gives light to everyone in the house.
In the same way, let your light shine before men, that they may
see your good deeds and praise your Father in heaven."

MATTHEW 5:14–16

My three-year-old grandson was right on my heels, following me closely as I walked across the lawn to the front door of our home. I took my shoes off at the door and turned around to help him, but he said, "I can do it, Papa." So I watched as he sat there, took off his shoes, and placed them right next to mine. Then he reached up to grab my hand and waited for me to lead him inside.

In the same way, God wants me to follow closely in his footsteps, doing those things I see him doing. The Bible calls that *sanctification*—becoming more like Jesus, one step at a time, which leads to one day at a time.

For those of us who have walked the steps in recovery, it's important to remember that many are watching us. They want to know if God can do for them what he has done for us. We walk in God's footsteps because that's what we need to do for ourselves, but it's also what we need to do for them. God is counting on us not to let them down.

— PRAYER —

Father, I am so happy to be following in your footsteps. Help me to remember that others are following in mine. In Jesus' name, Amen.

Laser Tag

What, then, shall we say in response to these things?
If God is for us, who can be against us?

ROMANS 8:31

A few years ago my daughter was invited to a laser tag birthday party. She was little, and the laser tag vest and gun were huge, which made it hard for her to play. The first time through, she didn't do well at all. She was an easy target for the more experienced players, and she got shot—a lot! She was pretty discouraged, but before the next round started, one of the dads handed me a vest and said, "Go get 'em, Dad." I got the message.

I followed close behind my daughter and picked off any kids foolish enough to come near her. By the end of the round, the kids knew that she was no longer an easy target. Her daddy was there, and he was not to be messed with. It was awesome. Her score that round vastly improved, bringing a big smile to her face.

When we go into the arena alone, it's easy to get picked on, singled out, and told that we are destined to fail. But when we go into battle with our heavenly Father's protection and covering, everything changes. Not only do we have a chance to stay alive, we have a guaranteed win.

PRAYER

Thank you, Father, for fighting for me, keeping me safe, and helping me come through as a victor. In Jesus' name, Amen.

Groundhog Day Revisited

*"I sought the LORD, and he answered me; he delivered me from all my fears.
Those who look to him are radiant; their faces are never covered with shame."*

PSALM 34:4–5

When you think of Groundhog Day, what comes to mind? The movie, right? Can you imagine living the same day over and over again? I can! Only in my life, I am the guy who kept walking around the corner and coming face-to-face with a guy holding a baseball bat. That guy took a swing at me and made contact every time. It didn't matter how many times I got hit. I always believed the lie that somehow "this time" he would miss. And yet, it kept happening over and over.

Of course, I'm not really talking about a guy with a baseball bat. I'm talking about getting knocked in the head by the same old hurts, hang-ups, and habits. Finally in my recovery, I realized the path I was taking was not working, and it was time for change. My pain had to become greater than my fear of change. I finally got tired of the bloody noses and emotional bruises inflicted on me by my poor choices. I had to come to grips with the truth that no matter how hard I tried, nothing was going to change until I changed my course and allowed Christ to fight for me.

We don't have to relive the painful consequences over and over again. Pain may be inevitable in our lives, but walking into a baseball bat is not. We can choose to go another way.

PRAYER

Heavenly Father, I surrender to you my bullheaded resistance to change. Show me how to walk away from the hurtful behavior of the past. In Jesus' name, Amen.

Son Protection Factor

Let all who take refuge in you be glad; let them ever sing for joy.
Spread your protection over them, that those who love your name
may rejoice in you. For surely, O LORD, you bless the righteous;
you surround them with your favor as with a shield.

PSALM 5:11–12

It was a rookie mistake. I had been doing some work outside on a sunny, summer day, and I ended up with a bad sunburn. I should have known better. It's hardly news that the sun can be a dangerous, formidable foe that can lead to cancer. At the very least, it can cause deep burns and great discomfort until the damaged skin heals. Fortunately, the sun's destructive rays can be easily subdued by a simple sunscreen.

It's foolish to work out in the sun without our SPF (Sun Protection Factor). In the same way, it's foolish to try to face any part of our new lives without our spiritual SPF. In that case, *SPF* stands for study, prayer, and fellowship. I also call it my SON Protection Factor. The more I stay in the Word and study what it says, the more I talk to the Father through prayer, the more I fellowship with God's people, then the more protected I am from dangerous and damaging behaviors. Why risk going out into the world without protection?

PRAYER

Thank you, Father, for giving me the tools to stay safe from the world's dangerous rays. In Jesus' name, Amen.

The Friend of Jesus

Jesus called in a loud voice, "Lazarus, come out!" The dead man came out,
his hands and feet wrapped with strips of linen, and a cloth around his face.

JOHN 11: 43–44

The story of Lazarus found in the gospel of John is all about the power of Jesus Christ to restore life to someone who has died. Although the story is about a real man who really died and was raised from the dead, I believe it serves as a powerful metaphor for what Christ can do for us in our lives.

When Jesus was teaching in the area, he often stayed with two sisters, Mary and Martha, and their brother, Lazarus. They were all close friends, so when Lazarus became ill, it wasn't surprising that the two sisters sent a message to Jesus, asking him to please come right away and heal their brother. By the time Jesus arrived, Lazarus had been dead for four days, and the situation seemed utterly hopeless. But Jesus was undeterred. First he prayed to his heavenly Father, and then he called, "Lazarus, come out!" And Lazarus did just that. Jesus instructed those around to remove his friend's grave clothes, and the rejoicing began.

Jesus specializes in the impossible and the hopeless. He is not intimidated by death. It would not be long before those who watched as Jesus was crucified would see him walk free of his grave as well. Jesus is uniquely qualified to breathe new life into those who invite him to do so.

PRAYER

Father, you gave me life and when I threw away the wonderful gift I had been given, you restored it to me. In Jesus' name, Amen.

Behind a Semi

One who trusts in the LORD is secure.

PROVERBS 29:25 NRSV

Last summer, my wife and I were taking Highway 1 toward Northern California. We were in the mountains and the scenery was beautiful. At one point, we approached a steep incline and realized there were about ten cars ahead of us. We were all stuck behind a slow-moving eighteen-wheeler.

As the truck slowly chugged up the hill, the driver stuck his arm out of the window and motioned when it was safe for a car to go around him. One by one, the drivers pulled out, and in blind trust, they went around the slow truck.

All of the sudden, it struck me—not the truck—that we trust our lives to complete strangers every day. We trust that oncoming cars will stop at intersections, that the hamburgers we eat at fast-food restaurants won't make us sick, that the medications we get at the pharmacy are the real thing. Why then is it so hard for us to trust our lives to the care of God, whose eyes are always upon us? I would rather walk with God in the darkest valley than walk alone or with a stranger in the light.

It's choice, not chance, that determines our destinies. Those choices require trust, putting our faith in action.

PRAYER

Lord God, I am trusting you to help me get around the slow-moving obstacles in my life and recovery. In Jesus' name, Amen.

Starstruck

The heavens declare the glory of God; the skies proclaim the work of his hands. Day after day they pour forth speech; night after night they display knowledge. There is no speech or language where their voice is not heard.

PSALM 19:1–3

Last night I looked up at a clear, high-altitude Colorado sky and was taken aback. My Father placed every one of those stars in the sky and then called them all by name! And that is just the beginning of our Father's handiwork. Beyond the Milky Way, there are many more galaxies, too many to count, all created and placed by our Father's hand.

It makes me wonder what there could be in my life today, next week, or ever that is too big for my Father in heaven to handle. The great God who set the stars in place surely wouldn't have any trouble with the complications in my life.

As I look up, I am amazed that the one who did all this loves *me*. I will never understand what he saw in my beaten-down, messed-up life. But I happily accept the mystery of it all. He has chosen me to be his child. He has redeemed me with the precious blood of his one, sinless Son, Jesus. He has invited me to lay all my troubles at his feet. Words cannot express my gratitude. I am completely starstruck!

PRAYER

Father, thank you for creating me in your own image, demonstrating that you care for me more than you care for all the stars in the heavens. In Jesus' name, Amen.

Loving One Another

*"A new command I give you: Love one another. As I have
loved you, so you must love one another. By this everyone will
know that you are my disciples, if you love one another."*

JOHN 13:34–35

When we consciously choose to surrender our lives to Christ's care and control, we are choosing to trust him, follow him, and make his plan our plan. He has given us his Word, the Bible, to tell us what he is like, what he wants from us, and how we can be more like him. Most of all, that comes down to one thing—love.

He asks that we love each other as he has loved us. That's a tall order, and one that is possible only as we allow his perfect love to flow through us. He asks that we show our love by supporting one another. This, he tells us, is how the world will know that we are different, that we are his followers. Bumper stickers, T-shirts, tattoos, and boycotts won't do. Only showing love will do.

It's not hard to show love, not really. Everyone around us needs love, so we just need to ask God to help us open the floodgates and let his love pour out through us onto everyone we see. It's a privilege and an honor to love someone God loves. It should be a pleasure indeed to obey his command.

PRAYER

My Father, thank you for loving me. Help me to let your love flow through me to others so that everyone will know that my life is in your loving hands. In Jesus' name, Amen.

Hitting the Wall

Since we are surrounded by such a great cloud of witnesses, let us throw off everything that hinders and the sin that so easily entangles, and let us run with perseverance the race marked out for us.

HEBREWS 12:1

A friend of mine ran a marathon. He told me it was one of the most difficult things he's ever done. He explained that at a certain point in the race, his mind began to tell him, "It's time to stop. You can't go on." Marathon runners call this "hitting the wall." Only by pushing through that wall are runners able to finish the race.

Being in recovery is a lot like running a marathon. At some point, we start to hear that old tape in our heads: *You can't go any further. This is just too hard for you.* That means we're about to hit the wall, and we're faced with the choice to push even harder or give up.

Experienced runners say they get through the wall by trusting their training and with the help of all the people on the sidelines cheering them on. That's the part our sponsors and accountability partners bring to our recovery—their encouragement means everything.

The difference between winning and losing, to a large extent, depends on who we choose to listen to. If we listen to the voices that tell us to give up because we're never going to make it, we'll never see the end of the race. But if we choose to push through the wall and go for that finish line, we will hear the cheers of men and angels.

PRAYER

Help me, Father, to push past the wall and finish my race. I know I can't do it without you. In Jesus' name, Amen.

Stay Away from Dark Places

*Everything exposed by the light becomes visible, for it is light
that makes everything visible. This is why it is said: "Wake up,
O sleeper, rise from the dead, and Christ will shine on you."*

EPHESIANS 5:13–14

My wife and I went bike riding with a group of Celebrate Recovery leaders. It was the first time in years, but the old saying is true: "It's just like riding a bike; you never forget how." Small problem, though. We didn't make it back to where we were staying before dark, and the group had only one flashlight. No big deal, I figured. Being a guy and a little competitive, I headed off in front of everyone else.

Who needs a light? I thought, until I got to the narrow, unlit, seventy-foot-long tunnel. I wanted to head on in, but I decided to wait for the light. Once the light arrived at the tunnel entrance, I could see clearly and raced right through.

Later, I was glad I'd waited instead of heading on into that tunnel. I could have been injured—and for what? Isn't that true of recovery as well? We don't go into dark places without a light. That would be taking an unnecessary risk. I also thought about why I get so focused on coming in first, especially when it means racing off on my own and leaving everyone else behind.

Isn't it great how God uses the little commonplace incidents in our lives to point out those areas that need attention? I'm so glad he does!

PRAYER

*Lord, help me to open my heart to every lesson you want to teach me. I know they
are all to make me a better person. In Jesus' name, Amen.*

Meditating on God's Word

I will consider all your works and meditate on all your mighty deeds.

PSALM 77:12

One of the most powerful tools we have to help us sustain healthy recovery is Bible memorization. Thinking about or meditating on Scripture is a great way to carry God's Word around with us, reminding us of the truth when we are faced with difficult situations and choices.

Meditating on God's Word simply means we commit it to memory. This can be done one verse at a time or one passage at a time. Either way, God's words are getting down into our souls where they can change us and make us more like him.

I've come up with a short process that has worked for me over the years. It offers an opportunity to form a new, beneficial habit to replace one of our old unproductive ones. Here's how it works:

- When you read a verse that stands out, highlight it.
- Write a note in the margin of your Bible or in your journal that says why this verse impressed you.
- Write the verse on a 3 x 5 card and put it where you'll see it.
- Repeat the verse out loud and in your mind throughout the day.
- Pray the verse back to God, thanking him for his Word.
- Tell others about the verse and why it's important to you.

When we do this, we are arming ourselves with God's Word. We will have it ready when we need it.

PRAYER

Thank you, Lord, for your Word that feeds us and keeps us. Quicken my mind as I work to make your words part of my heart. In Jesus' name, Amen.

Cracked Eggs

You can't heal a wound by saying it's not there.

JEREMIAH 6:14 TLB

As a young boy, I can remember going to the grocery store to buy eggs for my mom. Her instructions were clear: "Open the carton and check. If there's a cracked egg, put the carton back on the shelf and find one with a perfect dozen."

Yesterday, as I was buying a carton of eggs, I couldn't help but relate it to my younger days. For so long, I viewed God as the one who opens the carton and looks for cracked eggs. I was convinced he would see me, cracked and broken, sitting there among all the perfect eggs—those people who have it all together—and I would wonder, *Why am I so messed up? Why does everyone else have a perfect life?* I fully expected God to stick me back on the shelf to be disposed of later.

Looking back, though, I realize my thinking was distorted. God isn't examining each egg, looking for cracks. He knows we are *all* cracked eggs, imperfect in one way or another, and he values us anyway. Not only that, but he also has the power to restore, redeem, and renew us. He heals our cracks and makes us stronger than ever.

—————— PRAYER ——————

Father, thank you for loving this cracked egg, for seeing something beautiful and useful in me. Thank you for healing my cracks and making me strong. In Jesus' name, Amen.

Stay Away from Coyotes

"A new command I give you: Love one another. As I have loved you, so you must love one another. By this everyone will know that you are my disciples, if you love one another."

JOHN 13:34–35

I once witnessed an interesting encounter between a young elk and a group of coyotes. When I first noticed the coyote, the elk was about fifty yards ahead, running for his life. Then I saw three more coyotes trying to circle around in front of the elk. I was pretty sure this wasn't going to end well for the elk. But then the young elk got to the top of a small hill and stopped. Seconds later, a much larger, full-grown elk stepped up from the other side. Within seconds, a couple hundred more appeared. The coyotes immediately turned and ran in the other direction, in full retreat.

That is a familiar plan of attack that our enemy, the devil, uses on us. He tries to isolate us so that he can take us out. Unfortunately, this tactic often works. Wander out there on our own and we're likely to be history. Especially in recovery, it's so important to stay connected to family and supportive friends. There really is safety in numbers.

When we realize that the enemy is trying to surround us, the best thing we can do is run to church or to a meeting. Reach out to someone for help, but never try to go it alone. When we stand together, we put the enemy in full retreat.

PRAYER

Father, thank you for those you have placed in my life to stand with me in my recovery. In Jesus' name, Amen.

Mustard Seeds

*"Truly I tell you, if you have faith as small as a mustard seed,
you can say to this mountain, 'Move from here to there,' and
it will move. Nothing will be impossible for you."*

MATTHEW 17:20

Unfortunately, most of us allow our hurts, hang-ups, and habits to define us. We see them as immovable mountains, so much so that we often can't imagine what our lives would look like if we were to find ourselves completely free of them.

One of the reasons Celebrate Recovery has helped so many is that it provides a ladder to hope. As we begin to climb the ladder, freedom seems more and more possible because we are going about it one step at a time. We begin to believe that God is bigger than the mountains in our lives, more certain than our greatest uncertainties, and completely faithful. In other words, we begin to have faith in God. We begin to believe that we can be free, we can be whole.

It's true that a mountain represents a huge obstacle, but it can be moved. Not because our faith is huge, but because we serve a huge God who is capable of doing more than we could ever think or imagine. Anyone who wants to find out what God can do should come join us at Celebrate Recovery. We know because we've seen the mountains in our lives moved.

PRAYER

Lord God, thank you for a place where the power of God is demonstrated. Give me the words to share what you've done in my life with someone who is facing a mountain. In Jesus' name, Amen.

The Sixth Step

Humble yourselves before the Lord, and he will lift you up.

JAMES 4:10

In some recovery material, Step 6 has been referred to as the step that separates the men from the boys. Make no mistake, it also separates the women from the girls. One of the reasons the sixth step is so daunting is that it asks us to allow God to remove *all* our defects of character. Not *some*, but *all*!

> *Step 6: We were entirely ready to have God remove all these defects of character.*

Most of us would be more than willing to have certain character defects go away—and the sooner the better! But let's face it, there are others that are hard to give up. I'm an alcoholic, but there came a time in my life, a moment of clarity, when I knew I had hit bottom and was ready to stop drinking. But was I ready to stop lying? Stop being greedy? Was I ready to let go of resentments, impatience, selfishness? I had been indulging these things for a long time. Like weeds in a garden, the roots went deep! Sure, I could see what needed to be done, but could I allow the changes to occur? Each of us must find the answers to these questions.

That place between recognition and willingness can be filled with fear, and fear can trigger old dependencies. It's essential that we accept God's help throughout this step.

--- PRAYER ---

Father, I admit I am fearful and anxious about dealing with my character defects. I ask again for your help as I take this important step. In Jesus' name, Amen.

Superman

*He said to me, "My grace is sufficient for you, for my power is made
perfect in weakness." Therefore I will boast all the more gladly
about my weaknesses, so that Christ's power may rest on me.*

2 CORINTHIANS 12:9

My son-in-law told me that when he was a kid, he loved Superman. He had a cape, a shirt with a big S on the front, and tights. At one point, he confessed, he actually thought he *was* Superman. That all changed when he jumped off the roof of his house, thinking he could fly. Reality set in when his face met the ground.

When I try to do things that God never intended for me to do, the results are about as successful as my son-in-law's flying experience. I end up falling flat on my face. In Celebrate Recovery, I learn to listen as God speaks to me through his Word and through other people.

When I slow down enough to listen and meditate on God's Word, his plan unfolds for my life, and I come to realize there is only one Superman—and it isn't me! It's only in admitting my weakness that Christ's power can come to rest on me.

Today, I am joyfully dependent on Jesus Christ and his Holy Spirit who lives in me. Because of that I will be able to do things today I never thought possible, such as forgive, say "I'm sorry" and mean it, be totally honest, and look out for the interests of others.

PRAYER

Father, I will be the first to say that I don't have superpowers. I depend on you to bring power to my life— power to change and power to do what is right. In Jesus' name, Amen.

Perspective

This service that you perform is not only supplying the needs of the Lord's people but is also overflowing in many expressions of thanks to God.

2 CORINTHIANS 9:12

I'm writing this at a local coffee shop. At the next table, two teenage girls are drinking coffee, talking about life, and lamenting about all the things they have to face each day—tests, boys, etc. I'm not trying to listen, but they aren't keeping their voices down either.

From my perspective, the problems these girls are discussing are just silly. I'm a grown-up with real problems. But the truth is, I was a teenager once, and when I was at that age, the kinds of problems they're talking about seemed huge, life-shattering even. I can't help but wonder if this is how God views me when I complain about the problems in my life. To me they are life-shattering, but to him they could seem just plain silly.

The point is that each of us can see only one small portion of life, the portion that is in front of us right now. But God sees all. To him there are no huge problems—only those we think are huge. To him all things are doable, all things are possible. So . . . no reason to panic. It's just a matter of perspective.

PRAYER

Father, help me to trust you for the things I can see and the things I can't see because you see and understand everything. In Jesus' name, Amen.

How Do You Really Feel?

This is the day the LORD has made; let us rejoice and be glad in it.

PSALM 118:24 NKJV

We all have those days when it feels like the world is coming down around us. It could be a mood swing or a tough situation spinning out of control. It might be an overwhelming sense of guilt or sorrow. Whatever the case, the last thing we want to do is rejoice in the Lord.

A few years ago, my dad was sick and I had some rough days watching him struggle. Those rough days continued even after he went to be with the Lord. For example, I was going through some old pictures and saw my sweet dad's picture. All those painful emotions came rushing back. I missed him so much and felt deep sorrow in my soul. As I talked that out with the Lord, though, I was reminded of all the blessed days I was able to spend with my dad. My heart was filled with joy knowing that he is at peace with our Lord.

When I don't feel like rejoicing, I know I can and should tell God how I truly feel. The beauty is that he ends up giving me a reason to rejoice—even if it is just for another day to live and serve him. I have learned through Celebrate Recovery to embrace my feelings, rather than stuffing them down inside. God has given me a heart that hurts, but he has also given me a heart that loves.

PRAYER

You are my God, and I will praise you. No matter what I encounter in life, that will always be my song. In Jesus' name, Amen.

Take a Stand

*When the servant of the man of God got up and went out early the next
morning, an army with horses and chariots had surrounded the city.
"Oh, my lord, what shall we do?" the servant asked. "Don't be afraid,"
the prophet answered. "Those who are with us are more than those
who are with them." And Elisha prayed, "O LORD, open his eyes so he
may see." Then the LORD opened the servant's eyes, and he looked and
saw the hills full of horses and chariots of fire all around Elisha.*

2 KINGS 6:15–17

During WWII, General Creighton Abrams and the US Third Army
found themselves surrounded by the Germans to the east, west,
north, and south. General Abrams addressed his troops with these
words: "Gentlemen, for the first time in the history of this campaign, we
are in a position to attack the enemy in any direction!"

I know we all feel overwhelmed, outnumbered, and surrounded
by the enemy at times. When that happens, we need to remember two
important truths: First, there are more standing with us than there are
those standing with the enemy. Even when we aren't able to see them,
they are there, ready for battle. Second, those who have us surrounded
must be identified so we can engage the enemy on every side.

Our God has given us the victory, no matter what our eyes tell us.
Will we seize the opportunity to aggressively pursue the enemy that
surrounds us? The battle is great, but the Great One is fighting right
alongside us.

PRAYER

*Lord God, you are the one who gives me the strength to fight for my life. Open
my eyes to see the great army that is fighting alongside me. In Jesus' name, Amen.*

Pillow Spiders

"Do not worry about tomorrow, for tomorrow will worry about itself. Each day has enough trouble of its own."

MATTHEW 6:34

Daddy, help! There's a huge spider on my pillow!"
There's nothing like being ripped from sleep by a panicked, screaming child. I jumped out of bed and ran into her room, where I found her frozen and staring at her pillow. Her finger shaking, she pointed to a big black spider crawling across her pillow. I walked over to kill the spider (it's in my job description) and picked up a big, black ball of fuzz, probably from the stuffed penguin on her bed. There was no threat, there never had been, but my daughter didn't know it. She saw something and drew a conclusion: Spider! Danger!

To be honest, I have a tendency to do this myself. Not with spiders, but with my everyday life. I see something, hear something, and jump to a conclusion. That kind of thinking is dangerous because it can cause us to worry about things that aren't real, try to fix situations that don't need to be fixed, or strive to please people who might not even be upset.

To make good decisions, we need to get all the information before we rush to worry, stress out about a confrontation, or decide recovery is too difficult. We will do better if we can calmly assess the situation and then ask God to help us find the right solution.

--- PRAYER ---

Father, thank you for giving me the patience I need to rightly assess the situations I encounter without panicking and jumping to conclusions. In Jesus' name, Amen.

Hurt People, Hurt People

"Let us fix our eyes on Jesus, the author and perfecter of our faith, who for the joy set before him endured the cross."

HEBREWS 12:1-2

In recovery we hear that "hurt people, hurt people." We've all experienced this, and sometimes, we see it happen to others. It's heartbreaking. School shootings, for example, are a grotesque display of true evil that has brought heartbreak and pain to so many lives. How are we to deal with such deep pain? Where is the hope in a tragedy such as this?

The answer is that we have no hope apart from Christ. Without him, such tragedies just spawn more hurting people who go on to lash out at others in a futile effort to quench their own pain. Jesus is the only source of comfort and light capable of guiding us through our pain to a better place.

When our hearts are breaking and we have questions swirling around in our heads—questions we fear have no answers—God invites us to come and talk it out with him. Many of the answers may be past our comprehension, but knowing the answers are safe with him allows us to hand our questions—burdens too great for us to bear—over to him. God cares about everything that concerns us, everything that grieves our hearts. In the midst of the darkness, he is our hope, the one we can trust.

PRAYER

Lord, my heart is breaking as I see hurting people hurting people all around me. Help me to leave my unanswered questions with you. In Jesus' name, Amen.

Take It to the Father

My God will meet all your needs according to the riches
of his glory in Christ Jesus. To our God and Father be
glory for ever and ever. In Jesus' name ever. Amen.

PHILIPPIANS 4:19–20

My wife and I were traveling from Colorado to Louisiana with our two grandsons, ages two and four. I didn't know it was possible for two little boys to ask so many questions.

"How many people can fit on this plane?"

"How fast do we have to go before we fly?"

"Why don't the windows open?"

"How much does the apple juice cost?"

"Why can't I sit where I want to?"

You get the picture and believe me, this was just the tip of the iceberg. But the thing is that I didn't mind them asking all those questions because I'm their Papa. Our heavenly Father doesn't mind us asking questions either. So why don't we? Are we afraid we will bother him? Interrupt his busy schedule? He might think my question is dumb or silly? Or maybe we think he won't answer us anyway.

The Bible tells us that Jesus gave his life as a sacrifice for our sin, removing the wall that once stood between us and our Creator. Now we can talk to God anytime we want, about anything we wish. He's looking forward to hearing our questions because he's our loving Father in heaven.

PRAYER

Heavenly Father, thank you for letting me bring my questions to you. I know that you may not choose to answer them all because some are just beyond my comprehension, but I thank you for listening just the same. In Jesus' name, Amen.

Plans for You

"I know the plans I have for you," declares the LORD, "plans to prosper you and not to harm you, plans to give you hope and a future."

JEREMIAH 29:11

It takes a little time for our minds to grasp this awesome truth: The God who spoke the universe into existence is on our side. He's standing by, ready to help us recover from our hurts, hang-ups, and habits. Sometimes it might feel like we are on our own—but we aren't. We have a big God, a loving God, a faithful God, who invites us to call him Father.

Not only does God love us, not only is he on our side, but he also has plans for us, good plans, exciting plans. Our enemy would like us to think that God's aim is to take our freedom away, strip us of the things we love to do. But the opposite is true. When we surrender our lives to God, we gain the privilege of living out his plans for our lives. Not only does God's plan give us freedom, but also hope and a future.

Once we've given ourselves to God, it's time to start working on his plan for our lives. Typically, that's another one-step-at-a-time process, and we know by now that we can achieve anything if we tackle it a little at a time. All along the way, we will know that we are at the very center of God's will, a place where miracles happen.

PRAYER

Father, I desire to know your plan for my life. As I begin my journey, I want to thank you for revealing it to me one step at a time. In Jesus' name, Amen.

Bee Stings

*We know that in all things God works for the good of those who
love him, who have been called according to his purpose.*

ROMANS 8:28

As a child, I ran across a downed tree one day while playing in our
backyard. Like most boys, I couldn't resist hopping up on it and
walking down its long trunk. I'd been balancing pretty well until my foot
slipped and I fell to the ground. That's when the trouble started. As I fell,
my foot kicked a hive of bees hidden in the brush next to the tree. By the
time I got to the house, I had fifteen bee stings. Ouch! To this day, I am
very aware of bees around me.

We will always have slips in our journey to recovery. We try to keep
our balance, but every once in a while, we take a tumble. When that happens, our enemy rises up like a hive of angry bees bent on destroying us.
That's when we must pick ourselves up and run to God and the safety
of his presence. Just as my mom did so many years ago, he will calm us
down, doctor our stings, forgive our carelessness, and then wrap us up in
his loving arms.

It's important to be aware that our enemy, the devil, has been known
to lie hidden in the brush, waiting to do us harm. But we can't let the
fear of bee stings steal our confidence or keep us from adventures in
the woods.

PRAYER

*Father God, thank you for making me aware of the dangers around me. I know,
though, that even if I get stung, you are there to help and comfort me. In Jesus'
name, Amen.*

Taking Out the Trash

You were taught, with regard to your former way of life, to put off
your old self, which is being corrupted by its deceitful desires; to
be made new in the attitude of your minds; and to put on the new
self, created to be like God in true righteousness and holiness.

EPHESIANS 4:22–24

My wife and I both woke up before the alarm went off. We were excited about the trip we were taking later that morning. As we prepared to leave, I threw a garbage bag full of trash onto the back of my flatbed truck, thinking I would drop it into the garbage dumpster on our way out. Unfortunately, I got so busy that I forgot.

Twenty miles down the road, I remembered and shouted, "Oh no, the trash!" I was just sure it had fallen off on the highway where the police would find it, locate our address on some piece of discarded mail, and stick us with a big fine. I pulled over, rushed around to the back of the truck, and to my great relief found that the bag was still there. I immediately disposed of it in a nearby dumpster.

Remembering to get rid of the trash right away is important in recovery also. If we set it to the side and forget about it, some significant consequences might come to bear on our lives and the lives of those we love. It's so much better to take care of the trash right away.

PRAYER

Father, help me to keep the refuse in my life taken care of so that it won't cause
trouble for me or those I care about. In Jesus' name, Amen.

Playing Pretend

*"There is nothing concealed that will not be disclosed, or hidden
that will not be made known. What you have said in the dark
will be heard in the daylight, and what you have whispered in the
ear in the inner rooms will be proclaimed from the roofs."*

LUKE 12:2-3

My kids like to play pretend. It's a game in which everyone gets to choose who they want to be. That might be a superhero, a princess, a teacher, anything they want. Right now their pretending is focused on an office setting. My middle daughter is challenging my son to "pick up production!"

I can remember playing pretend when I was a child. I'd like to say that I don't play that game anymore now that I'm an adult, but that wouldn't be true. I play pretend all the time. I pretend something doesn't hurt or scare me. I pretend a situation doesn't need my attention. I pretend everything is fine in my relationships so I don't have to confront anyone. I pretend things will be all right if I just ignore them. As adults, we don't call this playing pretend: we call it *denial*.

Breaking out of denial isn't a one-time thing; we have to do it again and again. Denial always ends up causing us more pain. Ultimately, denial keeps us stuck and unable to get the healing we need.

Making the decision to step out of denial and into God's truth can be uncomfortable, even painful. But in the end, dealing honestly with the issue will be a key part of recovery in that area of our lives.

PRAYER

Thank you, Lord, for helping me face my problems and deal with them rather than bury them and pretend they don't exist. In Jesus' name, Amen.

Drinking Buddies

A righteous man is cautious in friendship, but the
way of the wicked leads them astray.

PROVERBS 12:26

I shall stay until the wind changes." That's what Mary Poppins said, and it reminds me of some of the friends I had before I got into recovery. When we get serious about asking God to help us begin to change our hurts, hang-ups, and habits, we may receive an unfavorable reaction from some of those friends we believed would always be there for us.

I referred to some of my old friends as my "drinking buddies." They were always there for me when I was practicing my addiction and compulsions. But when I told them I had finally had enough, they were less than supportive. They would call me from a bar and ask me to come over to shoot pool. I explained to them that I couldn't hang out in a place where people were drinking, but they didn't seem to get it. When I asked them to meet me for a cup of coffee instead, they thought I was kidding. Slowly we lost contact. I call those guys my Mary Poppins friends. When the wind changed, they were gone.

I did find the support I needed, though. The men in my recovery group reached out to me and would ask, "John, how are you doing?" As the days passed, they became my accountability team and my sponsor.

Most of us have lost friends when we decided to put God and sobriety first in our lives. But new friends, friends who truly understand what we are going through, are a gift from God.

PRAYER

Father, I thank you for the new friends you have placed in my life. In Jesus'
name, Amen.

The Charges Are Dropped!

When you were stuck in your old sin-dead life, you were incapable
of responding to God. God brought you alive—right along with
Christ! Think of it! All sins forgiven, the slate wiped clean, that old
arrest warrant canceled and nailed to Christ's cross. He stripped
all the spiritual tyrants in the universe of their sham authority
at the Cross and marched them naked through the streets.

COLOSSIANS 2:13–15 MSG

As I sat in a circle of people, waiting for the share group to start, some-one asked this question: "What's the best news anyone ever told you?" Without hesitation, one of the men shouted out, "The charges are dropped!" We all laughed but we knew exactly how good those words were. In reality, those should be the words we all long to hear. Those old arrest warrants with our names on them have been canceled by the redeeming work of Christ.

It can be shocking when we realize that none of us—not even one—was good enough to be in the presence of Jesus. The Bible says that even those who led really good lives are separated from God by their sin. We are all in need of a Savior.

Every one of us must make the decision to become a follower of Jesus Christ. And when we do, regardless of how we've lived our lives, the message we receive is, "The charges are dropped!" Forgiveness is instant and complete! Now that's real freedom.

PRAYER

Thank you, Father, for sending Jesus to arrange for the charges against me to be dropped. You have given me a new chance to live my life in a way that is pleasing to you. In Jesus' name, Amen.

Welcome Home

"The father said to his servants, 'Quick! Bring the best robe and put it on
him. Put a ring on his finger and sandals on his feet. Bring the fattened calf
and kill it. Let's have a feast and celebrate. For this son of mine was dead
and is alive again; he was lost and is found.' So they began to celebrate."

LUKE 15:22–24

In the parable of the prodigal in Luke 15, a man had two sons. At the request of his younger son, the man divided his estate and gave the younger son his portion. The son quickly squandered his wealth by living in a wild and ungodly manner. Finally, he found himself hungry and homeless. In desperation he went to work caring for pigs. Realizing that even his father's servants were well fed, he determined to return and ask his father to receive him, not as a son but as a hired servant. Arriving at home, he was surprised to see his father waiting to welcome him with open arms.

When we finally reach bottom, our heavenly Father is waiting to receive us again, not as servants but as sons. He has prepared places like Celebrate Recovery through which we can leave our past behind and experience the joy of being welcomed home.

H is for healthy. **O** is for open. **M** is for maturing. **E** is for encouraging.

PRAYER

Father, thank you for welcoming me back with open arms, and thank you for preparing a place for me to come home to, a place that is healthy, open, maturing, and encouraging. In Jesus' name, Amen.

The Last Day

We know that if the earthly tent we live in is destroyed, we have a building from God, an eternal house in heaven, not built by human hands.

2 CORINTHIANS 5:1

What if we knew that today was the last day we would live here on earth? What would we do? How would we choose to live it? Life has no guarantees. We are all here for just a short time, about 78 years on average. The following helped me settle the question in my own mind.

1. Have you ensured your eternal life by inviting Jesus Christ, the only true Higher Power, into your life as Lord and Savior?
2. Have you made amends to those you have hurt?
3. Have you offered your forgiveness to those who have hurt you?
4. Have you spoken with the people who are most important to you and let them know the significant impact they have had on your life?

Now think about what a difference it would make if we lived each day here on earth as if it were our last—each day, surrendering to God's will, making amends to those we have hurt, forgiving those who hurt us, and spending time with those we love. Then the real last day would be business as usual, wouldn't it? And all the days in between would be days of significance lived with meaning and purpose.

PRAYER

Father, I want to live each day as if it is my last—spending my days preparing for the eternity I will be spending with you. In Jesus' name, Amen.

The Hammer

The fruit of the Spirit is love, joy, peace, patience, kindness, goodness,
faithfulness, gentleness, self-control; against such things there is no law.

GALATIANS 5:22–23

In Galatians 5, we are given a list of the fruit of the Spirit that now lives in us. Part of that new fruit is gentleness, something I rarely experienced as a child. I was raised to be a man's man, rough and ready for anything. So being a "gentle-man" is something I have to work on daily. That may be why this quote from Abraham Maslow hit home for me: "If the only tool you have is a hammer, then every problem is a nail."

For many of the people in recovery, this quote describes how they deal with the relationships in their lives. For example, a woman shared how growing up with an alcoholic father taught her to believe that yelling is the way to handle spilled milk, misbehaving children, a husband coming home late, and friends not meeting one's expectations. She wondered why her relationships didn't last.

In Celebrate Recovery, we have a whole toolbox full of principles taken from Jesus' teachings of the Beatitudes in Matthew 5. We also have support groups in which we share our faulty ways of thinking and what we've learned from our mistakes. We discover a whole new way of handling problems, and we are learning to become a part of the solution rather than the problem. We learn to redirect the energy we spend hammering ourselves and every other person in our lives into a new way of living.

PRAYER

Father, a hammer didn't work in my life, but your love did. Thank you for teaching
me how to live a better life. In Jesus' name, Amen.

Action Packed

*Prepare your minds for action; be self-controlled; set your hope
fully on the grace to be given you when Jesus Christ is revealed.*

1 PETER 1:13

Recovery is not a passive lifestyle; it's action packed. To find the life
change we desire, we must trust that God will do his part, and be
willing to do our part by preparing our minds for action. What does that
mean? It means that we "get in the game."

With any sporting event, we know that watching a game and playing
in a game are two different things. Playing in a game takes focus and a
mind-set of readiness. On the sidelines, things are different. We can go
to the snack bar, carry on a conversation with a friend, text, or talk on the
phone. We can even leave early. But when we're playing, we have to be
alert and mindful of what's going on around us.

We need to have that same presence of mind while in recovery. It's
our life at stake, our wellness. We have to play the game rather than just
watch it. Then, while we are doing our part, we can depend on God to
do his. While we offer forgiveness and make amends, God heals relationships. While we attend meetings and commit to the process, God
gives us the power to find freedom from our hurts, hang-ups, and habits.
While we serve others, God recycles our pain to help those who are hurting. It's all about action!

PRAYER

*Father, thank you for faithfully doing your part while I do mine. In Jesus' name,
Amen.*

It's Just Rain

"Do not let your hearts be troubled. Trust in God; trust also in me."

JOHN 14:1

I woke up one morning to a steady rain and a moaning, whining, terrified dog. She has always been frightened by rain, maybe because she's associated it with thunder and lightning in the past. I tried to comfort her by saying, "Beulah, lie down! It's just rain, so quit stressing out, girl." Then it hit me. Like Beulah, I often let the most harmless things stress me out.

Beulah was doing a perfectly natural thing—she was looking to her daddy for comfort. I wondered why I don't do the same when I feel anxious and stressed out. Why it doesn't seem natural for me to go to my heavenly Father for comfort. I know that his response would be much like mine: "Calm down, son, it's just rain."

In the same way I provide peace and comfort for Beulah, God provides peace and comfort to me through his Holy Spirit. It's a much greater peace than I could ever provide for Beulah; it's a peace that passes all understanding. It's waiting there for me whenever I need it.

I read that 75 to 90 percent of all doctor visits are stress-related. It seems that we could all use the peace that only our Father God can bring.

PRAYER

Father God, thank you for giving me your comfort and peace whenever I come to you. In Jesus' name, Amen.

A Hole in the Sky

God was reconciling the world to himself in Christ, not counting
men's sins against them. And he has committed to us the message
of reconciliation. We are therefore Christ's ambassadors,
as though God were making his appeal through us.

2 CORINTHIANS 5:19−20

Not too long ago I cut down a tree, and as it fell to the ground, I
turned to survey the situation. What I noticed was not the tree on
the ground, but the huge hole in the sky where the tree had been. There
were plenty of other trees around, but nothing would fill the space where
that tree had been.

I immediately thought about leaders I've known in Celebrate
Recovery, those who for one reason or another stepped out of leadership. There are plenty of other leaders still around, but now there's a hole
where those who left once served. They may have grown weary, burned
out, or relapsed. Whatever the reason, they are missed. That's why it is so
important to let our ministry leaders and pastors know what great value
they are, not only to us, but also to the Kingdom of God.

Our Father is counting on leaders like us to take the message of hope
in Jesus Christ to others whom he is calling. Together we can do this!

───────────── PRAYER ─────────────

Thank you, Father, for those who have served and remained faithful. For those who
have not, I pray you would raise them up again for your glory. In Jesus' name, Amen.

Power and Praise

Let all who take refuge in you be glad; let them ever sing for joy. Spread your protection over them, that those who love your name may rejoice in you.

PSALM 5:11

One of my favorite things about Celebrate Recovery is that it's for everybody. It isn't just for addicts and alcoholics, though it certainly is for them too. It's for anyone struggling with hurts, hang-ups, or habits. God's life-changing power is available to everyone, no matter who they are or where they come from.

God's power covers each of us as we walk down the road to recovery. He is there to guide us, to help us, to pick us up when we fall, to protect us when we are attacked, to be there for us when we feel alone, to give us the power to change. And he uses our Celebrate Recovery family to achieve much of that.

We don't have the power to change on our own, but God can use our Celebrate Recovery family to help us stick with the plan until we win. Through our accountability partners, he makes himself known to us and assures us that he is right there, ready to act on our behalf. Let's thank God for giving us the love and support we need to succeed.

PRAYER

Dear Lord, thank you for my Celebrate Recovery family. You have used them to do great things in my life. In Jesus' name, Amen.

Keep Breathing

By the word of the LORD were the heavens made,
their starry host by the breath of his mouth.

PSALM 33:6

During a flight to Denver, the flight attendant was explaining what to do in case of an emergency. I have heard the talk dozens of times. I listened as she described the oxygen masks and noted, "Even though the oxygen is flowing, the bag may not inflate."

Wow! Isn't that the truth with life? Sometimes we are moving forward and changing without even realizing it. I have to remind myself that just because I don't "feel" like I'm breathing and changing, I am, with my heavenly Father's help. All I have to do is keep breathing and seeking his will.

We must never forget that we have only one true source of "oxygen." Even in dire circumstances, when it doesn't look like he is doing anything to help us, he has never left our side. He will never give up on us, never leave us, never desert us. His hand in our affairs may not be obvious or observable, but we can be certain that he is still there supporting, strengthening, and sustaining within us the breath of life.

PRAYER

Lord, you are the air that I breathe. Without you I am nothing. Thank you for never leaving or forsaking me. In Jesus' name, Amen.

Storm Warning

*My frame was not hidden from you when I was made in the secret
place. When I was woven together in the depths of the earth,
your eyes saw my unformed body; all the days ordained for me
were written in your book before one of them came to be.*

PSALM 139:15–16

My wife and I were sitting on a plane in Jackson, Mississippi, only one hundred miles from home. We couldn't take off because of severe thunderstorms. The pilot told us that a large storm cell was right on top of us, but from the window, it didn't look that bad.

I wonder how many times my Father has diverted my plans because of storms that I didn't even know about? The next time I'm late because a train is stopping traffic or my wife has to go back into the house for one more thing or I have just missed an elevator—whatever the delay—I will remember that maybe God is saying, "Sorry, but the purpose for this delay is to keep you from crashing."

This much we can know for certain: Our God is supremely interested in what is best for us. Even when I don't have eyes to see what's going on around me, I will trust him to keep me safe and show me the way.

PRAYER

Thank you, Father, for keeping me safe from the storms that pass through my life. In Jesus' name, Amen.

Stop and Pray

*Do not be anxious about anything, but in every situation, by
prayer and petition, with thanksgiving, present your requests to
God. And the peace of God, which transcends all understanding,
will guard your hearts and your minds in Christ Jesus.*

PHILIPPIANS 4:6−7

I've decided that, today, I'm going to stop and pray. I'm going to do what God's Word says I should do when I have a problem. He instructs me to bring every situation, every circumstance, every struggle to him. So I'm going to just stop and get quiet before him. I'm going to resist the urge to rush through my day. Today, I'm going to slow down and listen for God's voice. Today, I'm going to stop and pray.

First, I'm going to talk to God about all the things that are worrying me. I'm going to tell him what's on my mind. I'm going to let him help me see why I've been losing sleep. I will bring everything to him. I will thank him for the answers yet to be provided. Then I'm going to thank him for the peace that is flooding my heart and mind. Before I go, I'm going to ask God to be with me in every meeting, to assist me with every task, to be present in every conversation.

Throughout the day, I will soak up the peace, and should it begin to drift away, I'll stop, pray, and bring my worries to God again. And I'll keep on bringing them to him until his indescribable peace returns.

PRAYER

Thank you, Lord, for your peace that passes my understanding. I give you my worries and my concerns. Thank you for reminding me to stop and pray. In Jesus' name, Amen.

Keeping Priorities Straight

*Thank GOD! Call out his Name! Tell the whole world who he is and what
he's done! Sing to him! Play songs for him! Broadcast all his wonders!
Revel in his holy Name, GOD-seekers, be jubilant! Study GOD and his
strength, seek his presence day and night; remember all the wonders he
performed, the miracles and judgments that came out of his mouth.*

I CHRONICLES 16:8–12 MSG

In my younger years, my priorities were way out of whack. I thought
that if I had a new house or new car or the latest technology, I would be
happy. All I needed was more money, new clothes, expensive furniture,
and life would be rosy.

When I realized that these things brought only temporary highs,
I began to fill the void and stifle my disappointment with alcohol.
That made matters worse, and soon fear and anxiety were chasing me
through life.

God reached out to me. He taught me that only my relationship
with Jesus Christ could fill my empty heart. Only his presence in my
life could relieve my loneliness, fear, anxiety, and hopelessness. He has
made me a better husband, father, grandpa, and leader. God loved me
enough to let me see the futility of my own priorities and the abundance
that comes with his.

When we have had enough of our own ways, he will be faithful to
show us how to live lives that bring real joy and happiness.

PRAYER

*Father, I have had enough of my own twisted priorities. Show me how to live my
life in a way that will bring true joy, peace, and happiness. In Jesus' name, Amen.*

Love and Laughter

Our mouths were filled with laughter, our tongues with songs of joy. Then
it was said among the nations, "The LORD has done great things for
them." The LORD has done great things for us, and we are filled with joy.

PSALM 126:2−3

After a week of camping, my wife and I were on our way to pick up five of our grandkids so they could spend the weekend with us before we headed home. Our camper had been neat and quiet all week, but within thirty minutes of the kids' arrival, everything had changed. There were clothes, sleeping bags, and backpacks everywhere. Within the first few minutes, there was also spilled milk, cookie crumbs on the sofa, and much more. There was also a lot of love and laughter. My wife and I went to bed with smiles on our faces and hearts full of love.

I thought about this and how much it parallels our Celebrate Recovery group. People come into our group, into our lives. They're loud, and they make messes. But as we love them into our family and clean up a few messes, they learn to laugh, their hurts begin to heal, they come to know Jesus, and it's all worthwhile.

The love and laughter we share with family and friends is all we will take to heaven with us. Those relationships are the most important thing of all.

PRAYER

Lord God, thank you for giving us the ability to laugh even when faced with messy
campers and messy people. It reminds us of what is truly important. In Jesus'
name, Amen.

Pumpkin Vines

*"I am the vine; you are the branches. If you remain in me and I in you,
you will bear much fruit; apart from me you can do nothing."*

JOHN 15:5

A few years ago I took a portion of my small backyard and planted pumpkins. The kids helped me place the seeds, and they were excited as we watched them grow and grow and grow. What I hadn't realized is that pumpkins grow on vines, and vines spread. Pretty soon our whole backyard was covered in pumpkin vines.

I worked hard to keep the vines under control by pruning them. I was amazed to see how fast the vines shriveled up and died once I had separated them from their source. Without water and nutrients, they had no life force. The vines died, and any pumpkins attached to them stopped growing.

The same thing happens to us when we are separated from our life force—Jesus. Without him, our spiritual life, our recovery, will shrivel up and die. We must stay connected to him if we are to see victory and freedom from our hurts, hang-ups, and habits. So how do we stay connected? We do that by spending time in fellowship with God, reading and meditating on his Word, the Bible, and by allowing him to use us to bless others.

— PRAYER —

Father, your Word says that you are the vine. Help me to stay connected to you, for I know that is the only way that I can grow strong. In Jesus' name, Amen.

Washing Socks

He was crushed for our iniquities; the punishment that brought
us peace was upon him, and by his wounds we are healed.

ISAIAH 53:5

One Christmas, I was watching the movie *Santa Claus Is Coming to Town* with my grandchildren. One of the scenes has a young Kris Kringle talking with some kids at a washing station where they are washing their socks. Kris asks them what they are doing, and they answer that they are washing socks. "We are judged by how much work we get done and how clean our socks are," they told him.

I used to believe this is how life works: we are judged by how hard we work at being good and doing things in a perfect way. Today I know that's wrong. This thinking is guaranteed to leave us exhausted and defeated. It's so much better to surrender our lives to God and let him cleanse our hearts and minds. He doesn't judge us; he heals us. No matter how hard we try, we simply cannot clean our socks and keep them clean on our own. But because he takes our feeble efforts and makes them right, we are judged worthy and perfect in his sight.

We can spend our lives like those kids, working for what we will never achieve. Or we can surrender to God and walk away whiter than snow.

PRAYER

Father, you are the master, the one who cleans our soiled hearts whiter than
snow. Take my life and make it what it should be. I surrender all to you. In Jesus'
name, Amen.

Always Grateful

*Just as you received Christ Jesus as Lord, continue to live your
lives in him, rooted and built up in him, strengthened in the faith
as you were taught, and overflowing with thankfulness.*

COLOSSIANS 2:6–7

Our God is so good to us, so generous, so loving, so kind. How could we go even one day without verbalizing our gratitude? Having an ongoing list helps us keep our focus on all the good things our heavenly Father has done, is doing, and will be doing in our lives.

These are the Top Ten things I am thankful for:

1. Salvation—the price Jesus paid for me.
2. Hope—the belief that God will work out all things for my good.
3. Forgiveness—freely given and freely received.
4. God's unconditional love—despite my shortcomings, which are many.
5. My godly wife—she is undeserved, a gift from God.
6. My children and grandchildren—reminders of how much God loves me.
7. My forever family—those who continue to point me to God.
8. Celebrate Recovery—a program that reminds me that every life is valuable.
9. Peace of mind—a constant in the midst of a chaotic world.
10. Friendship with God—something I never imagined possible.

These are just my Top Ten. God has given us so much to be grateful for, no tablet or notebook could possibly be big enough to hold them all. But there is much benefit in trying. God is great and unswervingly gracious. My heart overflows with thankfulness for all he has done.

PRAYER

*Father God, as I list the things I'm grateful for each day, may they be a suitable
tribute to the grace and goodness you bring to my life. In Jesus' name, Amen.*

Recycled Pain

We know that in all things God works for the good of those who
love him, who have been called according to his purpose.

ROMANS 8:28

I don't know anyone whose life has gone exactly as they wanted it to. I don't know anyone who has managed to escape pain of some kind, whether that pain was caused by someone else or they brought it on themselves. We've all been hurt, and we've all hurt others. The good news is that God never wastes a hurt. He can make good from everything that happens to us, both the good and the bad. There is one condition, though.

God brings good from the bad in our lives when we give it to him and allow him to use it to help someone else. Though we might wonder how that is possible, we must remember that we're talking about God—the author of what is possible. He can redeem our pain and use our experiences to encourage others as they are walking through the fire.

Of course, this doesn't take the pain away from our lives or make it any less difficult to deal with. But God does give our pain a purpose, a mission. He uses our greatest weaknesses to strengthen and encourage others. Pain is just plain no good, but God can bring good out of the good and the bad.

PRAYER

Father, I'm amazed to learn that you can use my pain to help someone else. Thank you for giving my pain a purpose. In Jesus' name, Amen.

The Seventh Step

*If we confess our sins, he is faithful and just and will forgive
us our sins and purify us from all unrighteousness.*

1 JOHN 1:9

Once we ask God to remove our character defects and shortcomings, we begin a journey that will lead us to new freedom from our past. We shouldn't look for perfection, but instead rejoice in steady progress. In other words, patient improvement. God has promised to keep right on helping us until the work within us is finished (Philippians 1:6). He's in it for the long haul.

Step 7: We humbly asked him to remove all our shortcomings.

If we cling to self-reliance, we will never go beyond this step, but victory is ensured as long as we truly place our reliance on God. We must voluntarily submit to every change he wants us to make in our lives and humbly ask him to remove every shortcoming. We must be fully committed to allowing God to be the life-changer!

We are not the "how and when" committee. We are the preparation committee—all we have to do is be ready! And if there is suffering in the process, it won't be wasted. God will use everything, even tears of pain, to turn our weaknesses into strengths. All we need to do is humbly ask for his help and be willing to follow his lead. He won't quit until the job is done!

PRAYER

My loving Father, help me prepare my heart for the change you are bringing to my life. I trust that you will continue your work in me until all my weaknesses have been turned into strengths. In Jesus' name, Amen.

Hidden in the Baggage

When they looked for him, he had disappeared! So they asked the LORD,
"Where is he?" And the LORD replied, "He is hiding among the baggage."

1 SAMUEL 10:21–22 NLT

Our team was on the way home from an international mission trip, and each of us had been assigned a task to complete before we could proceed through airport customs. My task was to check on the status of our flight. My wife, Mary, was asked to watch all the bags (about thirty). I headed off to take care of business, and when I returned, I saw Mary sitting, almost hidden, in the middle of all those bags. It was a funny sight.

Later, though, as I rested in my seat on the plane, I reflected on my former way of life. When God first found me, I must have been almost hidden in the baggage. Certainly, I was trying to manage a life filled with it. I would tell myself I was doing a good job, while the truth was that I was losing myself in the baggage.

It was only through recovery and finding a relationship with Jesus that I was able to get rid of all the baggage and find true freedom. Jesus was more than willing to help me through the process, and today I don't even carry a backpack!

I had to laugh at the sight of my wife hidden in all that baggage, but the reality is no laughing matter. God wants us to be free to pursue his perfect will for our lives.

PRAYER

Father God, thank you for freeing me of my baggage and showing me how to keep
my life unfettered by burdens of life. In Jesus' name, Amen.

Fleeing Temptation

*"If your hand or your foot causes you to stumble, cut it off and throw
it away. It is better for you to enter life maimed or crippled than to
have two hands or two feet and be thrown into eternal fire."*

MATTHEW 18:8

I had a conversation with a friend over coffee about how he just can't
seem to get any victory over sexual addiction when he goes online.
Another time, I met with a woman who couldn't seem to stop spending money when she went to the mall. Still another man told me that
he couldn't say no to sweets if they were in the house. Then there was
the woman who didn't think sobriety was possible for her because she
worked at a bar.

These people and many more, including me, are stumbling because
of an area of their lives they'd be better off without, at least for a while. If
going online causes us to stumble, we can install accountability software
or take a break from the Internet. If we're spending too much money, we
can stay away from the mall. If food offers temporary comfort but causes
long-term ill effects, we shouldn't bring it into the house. If we work in a
place that makes sobriety difficult, we can remove ourselves from that
environment.

Some of these can be temporary changes, while others need to be
permanent. If we know what is making us sin, we can distance ourselves
from the temptation. That just makes sense. Once we've done that, God
can help us find wholeness.

--- PRAYER ---

*Father, thank you for showing me that I sometimes sabotage my own recovery. I
know that with your help and my common sense, I can find my way to wholeness.
In Jesus' name, Amen.*

Home-Baked Cookies

You are the body of Christ, and each one of you is a part of it.

1 CORINTHIANS 12:27

A while back my wife attended a women's retreat, and I decided to surprise her by making homemade chocolate chip cookies, her favorite. I found the recipe and looked over the list of ingredients. I had everything I needed—except flour. *No problem*, I thought. *I've got wheat flour. That should work.*

As I put the ingredients in the bowl and mixed them up, I could practically taste the cookies to come. But that was nothing compared to my excitement when I took them out of the oven. I let them cool and then took a bite of one of my masterpieces. Yuck—talk about disgusting! My wife suggested I leave the cookie baking to her. I don't mind because I realize baking cookies is one of her gifts, not one of mine.

I'm grateful for all the gifted people in my life. All the people who can do what I cannot. All the people who come alongside to help me. One of the great things about Celebrate Recovery is that it's a place where God's gifts are used and appreciated. We lift one another up and help one another, using what God has given each of us. That's how the body of Christ at large should work. And all over the world, it is working, with each person bringing his or her gift to be used for the sake of others.

PRAYER

Show me what gift or gifts I have been given to use on behalf of others. Help me also to gladly receive the help of others as they bring what you have given them. In Jesus' name, Amen.

Do You Hear That?

You are a chosen people, a royal priesthood, a holy nation,
God's special possession, that you may declare the praises of him
who called you out of darkness into his wonderful light.

1 PETER 2:9

We were camping in Colorado when my wife was awakened at 2 a.m. "Do you hear that?" she asked. "Hear what?" I answered. "I hear a scratching sound right outside my window! And I can hear something breathing hard! I think it's a bear!"

"I don't think it's a bear," I told her. "Let's go back to sleep."

That's exactly what I did, but my wife kept thinking about what the ranger had told us earlier in the day about bears tearing the lids off metal dumpsters. She was sure there was a bear and that our camper would be no match for such a beast.

My wife was up at first light after a fitful night. She woke me up and asked me to go with her to see what damage the bear had done. As soon as we left the camper, we saw a pine branch pressing against the window, rubbing back and forth with each breeze. The true identity of the scratching sound had been revealed by the light of day.

All of us who have been in recovery know that we can be confused about who we are while the darkness lingers. But in the light of day, our true identities are revealed. We are:

- A person chosen by God.
- A member of God's royal priesthood.
- A citizen of a holy nation.

PRAYER

Father, thank you for shining the light on my true identity. In Jesus' name, Amen.

A Light to My Feet

Your word is a lamp to my feet and a light for my path.

PSALM 119:105

As we walk the road to recovery, we often find ourselves wondering if we are on the right path. There are times when it seems we have far more questions than answers. Am I going the right way? Is this working? Should I keep going, or should I turn around and go back? Does anyone notice how much I've changed?

When we are faced with these questions, we need to go first to God's Word, the Bible. Our accountability partners and sponsors can offer insight, but only God has the truth we need to make our recovery succeed. In the book of Psalms, we read that God's Word serves as a light to our feet. All of us have experienced times of real darkness—no flashlights, no streetlights. When we walk in a world full of darkness, we need a lamp to show us where to take our next step.

The Bible is that lamp. Step-by-step God leads us, showing us what to do. He may not show us his entire plan for our lives, but through his Word, he shows us one step at a time. The truth is, we don't need all the answers. Not right now anyway. Instead, we need just enough light for our feet.

PRAYER

Thank you, Lord, for giving me your Word to light the path along my journey. Help me to take one step at a time. In Jesus' name, Amen.

Look Up!

*"The Spirit gives life; the flesh counts for nothing. The words I
have spoken to you—they are full of the Spirit and life."*

JOHN 6:63

The film *Les Misérables* contains a compelling scene where a prison guard says to Prisoner 24601, "Your time is up, and your parole's begun. Do you know what that means?" The prisoner responds, "Yes, it means I'm free." But the prison guard harshly replies, "No! It means you get your yellow ticket of leave. You are a thief. Look down, you will always be a slave. Look down, you are standing on your grave."

As I watched this scene unfold, I could not help but think about what my life was like when Christ came into it. I was a slave to my junk and looking down in shame. He gave me more than a "ticket of leave." He gave me a new identity and an eternity of true freedom. Sometimes the enemy will come to me and try to make me believe that I'm still that old person, but I know better.

What a gift we have been given! The past is forgiven, our old identity erased. We are free to be who God created us to be, servants of the Most High God. No longer are we the subjects of shame and abuse. No longer are we sitting in the darkness shackled by our past hurts, hang-ups, and habits. We are free! God has changed my name from Worrywart, Shamed One, Addict, Disappointment, Failure, and Lost Soul to Beloved Son, Redeemed Soul, and Blessing. We no longer have reason to look down. Instead, we look up into our Savior's face.

PRAYER

*Thank you, Father, for setting me free. I will look down no more. In Jesus'
name, Amen.*

Ability Versus Availability

We loved you so much that we were delighted to share with you not only the gospel of God but our lives as well, because you had become so dear to us.

1 THESSALONIANS 2:8

It's easy to buy into the lie that our Father uses only the really gifted people he has created—the best looking, most talented, most creative people we see in our churches. But that just isn't true. God uses whomever and whatever he wants to accomplish his will and purpose.

- He used a donkey to speak his words (see Num. 22:28).
- He told the people that if they kept quiet, the stones would cry out with praise for him (see Luke 19:40).
- He taught that those who are faithful with a little will be given more (see Matt. 25).

God's plan has been, and always will be, to use whoever is bold enough to speak for him. God is not really concerned with our ability—after all, he gave it to us in the first place. What he cares about deeply is our *availability*. That is our own choice.

Let's make sure as we plan our days and weeks that we leave room for those inconvenient moments when God sends someone our way because he wants them to hear that he loves them. That's something we all have the ability to do if we choose to.

───── PRAYER ─────

Father, use me as you see fit. I will tune my heart to you, and when you speak, I will obey because I love you. In Jesus' name, Amen.

Becoming a Runner

Though one may be overpowered, two can defend themselves.
A cord of three strands is not quickly broken.

ECCLESIASTES 4:12

A couple of years ago, I decided I was going to run a half-marathon. Since I hadn't run a mile since high school, I called my brother-in-law—a runner—and asked him to help me come up with a training plan. This is what he told me: "Start with a mile a day and increase over time."

Were I a reasonable person, I would have listened to what this experienced runner told me, but instead I decided I'd improve on it. If running one mile a day is good, isn't running three miles a day even better? I found out the hard way that running longer without building up to it is a very bad idea. I blew out my knee and injured my foot. I'd run 120 miles in six weeks, but now I couldn't run at all. I wasn't able to finish my marathon.

We all need people in our lives who are willing to tell us that we need to slow down or speed up. In recovery, it's tempting to skip important steps and find out too late that our bid for wholeness and healing has been short-circuited. The road to recovery is not meant to be traveled alone. We are better together. Whatever we do in life, we should not do it alone. We not only need someone to help us come up with a plan, but we also need someone to help us stick with the plan.

— PRAYER —

Thank you, Father, for putting people in my life who can help me reach my goals. In Jesus' name, Amen.

Making Things New

*You have begun to live the new life, in which you are being made
new and are becoming like the One who made you.*

COLOSSIANS 3:10 NCV

One day my daughter, Taylor, and I were jogging through the neighborhood. The beautiful springlike day was a nice break from the hot days we had been having. Taylor had her iPod playing, and she was singing along in a very animated way. I had my own iPod, and I was listening to a new song I had discovered a few weeks before.

I looked over at my daughter as the words of this new worship song I was listening to began to sink into my consciousness. The song "Beautiful Things" by Gungor brought me to an unexpected worship moment. The lyrics spoke about finding one's way through pain and whether life could ever change. Can everything we have lost be found again?

The words made me think about what God had brought me through as a messed up young man chasing wealth and possessions rather than God. I thought I would always be a dysfunctional mud puddle. But here I was enjoying the day, jogging next to my amazing daughter. God had taken the ruins of my life and replaced them with beauty. That's the promise he gives us when we surrender our lives to him.

PRAYER

*Holy Father, I thank you for your grace, forgiveness, and the beauty you've brought
to my life. In Jesus' name, Amen.*

Tie a New Knot

*Sin shall no longer be your master, because you
are not under the law, but under grace.*

ROMANS 6:14

I hate it when I wake up and things start going wrong right off the bat. It's like my day has already been defined for me. The other morning, I woke up as usual and got ready to go for my workout. I put on my tennis shoes, pulled the laces tight—and my lace broke. I thought to myself: *Great, I can see this is going to be a crappy day!*

I could have let that little shoelace incident ruin the day for me and everyone I encountered. But as soon as I thought about the crappy day ahead, I remembered that Jesus Christ defines my life now, not my shoelaces. He has given me the grace to make a good choice rather than react to everything that happens.

I decided to forget about the top holes, pull up the slack in my laces, and tie a new, smaller knot. After that, I was ready to work out and have a glorious day. It's all about choosing to *act* rather than *react*. We can't change the things that happen to us. But we can choose to be a victim of them or a victor over them!

PRAYER

Lord, thank you for teaching me that I don't have to be a victim of my circumstances. I can choose how I will face each one. In Jesus' name, Amen.

I'm Right Here

I sought the LORD, and he answered me; he delivered me from all my fears.

PSALM 34:4

D addy, I'm afraid. Where are you?"

"I'm right here. Squeeze my hand, so you'll know for sure."

"But I don't like this. I'm scared."

"I know, but it's okay, baby. I'm right here. I'm not going anywhere."

"Is it going to hurt?"

"Probably, but only for a second, and I'm right here."

"You won't leave, will you, Daddy?"

"I'm not going anywhere."

"*Ouch*! That didn't hurt as bad as I thought it would."

"It's all over, you're okay, and I'm still here."

"Thanks, Daddy."

A shot in a doctor's office is a scary thing for a five-year-old. Sitting on my lap, my daughter tried to prepare herself for what was coming. She'd had shots before, but she always hated them, always made them a bigger deal in her head. The only way she would go through with it was if I was with her. Yes, it still hurt, but she got through it. And even though there was a little pain, in the end, she would be stronger.

Many times we make things bigger in our heads, fearing what we know is coming—confrontation, the future, making amends, following through on commitments. There is no reason to go through it alone. Your Father is with you. Stay connected to him and hold on tight to his love. He's right there, and he isn't going anywhere.

—— PRAYER ——

Father, I'm so glad that you are with me no matter what circumstance I encounter. Thank you for holding my hand, encouraging me, and never leaving. In Jesus' name, Amen.

A Faith Killer

God did not give us a spirit of timidity, but a spirit
of power, of love and of self-discipline.

2 TIMOTHY 1:7

Imagine how many hours we waste each year worrying about things that never happen, things that are out of our control. Worry is not an emotion, but a mental obsession. It causes lack of sleep, irritability, strain on relationships, and the feeling that life is floating out there just beyond reach. I am learning that worry is the direct opposite of faith—and fear in disguise.

I want to live smarter, understanding what I can and cannot control. I can't control the lives of others or the circumstances I will have to face. But I can control how I respond to them. Will I allow myself to become obsessed? Will I allow my fear to create enormous monsters in my mind, monsters intent on pulling me down and away from my faith in God?

With God's help, I won't let that happen. Instead, I will seek God daily, saturate my mind with God's Word—the Bible—and immerse myself in prayer. I will turn my worries over to God before they can become obsessions. Then I'm going to record it in my journal. Finally, I'm going to reach out to the people God has placed in my life. I will invite them to tell me if they see something in my life that I need to deal with. I'm going to live the next year free of mental obsessions by seeing that God is in control of my life.

PRAYER

Dear Lord, you are the only one who controls the affairs of this life. Help me as I work to cast off mental obsessions and take on your peace. In Jesus' name, Amen.

Too Big—Too Small

*There is now no condemnation for those who are in Christ
Jesus, because through Christ Jesus the law of the Spirit who
gives life has set you free from the law of sin and death.*

ROMANS 8:1–2

The enemy of our soul would like nothing more than to make us believe that some of our sins are unforgivable, and we are destined to carry the burden of them for the rest of our lives. Maybe it's a big sin, the one we think God wouldn't want to get his hands dirty with. Or it could be one of those small, nagging sins that we think God wouldn't have time for. Either way, we end up hanging onto sins that make us miserable and take up space in our minds that could be used for good, beneficial thoughts.

Years ago my sponsor told me that if I was hanging out with these thoughts, I was in a bad neighborhood, and it was time to move. Good advice. The belief that some of my sins are unforgivable robs me of the peace that Jesus gives me, and his Word tells me that God's forgiveness is absolutely complete.

Once we have been washed in the blood of Jesus, *all* our sins are gone—every last one! There is *no* condemnation for those of us who have been forgiven. God sees us as his perfect, holy children. Why let our sins hold us hostage when we can be free and at peace?

PRAYER

*Thank you, Father, for forgiving all my sin. You've taken care of the guilt and the
shame so that I can walk in holiness before you. In Jesus' name, Amen.*

Sleep in Peace

In peace I will lie down and sleep, for you alone,
LORD, make me dwell in safety.

PSALM 4:8

Sometimes I have trouble sleeping. Well...I always have trouble sleeping. Some nights are just worse than others. Of course, sometimes it's just because I drank coffee too late in the day. But there are some nights when I lie awake thinking about the other day when I really blew it. Or my mind is full of worry about what's coming tomorrow. There are the nights when my mind won't stop working on a problem, and there are nights when I'm struck with regret over past bad choices that have lingering consequences.

The thing is, my mind is often my enemy at bedtime. And I know that I won't be at my best in the morning if I don't get sleep. When this happens to me, I usually toss and turn for a few hours before it dawns on me that there is only one course of action to take—prayer. I visualize myself taking each worry, each failure, each regret, each fear and turning it over to Jesus.

On the nights when I do this, a funny thing happens: I begin to feel peace. I might not fall asleep immediately, but the power of those negative thoughts is broken. Their weight is lifted because I'm not the one carrying them anymore. After that, I just talk to my heavenly Father for a while until I finally drift off.

PRAYER

Thank you, Lord, for taking all my anxious thoughts and carrying them for me so that I can rest peacefully. In Jesus' name, Amen.

Not the Same Thing

Delight yourself in the LORD and he will give you the desires of your heart.

PSALM 37:4

Last summer, I went to the concession stand during a baseball game. I asked the lady at the counter, "Do you have Coke or Pepsi?" Her response? "No, but we have water." Did she really think water was a reasonable substitute for a soft drink? Who knows, maybe she did. But I sure didn't.

It's strange how we try to substitute one thing with another that doesn't even come close. In my life, there are many times when I try to substitute something else for my relationship with God. Even though I've learned the lesson over and over again, I still try to find happiness in possessions. It's ridiculous, and I know that. But I still get caught up in it.

The Lord wants us to seek him, not some ridiculous substitute. He wants us to allow him to fill us up and satisfy our souls. And yet, we can become that waiter behind the counter trying to convince ourselves that "something else" is an acceptable option. Let's drink in God's love and allow him to quench our thirst with his living water. It's the only thing that will satisfy.

PRAYER

Lord, thank you for loving me and filling me with the water of life. Nothing else can quench my thirst and satisfy my yearning. In Jesus' name, Amen.

Twice the Work

*Do not be anxious about anything, but in every situation, by prayer
and petition, with thanksgiving, present your requests to God.*

PHILIPPIANS 4:6

Before one of our trips out of town, I decided to put in a septic system for our camper. I had only one day to get it done, and the weatherman was predicting heavy rain. But I thought I could get it done before the bad weather set in. I had the tank and the lines in place when the rain started, so I covered them with dirt and left, thinking I had done enough to protect the system.

When we returned two weeks later, I found that mud after the heavy rains had crushed the tank. I should have waited until I had time to do the job right. Now I had to dig it up and start over. I had twice the work because I had been in a hurry.

In recovery, we can be in such a hurry to work through the principles and steps that we end up cutting the healing process short. Then we have to do the work again in order to regain what we lost. It never pays to rush through the work God is doing in our hearts and minds. Let's choose to slow down and do the job right.

PRAYER

---

*Father, it's tempting to rush through those painful areas in my life, but I want to
be fully healed. Help me to be patient and do the job of recovery in the right way.
In Jesus' name, Amen.*

Stand Firm

Brothers and sisters, stand firm and hold fast to the teachings we
passed on to you, whether by word of mouth or by letter.

2 THESSALONIANS 2:15

Every day is a decision. Will we continue to go down the road to recovery God's way, or will we choose to go our own way? If we've experienced any change, any growth, any freedom from our hurts, hang-ups, and habits, we know that the power to change comes from God alone. But every day we must decide again if we will keep trusting God, living the truth found in recovery, or turn back to our old ways.

When we are tempted to go the wrong way, we must stand firm and keep trusting God. We should never give up one inch of ground. Why would we want to waste the struggle it took to get here? If we turn back, we lose everything we've gained.

The power to change comes from God. In order to grow and keep on growing, we need to keep our focus on him. We must never turn back and begin to walk by our own power. It is so tempting to try and go our own way, to do it on our own, to think we have it from here, but stand firm.

PRAYER

Lord God, thank you for keeping me on the right path. I want to finish what you've
started in my life. I want to make you proud of me. In Jesus' name, Amen.

Multiplication

*Be kind and compassionate to one another, forgiving
each other, just as in Christ God forgave you.*

EPHESIANS 4:32

Multiplication! The word jumped out at me at a dinner I was attending. We were celebrating the completion of a Celebrate Recovery
step group. What an incredible blessing it was to hear these men talk
about where they were a year ago and where they are today! These men
were now grounded in Christ, becoming the spiritual leaders in their
homes, and living in freedom from a host of hurts, hang-ups, and habits.

But the most exciting thing I saw in these men was a desire for multiplication. Three new men's step groups had formed, led by men from
this one group. These men had caught the vision. Heal and grow, and
when we are well on our way to wholeness, let others know that they can
do what we've done. As we share with others and teach them what we
know, they will find freedom, and we will find strength and resilience.
I am reignited in my vision to create a culture that challenges me to ask,
"Who will you share your recovery story with today?"

Multiplication, in this case, is what happens when we take what the
Lord has done in us and share it with other hurting people. Let's make it
happen every time because when it does, everyone wins big!

PRAYER

*Father, I want to thank you for what you've done in my life by sharing it with oth-
ers who are still hurting and in bondage. In Jesus' name, Amen.*

Uncharted Territory

*Trust in the LORD with all your heart and lean not on
your own understanding; in all your ways acknowledge
him, and he will make your paths straight.*

PROVERBS 3:5–6

When a friend of mine received his one-year recovery chip, he told me that he felt he was now in uncharted territory. My friend is thirty-five, but he hasn't been sober for this long since he was ten years old. This can be a scary place—and many of us have been there.

It occurs to me, though, that uncharted territory could be a great place to be. It just means that we are exploring places we haven't been before. And we can do this because Jesus is with us.

I'm reminded of the Bible account of the apostle Peter walking on the water. He was the only one brave enough to step out of the boat and into uncharted territory when Jesus said, "Come to me." Peter took a few steps before losing his courage and starting to sink. But Jesus was there to take his hand and pull him up.

We shouldn't hesitate to step confidently into our new lives. As long as we are strong and courageous, we might even walk on water as long as we keep our eyes on Jesus. But even if our courage deserts us and we begin to sink, Jesus is there to both save us and keep us safe.

—————————— PRAYER ——————————

*Lord God, I turn my face to you as I walk into the new life you have given me.
Thank you for keeping me safe as I step out of the boat and onto the water. In Jesus'
name, Amen.*

Stay Connected

Rejoice always, pray continually.

1 THESSALONIANS 5:16–17

I love technology and gadgets. My favorite gadget is my phone because it allows me to stay connected to my wife. We can text, video chat, and send each other pictures of our kids or funny things we see. We can even do this weird thing where we actually talk over the phone.

The point is, we can check in with each other throughout the day. Each of us can each see how the other is doing, tell each other if we need something, and check to see if we can do anything for each other. We have an ongoing dialogue.

This reminds me of how prayer works for me. I used to think it had to be formal, every word thought out before it was spoken, but that has all changed for me now. Instead, prayer for me is an ongoing conversation. There is no "amen." I'm not saying there isn't a time for formal, concentrated prayer. I'm saying I like being so connected to God, just as I am with my wife. I love being able to speak his name and feel his presence.

PRAYER

Father, thank you for allowing me to speak with you whenever and wherever I am. I love our long talks and knowing you are as close as my own breath. In Jesus' name, Amen.

Nail It!

"I am making everything new!... Write this down,
for these words are trustworthy and true."

REVELATION 21:5

A friend of mine used to shingle houses for a living. Any time the shingles were straight and looked good on the house, the phrase he would use was, "We nailed it!"

That's always what we want when we start out, but we don't all make it on the first try. Sometimes we mess up, go down the wrong path, become isolated, return to unhealthy relationships, or relapse. Then that old voice starts telling us that we can never go back. God no longer wants us.

That's a lie! But what else would we expect from the enemy of our souls? He is a liar!

God loves us, and he always wants us to come back to him, no matter what poor choices we've made. No matter how long we've been away. Every moment is a chance to start again. We don't have to have it all figured out. We don't have to belabor our mistakes. God simply says to repent, which means to turn around and go in the opposite direction. When our backs are to our sin, we will always be facing God. He is eager to forgive us and give us a brand-new start—another chance to "nail it."

--- PRAYER ---

Heavenly Father, thank you for always welcoming me back, giving me a second chance and a third and a fourth—and a fifth. I can see that you will never give up until I nail it! In Jesus' name, Amen.

Victory Is Ours

You give me your shield of victory, and your right hand
sustains me; you stoop down to make me great.

PSALM 18:35

Sometimes it feels like winter will never end. That's what I was thinking as I left the house to cut more firewood, and it was making me a little grumpy. After all, I had other things to do on this cloudy morning. I was still complaining under my breath as I went up the hill behind the house to start cutting. After the first tree came down, I set my chain saw to the side and turned around to an amazing sight.

The clouds had lifted, revealing a 14,000-foot, snowcapped mountain! As I stood looking at this magnificent example of my heavenly Father's creative genius, all my complaining was replaced with thoughts of gratitude and appreciation. I was healthy, my chain saw was working, I was surrounded by beauty, and there was an abundance of trees to be cut in order to warm our home.

I thought back to my recovery and remembered how God had helped me climb the mountain of my past failures and overcome obstacles that once had defeated me. Complaining has no place in one so redeemed.

PRAYER

Father, thank you for giving me new eyes to see that you have surrounded me with beauty and given me a life of joy, peace, and love. In Jesus' name, Amen.

Outpatient Surgery

*Do not lie to each other, since you have taken off your old self
with its practices and have put on the new self, which is being
renewed in knowledge in the image of its Creator.*

COLOSSIANS 3:9–10

A while back, my son was getting colds all the time and having trouble breathing through his nose. The doctor told us adenoids were taking up almost 85 percent of his breathing space, but a common outpatient procedure would take care of the problem. We woke up early on the day of the surgery and hurried off to the hospital. A few hours later, it was over. Everything went as planned.

In the grand scheme of things, this was not a big deal. But for me, it seemed huge. This was my little boy, and he was in pain. It was difficult to watch, especially when the doctor said we had the option to leave the adenoids alone. Of course, that would mean my son probably would get sick every time someone around him sneezed. We had to weigh the short term with the long term.

Truth works this way in our lives. When we're going through the process to remove our hurts, hang-ups, or habits, it hurts. But we have to weigh the short term with the long term. Despite some temporary discomfort, it's always better to be free and whole and healthy.

— PRAYER —

Father, I know you don't like to see me hurting, but you allow it because you know it's necessary in order for me to walk in freedom and wholeness. Thank you for loving me so much. In Jesus' name, Amen.

In Need of Encouragement

Encourage one another daily, as long as it is called Today, so
that none of you may be hardened by sin's deceitfulness.

HEBREWS 3:13

Encouragement means a lot, especially when we're working hard to stay on top of our recovery. A simple, encouraging comment can sometimes make the difference between staying on the path and slipping into old habits. We should all realize the importance of encouragement in our own lives and be willing and ready to encourage others. Here are some thoughts that can help us encourage others:

1. Everyone deserves honest praise and recognition.
2. Encouraging others may not come naturally, but practice makes it easier.
3. We should speak words of encouragement only when we really mean them.
4. Encouragement comes easier if we look for the good in others.
5. Like anything else in our lives, encouraging others must be intentional. It requires a decision to do something for someone else.
6. When we encourage others, we are also praising God and strengthening ourselves.

No one knows better what it takes to tackle our hurts, hang-ups, and habits than those who have been there. We understand because we've struggled with the same issues. It helps to remember those times when someone encouraged us, a time when we were down and low and close to losing it. Now we have the privilege to pass that along to someone else.

PRAYER

Father in heaven, you are encouragement personified. Every moment with you I feel my heart brighten and my resolve strengthened. Show me how to share that encouragement with others. In Jesus' name, Amen.

Wait and Listen

*"When he, the Spirit of truth, comes, he will guide you into
all the truth. He will not speak on his own; he will speak only
what he hears, and he will tell you what is yet to come."*

JOHN 16:13

Recently, on my way to a recovery meeting, I stopped at a convenience store to get something to drink. As I was walking in, a man in a pickup drove by, suddenly put on the brakes, and turned into the parking lot. I knew the man because he had once attended our church and recovery group, but he had burned some bridges there and with me as well. When I came out of the store, he and his teenage daughter were standing beside my truck. My first thought was a negative one: *I don't have time for this.*

Immediately, however, I heard the Spirit of God tell me to be quiet and listen to what the man had to say. "I've been looking for you," he said. "I need to tell you how sorry I am for all the things I did. What can I ever do to make things right?" With tears streaming down my face, I hugged the man and told him I was headed to Celebrate Recovery and would sure like him to come with me. He did come that night and brought his family with him. He's been attending faithfully ever since.

It's not easy to push our fleshly thoughts aside, but it's the only way to hear the voice of the Holy Spirit, from whom healing flows.

--- PRAYER ---

*Father, thank you for getting through to me so that I could put my flesh aside and
be part of the miracles you are performing in human hearts. In Jesus' name, Amen.*

Taking Action

Do not merely listen to the word, and so deceive yourselves. Do what it says.

JAMES 1:22

I love going to the movies. I like to get there early so I can choose my snacks, get a good seat, and watch all the previews. I especially like action movies, with their amazing car chases and big explosions.

Imagine how boring these movies would be without the action. What kind of movie would it be if the hero just sat around and complained? Now, think about this: our recovery requires action as well.

- We take the action of accepting Jesus Christ as our Lord and Savior.
- We take the action of attending meetings and sharing openly and honestly at these meetings.
- We take the action of making amends for the things we have done that hurt others.
- We take the action of offering forgiveness for the things that have been done against us.
- We take the action of beginning healthy accountability relationships.
- We take the action of serving others.
- We take the action of applying the truth we learn at Celebrate Recovery to our lives.

Recovery is full of action! It isn't enough to sit on the sidelines wishing things were different—we have to get in the game. We take the next needed action to change. When we do, we begin an exciting journey of change that never stops.

PRAYER

Lord, thank you for endowing your people with options and for reminding us that we need to take action, doing those things that are pleasing to you. In Jesus' name, Amen.

New Name

*We are children of God, and what we will be has not yet
been made known. But we know that when he appears,
we shall be like him, for we shall see him as he is.*

1 JOHN 3:2

This morning I was reading about Jacob, Abraham's grandson, and how he wrestled with God. Jacob was one messed-up guy—a liar, deceiver, thief. He spent a good bit of his life carrying the weight of that identity. Imagine how amazing it was for Jacob when he finally quit wrestling with God and surrendered to his leadership. After that, the Bible tells us that God reached down and whispered these words: Jacob, Jacob, you're no longer going to be identified as Jacob. I have given you a new name. You will now be called Israel (Genesis 35:10).

Like Jacob, my name used to be Shameful, Guilty, Liar, Thief, Prideful, Selfish, and more. I also wrestled with God, and I'm happy to say he won. God also reached down and whispered in my ear: "John, I have given you a new name. You will now be called Forgiven and Beloved Child of God."

We all know that the best and most beautiful things in life cannot be seen or touched. They are felt by the heart. When we finally stop wrestling with God, when the struggle is over, we will be ready to hear him whisper to each of us, "I love you. I have given you a new name and a new identity. Come closer and I will tell you what you will now be called."

PRAYER

Father God, thank you for liberating me from the shameful identity I once carried. I cherish the new name you have given me. In Jesus' name, Amen.

Wake-Up Bumps

We have not received the spirit of the world but the Spirit who is from God, that we may understand what God has freely given us.

1 CORINTHIANS 2:12

We were about to drive home from New Orleans and decided to eat before we began the trip. With our appetites satisfied, we got on the road. My wife was soon napping, and my eyes were getting heavy too, but I was sure I could make it because I'm a man. I'm tough. I don't need help. At least that's what I tell myself.

About an hour into the drive, with that last meal settling in and my wife sleeping next to me, my eyes started to get heavy. But of course I didn't let on because I'm a man; I'm tough! Finally, my eyes closed for a second and the car veered to the right, running over those little wake-you-up bumps on the side of the road. The noise woke my wife, and she asked how I was doing. "I'm fine," I insisted—again. I urged her to go back to sleep, but instead she stayed awake and talked to me for the rest of the trip. With her help, we made it home safely.

I couldn't help but think about those days in recovery when I get full of myself and think, *I got this!* That's when I hit those little bumps the Holy Spirit places in my life to remind me that I can't do it alone. I need help. We are better together!

--- PRAYER ---

Thank you, Lord, for sending the Holy Spirit to wake me up and my family and friends to help me stay awake on my road to recovery. In Jesus' name, Amen.

Time to Read

Whose delight is in the law of the LORD, and who meditates on his law day and night. That person is like a tree planted by streams of water, which yields its fruit in season and whose leaf does not wither—whatever they do prospers.

PSALM 1:2–3

Reserving time for anything in our busy culture is a challenge. No wonder we aren't always faithful at reading our Bibles every day and letting God's Word soak into our souls and spirits. But Bible reading is an essential part of our spiritual growth and recovery. Here are some tips on getting started:

- Set a time every day.
- Put it in your calendar.
- Put away your phone and turn off any distractions. This time should be between you and God.
- Start by asking God to speak to you through his Word.
- Pick a place to start. There are lots of Bible reading plans available. Some are designed to help you read through the Bible in a year, while others focus on certain books of the Bible. There are lots of options—the important thing is to start reading.
- Keep a journal and a pen with you while you read so you can write down anything that stands out to you.
- Make it a habit. Do it every day. Make it part of your routine.

By spending time in God's Word daily, we will gain insight into our lives as followers of Christ. That's pretty important to our success.

PRAYER

Lord, help me to make a habit of Bible study and prayer so that I might grow spiritually and be pleasing to you. In Jesus' name, Amen.

The Eighth Step

"Do to others as you would have them do to you."

LUKE 6:31

In Step 6, we asked God to clear out the roots of our character defects. Then in Step 7, we humbled ourselves, freeing ourselves from pride. Now that we're free, God can begin to change us, as he has promised. Now we're ready for the next step.

Step 8: We made a list of all persons we had harmed and became willing to make amends to them all.

God forgave us for all our wrongs, all our sins. But we still have to deal with the trail of wreckage those wrongs have strewn along the path. That means making amends and restitution. As we reconcile ourselves with others, we are able to shed the shame and guilt that is impeding the progress of our recovery.

The list of those we've harmed should be both comprehensive and complete. No rationalizations, no hedging. That means old resentments have to come into the light, pride banished, and the truth embraced. It won't be easy, but it will be worth it. It does no good to bury the past. Some old dog will dig up the bones and bring them back to our door. The past must be dealt with and cleared, so that our new lives can be built on a firm foundation.

—— PRAYER ——

Lord, guide me as I make my list. I realize it will mean reliving painful memories, but, with your help and your presence here with me, I'm ready to do my best. In Jesus' name, Amen.

Weird Head Day

In the same way, the Spirit helps us in our weakness. We do not know what we ought to pray for, but the Spirit himself intercedes for us through wordless groans. And he who searches our hearts knows the mind of the Spirit, because the Spirit intercedes for God's people in accordance with the will of God.

ROMANS 8:26–27

I woke up in a funk. Around our house we call this a "weird head day." There was no real reason for this except that I just didn't want to feel better. My mood was telling me that I wanted to be miserable and make everyone around me miserable as well.

My wife saw what was happening and asked me what I could do to feel better. She was trying to get me to pick up some of my recovery tools. But I quickly answered, "There's nothing to do. I don't even think God wants to hear from me today." She responded by saying, "Really? God doesn't want to hear from you? Is that how you would treat your children when they're having a bad day?"

Her words woke me up, and I realized it was time to stop feeling sorry for myself. We prayed together, and before long the black cloud hanging over my head lifted. We are all in a spiritual battle, but God has given us spiritual armor to wear and recovery tools to help us. Prayer is the number one tool to use on those weird head days.

PRAYER

Father, thank you for giving me everything I need to live joyously every day. Forgive me when I choose to forget that and give way to moodiness. In Jesus' name, Amen.

Fish Crackers

A man's pride brings him low, but a man of lowly spirit gains honor.

PROVERBS 29:23

When my kids were little, it seemed like any problem could be quickly solved with fish crackers and a juice carton. But the reality of grown-up life is that we are powerless over many of the circumstances in our lives. When I try to grab one of those problems by the horns and fix it myself, it usually ends up in a tangled mess.

It's humbling to realize we have no power. The big man inside us wants to be able to take care of business. But no matter how bad things are, we can always make things worse by flexing our muscles and beating our chests.

Fortunately, there is a way to deal with the problems in our lives, though it seems opposed to what we've always been taught. The Bible tells us that the people who humble themselves will gain honor and find a solution to their problems. God has a unique and special purpose for each of us. But we must remove our pride and let him lead the way. Only then can we be infused with his wisdom and counsel. Only then can we see the big picture. Only then can we find permanent solutions rather than temporary fixes.

PRAYER

Father, I surrender my heart and life to you once again. Thank you for teaching me that I have no power over my life, but I am powerful when I live in full surrender to you. In Jesus' name, Amen.

What's That Smell?

Thanks be to God, who always leads us in triumphal procession in Christ and through us spreads everywhere the fragrance of the knowledge of him. For we are to God the aroma of Christ among those who are being saved and those who are perishing.

2 CORINTHIANS 2:14–15

People living in Louisiana typically love to cook. Whenever we plan anything special in our homes, the first question we ask ourselves is, "What are we gonna cook?"

Yesterday my wife and I took the day off, deciding to stay home and enjoy each other's company. Naturally the question about what to cook came up, and we decided on gumbo.

Making gumbo is a pretty complicated process. It starts with a roux, which is stirred for one and a half hours until it turns a rich, brown color. We then add a myriad of colorful vegetables. Next we cook duck meat and sausage with a multitude of seasonings. Finally, we prepare a large pot of rice. We started at 5:30 a.m. with that great aroma building throughout the day. About 3:00 in the afternoon, we sat down to eat. As a Cajun would say, "It was so good it would make your tongue slap your brains out."

Celebrate Recovery is a complicated process as well. All manner of lives go into it, making it a colorful mixture with a wonderful aroma as we are healed from a multitude of hurts, hang-ups, and habits. There's nothing God loves more than changed lives.

PRAYER

Father, thank you for making it possible for us to come together and help each other in our journey toward healing and wellness. In Jesus' name, Amen.

When I'm Tired

Truly my soul finds rest in God; my salvation comes from him.

PSALM 62:1

I don't think straight when I'm tired. When I don't get enough rest, I can't sleep well at night; my thoughts get seriously crazy. I'm pretty sure I'm not the only one who has to deal with this problem. The trouble is, we often bring it on ourselves by not making the best choices.

After all, life doesn't stop just because we need a nap. There are projects to complete, decisions to make, people to see, fires to put out, and so much more. Who's going to make all that happen if we sit down and take a load off? That truly is a dilemma, but especially for those of us walking the hard road of recovery, there is only one answer: We have to stop and rest whether we think we can afford to or not.

We can begin by asking God to bless our sleep at night and refresh our souls. Then we should ask others to help as well. Ask them to pray for us to rest adequately at night and when restful opportunities present themselves. Most of all, we should ask our friends and family to help us monitor our moods, so that we know when our resources are getting dangerously low, and we can take appropriate action. A little wisdom from others goes a long way.

PRAYER

Father, thank you for blessing my cycles of rest so that I can bring my best game to all those things you put before me. In Jesus' name, Amen.

Positive Habits

"When an evil spirit comes out of a man, it goes through arid places seeking rest and does not find it. Then it says, 'I will return to the house I left.' When it arrives, it finds the house unoccupied, swept clean and put in order. Then it goes and takes with it seven other spirits more wicked than itself, and they go in and live there."

MATTHEW 12:43–45

We begin recovery by focusing our attention on ridding ourselves of negative habits. We then learn that lasting change comes only through God's power. As the days pass, we became more and more free from our old hurts, hang-ups, and habits. We make fewer poor, unhealthy choices, and we grow closer to the one and only Higher Power—Jesus Christ. Reaching that point in our recovery is a great accomplishment as well as a dangerous place to be. It's a mistake to say we have arrived. Unless we keep moving forward, we risk relapse, which can actually leave us worse off than when we began.

We must always be hard at work making positive choices and adding new, healthy habits to our daily lives. And even more important, we must work to keep our relationship with God fresh and vibrant. We can do this by reserving a daily time with God for self-examination, Bible reading, and prayer. The more we know God and his will for our lives, the more we fortify ourselves against relapse, strengthen our relationship with God, and become empowered to reach out to others through our words and example.

PRAYER

Holy Father, thank you for rescuing me from my mess and empowering me to hold on to my freedom. In Jesus' name, Amen.

The Value of Integrity

Do not lie to each other, since you have taken off your old self
with its practices and have put on the new self, which is being
renewed in knowledge in the image of its Creator.

COLOSSIANS 3:9–10

I bought thirty sheets of tin to put on the roof of an old barn. I wrestled the first piece onto the roof, got it situated, and used my screw gun to put in a screw to hold it in place. Then I went to the other end of the piece of tin and realized it was five inches too short. I had built this barn myself years ago, and I thought I knew exactly how long the original tin was. Now I would have to return the tin to the store and get the next longer size. I could have avoided this setback if I had measured it rather than assuming I knew how long it was.

As if that weren't bad enough, I had another problem. I had already punched a hole in one of the sheets. Now there was a time in my life when I would have put that sheet in the middle of the stack and returned it to the store thinking no one would know the difference. Fortunately, I'm no longer that person. I have learned that my integrity is worth far more than the twenty-two dollars I would save by deceiving the clerk at the store.

Deceptive thoughts do come into my mind at times, but I have learned to take them captive and make them obedient to Christ.

PRAYER

Thank you, Lord, for showing me the value of integrity. I cherish the peace of mind that it brings. In Jesus' name, Amen.

Making a List

You have searched me, LORD, and you know me. You know when
I sit and when I rise; you perceive my thoughts from afar.

PSALM 139:1−2

I travel all the time, so imagine how surprised I was to find myself in a hotel room without a toothbrush. I couldn't imagine how I could forget to pack something I use twice a day. Then it hit me—I hadn't written it down on my packing list. That might seem kind of lame, but apparently I'm dumb enough to do it.

In the end, it wasn't that big a deal. I got a new toothbrush at the gift shop, and my teeth never knew the difference. But I decided to add the experience to a list of lessons I've learned. If we write things down, we are less apt to forget them. It is a small but important habit that can make one better prepared for a trip. It is also one of the reasons why it's important to take a daily inventory of our lives. If we don't, we may miss an unhealthy pattern that is beginning to emerge or find ourselves blindsided by a relapse or ill-prepared for an unexpected circumstance.

That daily inventory doesn't take long at all, but it could save us from some pretty big consequences. If it keeps us on track, it's more than worth the discipline it takes to make it a daily habit.

PRAYER

Father, I don't want even one day to go by without knowing I'm right with you and right with others as well. Each day as I take my personal inventory, help me to be alert and honest. In Jesus' name, Amen.

Praying the Scriptures

[Jesus said] "And surely I am with you always, to the very end of the age."

MATTHEW 28:20

As a pastor, my heart is broken daily when I see God's people carrying heavy burdens and living under negative circumstances. After listening to their stories, I try to encourage them to stand firm in their faith and let Jesus help carry their burdens. They smile and nod, but I can see that too often they don't know where to start.

When this happens, I often share with them what I have learned from my own experience. I take a chapter of Scripture—for me, it is Psalm 119—and then I begin by praying that Scripture back to the Lord as an act of worship. As I thank him for who he is and what he does, my belief in his promises and loving care are reaffirmed to my heart.

After we finish reading the Scripture, we continue to worship by thanking God for helping us, giving us his Word, walking with us through our circumstances, and helping us to carry our burdens. As we extol his greatness and thank him for the wisdom and knowledge he gives us each day, his peace flows over us.

The Bible is filled with praise for the Most High God. So let's dig in like hungry men and women who find themselves enjoying a great feast. Circumstances change and burdens become lighter as we feed on God's Word.

— PRAYER —

Heavenly Father, as I worship you, I believe that my confidence in your goodness will increase, and I will find rest and comfort in my time of need. In Jesus' name, Amen.

Two Are Better

Do nothing out of selfish ambition or vain conceit. Rather, in humility value others above yourselves, not looking to your own interests but each of you to the interests of the others.

PHILIPPIANS 2:3–4

I was backing up my camper and had to turn it sharply to get it into the space. I looked in the rearview mirror just in time to see the toolbox, which I had just put on the bed of my truck, tearing through the fiberglass on the front of the camper! My first thought was, *How dumb can I be?* There were men one hundred yards away in our cabinet shop who would have been happy to help watch and guide me as I backed up. But no! I got this, right?

God never meant for us to live our lives alone. Two are always better than one because we can watch out for each other. That's one of the reasons Celebrate Recovery works. We start looking out for others rather than just focusing on ourselves. I'm always glad to lend a hand when someone asks, so why is it so hard for me to ask for help?

Fortunately, my screwup can be pretty easily fixed. It's just a material thing. It's tougher when our messes involve other people. Maybe we can all learn from my mistake to swallow our pride and ask for help. It's the right thing to do.

PRAYER

Father, thank you for creating us with a need for you and for each other. Help me to put my pride aside and ask for help when I need it. In Jesus' name, Amen.

Total Package

*Praise be to the God and Father of our Lord Jesus Christ! In his
great mercy he has given us new birth into a living hope through the
resurrection of Jesus Christ from the dead, and into an inheritance
that can never perish, spoil or fade ... kept in heaven for you.*

1 PETER 1:3–4

When people tell me they don't believe in Jesus, I feel sad for them. I
don't mean that to sound judgmental. It's just that they are missing out on so much. Think for a moment about all he brings to our lives:
forgiveness; a new, full life; a purpose for living; the power to change; and
hope for the future. Add to that the promise that there are infinite life-
times ahead of us when we die.

All I can do is pray that God's Spirit will give life to my words when I
share what I've found in Jesus. I also pray that others' hearts will be open,
as mine was. The enemy of our souls has deceived so many, making them
think that relationship with God is a hard thing, that it requires us to sacrifice our own plans and let someone else run our lives. And fun is one
more thing that isn't allowed.

The truth is that God never strips us of our will. We retain the privilege and the responsibility for the lives we've been given. In addition, my
relationship with God has brought more fun, more humor, more fellowship with others, than I could have ever imagined.

PRAYER

*Father God, your Word says that you don't want anyone to miss out on the joyful
benefits of salvation. Take my words and use them to draw others to you, I pray. In
Jesus' name, Amen.*

Pride Check

Pride goes before destruction, a haughty spirit before a fall.

PROVERBS 16:18

Pride is a big problem that can derail recovery. But knowing why we act out of pride can sometimes help us reject that unhealthy thinking. These are some of the reasons:

1. Pride often masks insecurity. We feel that no matter how much we achieve, it will never be enough.
2. Pride may be the result of a lack of positive attention and affirmation in our lives. We think we have a right to this recognition even if we have to boast about ourselves.
3. Pride comes when we believe our achievements are our own doing.

The following acrostic is a check to help us rid ourselves of **PRIDE**:

P stands for prayer. Pray that God will show you where pride is present in your life.

R stands for reading your Bible. A word study on the word *pride* is a good place to begin.

I stands for involvement with others. Because it's hard to see things in ourselves, we need to ask others what they see.

D stands for developing a plan for getting rid of the pride in your life. This plan should include God and your accountability partners.

E stands for Ephesians 3:20–21, which says, "To him who is able to do immeasurably more than all we ask or imagine, according to his power that is at work within us, to him be glory in the church and in Christ Jesus throughout all generations, forever and ever! Amen."

--- PRAYER ---

Dear Father, I want my life to be free of pride, which can trip me up and keep me from being all I can be. Thank you for helping me as I fight this enemy of my soul. In Jesus' name, Amen.

Where Would You Be?

*As Jesus was getting into the boat, the man who had been demon-possessed
begged to go with him. Jesus did not let him, but said, "Go home to your own
people and tell them how much the Lord has done for you, and how he has
had mercy on you." So the man went away and began to tell in the Decapolis
how much Jesus had done for him. And all the people were amazed.*

MARK 5:18–20

A young man who was new to Celebrate Recovery, and to his relationship with Jesus, was at church one Sunday morning, bubbling
over with enthusiasm and telling everybody about the demons and
strongholds that have been removed from his life. His excitement was
contagious! He was experiencing positive things in his life, some for the
first time—like clarity of mind, restored relationships, and happiness.

After the service, I asked him how it was going. He replied very
excitedly, "Are you kidding? I don't know where I'd be—" He stopped in
midsentence and said, "Let me rephrase that. I know exactly where I'd be
without the love, acceptance, and guidance from this new family. I would
still be lost."

I was reminded by his words that we all need this family that God
has placed us in. I was also reminded where I would be if my Savior Jesus
Christ had not paid the price for me to be reunited with my heavenly
Father. We should always be telling the story of God's love so that others
can know the joy of wondering where they would be without him.

PRAYER

*Lord God, your love for me has made all the difference in my life. Thank you for
all you have done. In Jesus' name, Amen.*

Trash Day

*"You hypocrite, first take the plank out of your own eye, and then
you will see clearly to remove the speck from your brother's eye."*

MATTHEW 7:5

Trash day is Wednesday in our neighborhood, so every Tuesday night we drag our trash cans to the curb, and every Wednesday night we bring them back in. It's kind of a social contract we have with one another. It works out quite well, except for those neighbors who don't comply and leave their trash cans sitting on the curb until the weekend. I'll be honest, that drives me crazy.

Lately, I've been asking myself why this bothers me. Those trash cans are really no big deal in the grand scheme of things. Furthermore, they aren't even in my way, so why do I get so stirred up about them?

I don't know the answer, but it's the same feeling I get when I work hard to partner with God to remove my hurts, hang-ups, and habits while others stay stuck in theirs. In the end, we have to accept the fact that we can't bring in our neighbor's trash cans for them, and we certainly can't clean up people's lives for them either. All we can do is clean up our driveway and leave other people and the things they do in God's hands.

PRAYER

Lord, thank you for the assurance that I'm not responsible for the choices others make. That frees me to do what you ask me to do in the very best way possible. In Jesus' name, Amen.

Recalculating

Even when I am afraid, I keep on trusting you.

PSALM 56:3 CEV

I'm pretty challenged when it comes to navigation, so I carry my GPS with me. I was driving to the Dallas/Fort Worth airport to catch a flight home. I felt pretty confident with my GPS pointing the way until I realized there was construction going on all over the place.

On more than one occasion my GPS told me to turn, but there were concrete barriers blocking the way. Every time this happened, I heard the word "recalculating," as my GPS tried to make sense of the confusion.

Once I had finally made it to the airport and was safely on my flight, I began to think about what I had just experienced. My GPS was no match for the construction. All it could do was say "recalculating" and try to find an alternative route around the barriers. God is like a GPS in that he gives me directions and shows me the way. But the similarity ends there. God doesn't let a silly obstacle get in the way. He doesn't need to recalculate the plan he has for me. Instead he demonstrates his power and authority by simply pushing the obstacles out of the way, no matter how daunting they might be.

I used to become discouraged when I was faced with obstacles until someone said, "Refuse to be fearful about what will happen to you. God is faithful, and he will take care of you if you trust him." Now, when I know I'm in God's will, I push forward knowing that he will clear the way before me.

PRAYER

Father, thank you for opening the way before me, removing the obstacles from my path. I will always love and trust you. In Jesus' name, Amen.

White as Snow

"Come now, let us reason together," says the LORD. *"Though
yours sins are like scarlet, they shall be as white as snow;
though they are red as crimson, they shall be like wool."*

ISAIAH 1:18

I woke up one morning to a beautiful sunrise in the Rocky Mountains.
It was 50 degrees, so I decided it would be a great day to work on one
of my outside projects. Soon after I started, however, the wind started
blowing. It seemed to be getting colder, and dark clouds started rolling
in. Thirty minutes later a blizzard was underway. By 8:00 p.m. everything was covered in a fresh layer of snow.

I looked out the window in amazement. Nothing but pure, white
snow as far as the eye could see. No brown grass. No gravel driveway.
Everything disappeared under a beautiful covering of white.

That's how our heavenly Father sees us—pure, clean, unblemished,
holy, and perfect. We must never buy into the lie that we are worthless,
that we don't measure up, that God could never love us. God gave the
precious life of his Son so that we could be washed as white as snow and
be called his children.

PRAYER

*Oh Lord, how grateful I am that the pure and perfect blood of your Son has washed
me until I am whiter than snow. In Jesus' name, Amen.*

Trusting God

Trust in the LORD with all your heart and lean not on
your own understanding; in all your ways submit to
him, and he will make your paths straight.

PROVERBS 3:5–6

When we choose to go God's way, we are often asked to do the exact opposite of what we would naturally do:

- We want to get even, but God says to forgive.
- We want to get more, but God says to give more.
- We want to be served, but God tells us to serve others.
- We want to be the most important, but God says we must humble ourselves and become the least.

This reversal will seem odd for a while. It might even make us question our trust in God. But as we continue to admit that living life our way didn't pan out (in fact, it was a huge failure, just barely survivable), we will begin to see the wisdom in God's way of doing things. And later on we will even begin to see that God's way removes the striving from our lives and allows us to rest peacefully in his care.

It's always an adjustment when we decide to do something different. Our brains have to be retrained, reprogrammed. But if we are faithful to continue, trusting God, his ways will begin to overrule our own. That's when we can finally begin to relax and enjoy our new lives.

PRAYER

Father, sometimes it's difficult for me to understand why you ask me to do certain things, but I will be obedient knowing that each new thing strengthens and establishes my new life. In Jesus' name, Amen.

Reproducing Healthy Choices

*"I am the light of the world. Whoever follows me will never
walk in darkness, but will have the light of life."*

JOHN 8:12

There was a time in my life when I was completely wrapped up in myself. My selfish pride pushed me toward unhealthy choices— lying and manipulating situations, for example—and then reproducing them in my life. Soon those unhealthy choices became unhealthy habits and my life was headed for emptiness and destruction. I tried to white-knuckle my way through my hurts, hang-ups, and habits, but the same pride that brought me to that place, kept me there, even dug me in deeper.

My life was miserable until I finally surrendered myself to Christ. I learned that while unhealthy choices, once initiated, reproduce themselves in my life, so do healthy choices. Those good choices help me replace old destructive patterns with new life-giving patterns.

Pride blinded me and held me captive to the hurt and dysfunction in my past, but Christ opened my eyes, freed me from the past, and gave me hope. God repeats his wonderful acts of kindness, grace, goodness, comfort, courage, love, forgiveness, and so much more until a positive cycle is established. Then we begin to reproduce those same good acts on behalf of others. The key is to banish pride and live in a state of constant surrender to God.

PRAYER

Lord, help me to banish pride whenever it shows its ugly head. Instead, may I encourage humility and surrender to you. In Jesus' name, Amen.

Work in Progress

I thank my God every time I remember you. In all my prayers for all of you, I always pray with joy because of your partnership in the gospel from the first day until now, being confident of this, that he who began a good work in you will carry it on to completion until the day of Christ Jesus.

PHILIPPIANS 1:3–6

If there's one thing I know for sure, it's that I am a work in progress. We all are. Life becomes easier when we understand that we will never "arrive." There will always be areas of our lives that we need to work on until the day God takes us home to heaven.

My wife, whom I love more than anyone on this earth, and I have come to realize that we don't need to talk about any heavy problems after 9:00 p.m. We're just too tired. We've also learned that when she says something I strongly disagree with, I should wait at least ten minutes before responding. My response will be much nicer, and sometimes I've even been known to change my mind from what I was thinking at first. The bottom line is that there are still aspects of my personality and temperament that need improvement. God knows it, my wife knows it, and I know it!

It might be helpful for all of us to make a list of those areas that still need work in our lives. Then we can pray regularly that God will help us grow in those areas.

PRAYER

Father, I still need an awful lot of work. Thank you for loving me through all the work that still needs to be done. In Jesus' name, Amen.

Watch and Pray

"Watch and pray so that you will not fall into temptation.
The spirit is willing, but the flesh is weak."

MARK 14:38

When Jesus' disciples asked how they could help him as they waited in the Garden of Gethsemane, he answered them with two words: *watch* and *pray*.

By *watch*, he was telling them to keep their eyes open, be alert, pay attention to what was going on around them. That's good advice for us as well, especially if we are in recovery. We need to be aware of our surroundings, reading his Word, the Bible, and meeting with others who can help us unveil our blind spots. When Jesus told his disciples to *pray*, he was urging them to stay in tune with God's voice, listening and responding accordingly. He was instructing them to be aware of spiritual adversaries, to be ready to fight the good fight of faith.

Watching and praying are perhaps the two most important jobs we have as Christians. They are the best possible way to make a difference for God's Kingdom. They are also the most effective way to deal with adverse circumstances in our own lives. When Jesus spoke these words, he was only hours away from his crucifixion. Nothing in our lives could ever rival that.

PRAYER

Dear Lord, I ask for your help as I discipline myself to watch and pray for the sake of the Kingdom and for my own life. In Jesus' name, Amen.

Rip in My Sails

*"The Spirit gives life; the flesh counts for nothing. The words I
have spoken to you—they are full of the Spirit and life."*

JOHN 6:63

Call me silly but one of my favorite movies is *Tommy Boy*. Of course
there are many funny scenes, but one stands out for me. Tommy is
sitting in his sailboat going nowhere because there's no wind. Then he
says, "Hey, Dad, I sure could use some help down here. Could you give
me a little wind to get my boat moving?" And of course the wind picks up,
and his sailboat begins to move with the breeze.

In the past, I often made that same request: "Hey, God, how about
a little help down here. I can't seem to get moving." But unlike Tommy
in the movie, nothing changed for me. I was still dead in the water. I
finally realized why! My sails were ripped. Nothing happened until I was
willing to acknowledge the condition of my sails and surrender myself
to God. Once I did that, the Lord restored and rebuilt my sails, and the
Holy Spirit (God's holy wind) was able to get my boat moving again.

Sure, new rips happen from time to time. But I now have a daily
maintenance plan to repairing those rips and keeping my sails function-
ing properly. I do this because I want the full blessing of the Holy Spirit
in my life.

PRAYER

---

*Father, as I come to you each day, show me the rips in my sails and give me the
foresight to keep my sails maintained by daily confessing my sin and forgiving those
who hurt me. In Jesus' name, Amen.*

Corrupted Hard Drives

Everyone who calls on the name of the Lord will be saved.

ROMANS 10:13

My computer was moving slowly—so slowly that it was hard to get anything done. It finally froze up, so I called for help. The computer expert said my hard drive was corrupted, which was the last piece of news I wanted to hear. He asked me if I had backed it up, which I had. So it was just a matter of erasing my hard drive and restoring it to its original settings. This took about a day and a half and was well worth the time.

I couldn't help thinking about this later and seeing the parallel with my life. Because of bad decisions, poor choices, and outright rebellion, my heart and mind (my hard drive, if you will) had become corrupted. But when I made that one great choice to turn my heart and my will over to God, he restored me to my original settings.

Now it's kind of like we're all in customer service. We get to point people to Jesus, the Great Technician! He can erase their corrupted hard drives and straighten out their settings as well. That's the kind of news we all like to hear.

--- PRAYER ---

Father, thank you for restoring my life and for allowing me to be part of the healing process in the lives of others. In Jesus' name, Amen.

Jesus Is the Way

Jesus answered, "I am the way and the truth and the life.
No one comes to the Father except through me."

JOHN 14:6

Celebrate Recovery is a Christ-centered recovery program. Those aren't just words. We aren't putting a Jesus sticker on it and calling it Christ-centered. The cornerstone of this program is Jesus. Without him there is no life change. Without him there is no hope. Without him there is no future. With him, though, everything changes. He truly is "the way and the truth and the life." Let's look at it this way:

Jesus is the *way* to a changed life. He is the *way* to peace. He is the *way* to heaven. Jesus is the *way* to find freedom from our hurts, hang-ups, and habits. Jesus is the *way*—the best way and the only way.

Jesus is also the *truth*. Many teachers claim to have the truth, but only Christ claims to be the *truth*. In a world of pretenders and deceivers, he is the only one we can trust, the only one who can answer our questions and free us from the lies of the enemy.

Jesus gives us *life*. He pulls it from inside himself and offers it to us freely and abundantly. When we accept Jesus as our Savior, we find true life—a life free from hurts, hang-ups, and habits.

Jesus will show you the way. He will tell you the truth, and he will give you life.

PRAYER

Father God, thank you for lighting up the path before me, opening my eyes to the truth, and giving me eternal life. In Jesus' name, Amen.

New Problems

You know my folly, O God; my guilt is not hidden from you.

PSALM 69:5

Some problems we bring upon ourselves and some are handed to us by others. But one way or the other, life is full of problems and challenges that must be dealt with. We can't just pretend they don't exist. And yet, in recovery we learn that often, that's exactly what we do. We keep them hidden from ourselves and others.

But none of us can run forever. Sooner or later, we run out of steam; we can't go any further under our own power. When we reach that point, we're ready to receive God's help, and our recovery kicks into gear. We begin a new journey. There's just one more thing we need to remember: New problems are always coming along. Each day we need to ask ourselves how we are dealing with the new problems in our lives. Are we dealing with them God's way, sharing them with our accountability teams?

Failing to face up to our new problems has the potential to take us right out of the race, allowing old habits to surface once more. God wants us to begin each day open and ready to face life squarely.

PRAYER

You, Father, are my only hope of lasting peace and freedom. Help me each day to reject pride and the urge to run from my problems. Give me the courage to keep my life open to myself and others. In Jesus' name, Amen.

A Little Help

*If two lie down together, they will keep warm. But how can one keep
warm alone? Though one may be overpowered, two can defend
themselves. A cord of three strands is not quickly broken.*

ECCLESIASTES 4:11–12

One morning my wife casually said, "I wonder how you get your
computer keys unstuck."

A little distracted, I replied, "I don't know. That's never happened to
me. Google it."

A little while later she came in and said, "I found out what to do, but I
probably ought to tell you that when I was opening a jar of peanut butter
yesterday, some of the oil spilled out on my keyboard."

We looked at each other and started laughing. She didn't want to
give me too much information before she had found a solution.

This is how it is in recovery. Sometimes when we're going through
trials, we don't give out all the information. We hold back, thinking we
might be able to figure it out on our own. That usually takes longer, if it
works at all. In Celebrate Recovery, we come to understand that it's better to get everything out on the table right away. This allows us to get help
instead of having to fight alone. If we fall down, someone will be there to
help us get up.

PRAYER

*Father, thank you for knowing me better than I know myself. Thank you for sur-
rounding me with those who are willing to help me up when I fall down. In Jesus'
name, Amen.*

What Are We Worth?

He who did not spare his own Son, but gave him up for us all—how
will he not also, along with him, graciously give us all things?

ROMANS 8:32

How do we know how much something is worth? Well, I'm not an economist, but I think the simplest answer is, something is worth as much as someone is willing to pay for it. It doesn't matter if it's a house, a comic book, a vintage record, or anything else. Considering that, how much are *we* worth?

According to the Bible, God's holy Word, we are priceless because God was willing to pay an unimaginable price for us—the lifeblood of his own Son, Jesus Christ. We see this again and again in Scriptures, as in the following:

- "God so loved the world that he gave his one and only Son, that whoever believes in him shall not perish but have eternal life" (John 3:16).
- "This is how we know what love is: Jesus Christ laid down his life for us. And we ought to lay down our lives for our brothers and sisters" (1 John 3:16).
- "Even the Son of Man did not come to be served, but to serve, and to give his life as a ransom for many" (Mark 10:45).
- "God demonstrates his own love for us in this: While we were still sinners, Christ died for us" (Romans 5:8).

PRAYER

Father God, I can't imagine why you would pay such a price for me, but I'm so glad you did. Thank you for your inexplicable and incomparable love for me. In Jesus' name, Amen.

Tearing the Flesh

*A word out of your mouth may seem of no account, but it
can accomplish nearly anything—or destroy it!*

JAMES 3:5 MSG

Even the best of homes can sometimes become a battlefield. People living closely together, trying to hash out issues, tempers flaring, individuals in different stages of maturity. That conflict often leads to angry words and sarcastic jabs.

A friend shared with me that he grew up in a home where sarcasm was used often. In fact, it was the weapon of choice in family battles. He told me he was good at it, too, able to hold his own with anyone. He felt that sarcasm, because it has an edgy feel of humor, allowed them to say terrible things to each other and then follow it up with "I'm just kidding." He would walk away telling himself that he had done no harm, even though he could see that it often left deep and severe wounds.

Sarcasm has been defined by some as "biting of the lips and the tearing of the flesh in rage." In recovery, my friend learned that getting in his verbal jab left him with a temporary good feeling and a much longer bad feeling when he saw how his words hurt others. He has now learned to hold his tongue, choosing instead to use his words to encourage others. This is what God does—he uses his words to bless, strengthen, and teach us. Shouldn't we do the same?

PRAYER

Heavenly Father, I surrender my words to you. Help me to use my words to bless, comfort, and strengthen others. In Jesus' name, Amen.

All Hope Is Gone

*Train yourself to be godly. For physical training is of some
value, but godliness has value for all things, holding promise
for both the present life and the life to come.*

1 TIMOTHY 4:7–8

I was at a friend's home and noticed he had a room full of exercise equipment. I knew he hadn't worked out in quite a while so I asked, "Why do you keep that stuff around?"

He said, "As long as I keep it, there is hope. But if I get rid of it, all hope is gone that I will ever get back in shape."

I thought about myself. If I have the equipment/tools of recovery and don't use them, I can never hope to be spiritually fit. As a matter of fact, having the equipment/tools and not using them is even more frustrating because I know I could be in shape.

So what are some of the tools of recovery? How about that 500-pound phone that's so hard to pick up when we need to call somebody? Or that 300-pound pencil when we know we need to be working on writing our inventory or testimony? Or how about that forgiveness we need to extend that seems almost too heavy to carry? What about releasing the past that's weighing us down? How about picking up another weighty meeting this week? Making phone calls, writing about our recovery, forgiveness, releasing the past, and making meetings are just a few recovery tools.

When we aren't feeling spiritually healthy, it's probably because we aren't using the tools God has given us. It's time to pick them up and get started on a good spiritual workout.

PRAYER

Father, thank you for the recovery tools you've given to me through Celebrate Recovery. In Jesus' name, Amen.

Blowing It!

If we claim to be without sin, we deceive ourselves and the truth is not in us. If we confess our sins, he is faithful and just and will forgive us our sins and purify us from all unrighteousness. If we claim we have not sinned, we make him out to be a liar and his word has no place in our lives.

1 JOHN 1:8–10

We've all blown it at one time or another. We've all made mistakes, some more drastic than others. And we've all found ourselves in messes of our own making. For that reason, it's important to be aware of two dangers in particular as we begin to clean up after ourselves.

First of all, we sometimes give our mistakes too much power in our lives. We let them snag us and keep us stuck rehearsing them over and over. This way of coping can keep us so connected to the past that we can't go on to complete our recovery. We begin to feel that we aren't worthy of God's help or anyone else's, for that matter. Or we live crippled with fear that we will repeat our mistakes.

Second, we sometimes try to downplay our mistakes by pretending that they're no big deal. This is just another type of denial, and it's risky business because it keeps us from learning from the past and opens us up to deception in the future.

We've all blown it, but the good news is, Jesus already paid for all of it. We don't have to hold on to our mistakes, and we don't have to hide them. We can lay them at the foot of the cross and find forgiveness and grace.

PRAYER

Thank you, Father, for the power of your forgiveness. In Jesus' name, Amen.

Secrets

*"What you have said in the dark will be heard in the
daylight, and what you have whispered in the ear in the
inner rooms will be proclaimed from the roofs."*

LUKE 12:3

We start keeping secrets as children. A sixth-grade boy rushes home to beat his parents to the mailbox. He has to retrieve his poor report card before they see it. He has a secret! He lies awake, worrying if they are going to find out. They ask him why his report card hasn't come. He tells them that the office said there was a computer problem and report cards will be a little late. Now he has covered up his secret with a lie. His guilt grows daily. He tries to isolate himself from his parents by spending more time alone in his room.

Finally, he comes home from school, and his parents are sitting in the living room waiting for him! His mom tells him that she called the school, and they told her that the report cards were mailed out two weeks ago. Now, instead of just being in trouble for his poor grades, he has lost his parents' trust.

Whether we are young or old, keeping secrets always turns out the same way. We start out keeping a secret to escape possible negative consequences. Soon we must defend those secrets by telling lies. Guilt increases, and soon we find ourselves isolated and alone. In Celebrate Recovery we have a saying: "You are only as sick as your secrets." Secrets keep us in the darkness, but when we step out into the light, they no longer have the power to make us sick.

PRAYER

Father, give me the courage to abandon my secrets and step out into the light. In Jesus' name, Amen.

The Ninth Step

*"Therefore, if you are offering your gift at the altar and there
remember that your brother has something against you, leave
your gift there in front of the altar. First go and be reconciled
to your brother; then come and offer your gift."*

MATTHEW 5:23–24

In Step 8, we evaluated all our relationships. We became willing to offer forgiveness to those who have hurt us and to make amends for the harm that we have done to others. We agreed to do this without expecting anything in return. Now we must walk the talk.

*Step 9: We made direct amends to such people whenever possible,
except when to do so would injure them or others.*

As we grow in faith and pursue recovery, we want to follow the example Jesus set. As we get to know him better, we want to model his teachings and his ways. We want to become more like him. If we are to implement Step 9 to the best of our ability, we must learn to model God's grace.

Grace is a gift. It cannot be bought. We know this because God has given it to us without expecting anything in return. When we offer our amends in the same way, we are offering a gift to those we have harmed. On a human level, we might not feel that some of these people deserve such a gift, but neither do we deserve any of God's gifts to us. God showers us with his grace, and his strength is ours as we go and do likewise.

PRAYER

*Father God, I need your help as I set out to make amends with those I've harmed.
Endow me, Lord, with wisdom and courage to do what has to be done. In Jesus'
name, Amen.*

Are You Talking to Me?

*Train yourself to be godly. For physical training is of some
value, but godliness has value for all things, holding promise
for both the present life and the life to come.*

1 TIMOTHY 4:7–8

This morning I woke up before the sun rose to get in my morning workout. But I didn't want to go. The bed was so warm and comfortable. I kept lying there thinking about how good it would feel to hit the snooze button and go back to sleep for about thirty minutes. But a voice somewhere in my head kept saying, "Get up! You need to get up and go!"

I'm sure for all of us, there are days when we don't want to do the things we know we need to do. But God knows we can't afford to just lie there in bed, especially when it comes to our spiritual fitness. So when we hesitate, the Holy Spirit keeps urging us until we get back into our right minds. He reminds us to do the following:

- Read the Bible, God's letter to us.
- Contact members of our Forever Family to avoid isolation.
- Spend time talking to our heavenly Father in prayer.
- Think of someone we can serve.
- Start training ourselves to be godly.

A good place to begin your spiritual fitness program is the book of James. It reads like a manual for godly living. If we read part of a chapter each day and reflect on what we read, we are sure to see changes in how we are living our lives.

— PRAYER —

Lord, thank you for the Holy Spirit, who keeps me committed to doing those things that are best for me. In Jesus' name, Amen.

I Have a Story

*In your hearts set apart Christ as Lord. Always be prepared to
give an answer to everyone who asks you to give the reason for the
hope that you have. But do this with gentleness and respect.*

1 PETER 3:15

Without exception, God has a unique story for each and every
human being. For those of us who surrender our lives to Jesus
Christ, that story takes on a whole new significance and power. That
story, from start to finish, is our testimony, and throughout the New
Testament we are urged to share it with others. Because our story might
draw someone to God who does not know him, it has an importance and
urgency outside of ourselves. But sharing our story also has significance
in our own lives:

- It gives others hope to hear what has happened to us.
- It reminds us of the changes God has made in our lives.
- It lets people know that Celebrate Recovery is for more than just
  drug and alcohol issues.
- It gives us a way to invite others to attend church and Celebrate
  Recovery.
- It increases our sense of gratitude.
- It keeps us humble.
- It helps us maintain a good sense of balance as we remember who
  we are and where we came from.

Sometimes it's difficult to find the words to describe what God has
done for us. Writing it down can be a big help. No matter how we choose
to do it, telling our stories is a wonderful way to thank God for what he
has done for us.

PRAYER

*Thank you, Father, for writing the story of my life. I will never forget what you've
done for me. In Jesus' name, Amen.*

The Little Boy Inside

He was pierced for our transgressions, he was crushed
for our iniquities; the punishment that brought us peace
was upon him, and by his wounds we are healed.

Isaiah 53:5

A man once told me that he felt like a little boy in a man's body. When things got tough, he would always revert to that little boy and run away to hide. This man had suffered some pretty traumatic stuff in his life, especially from men. When he felt threatened or challenged, he would isolate himself or even lash out at others. Even in the best of times, he kept a distance from others. In an effort to protect himself, he formed no real relationships.

The man said that for many years, he listened to Satan's lies and even carried them into his marriage. All that unresolved junk from his past kept him handcuffed emotionally to a frightened little nine-year-old boy.

Today, this man is no longer bonded to the boy. He has finally found the courage to reach out for help. In recovery, God gave him the courage to face the past and deal with it. He says that when things get tough, he's still tempted to shrink back into defense mode. He can still hear the little boy saying, "Run and hide and it will all go away!" But now he heeds Christ's words instead: "Come to me, and I will lead you through this fiery trial." Instead of running to hide, he runs to God and finds grace, mercy, love, and strength enough to face his past and be the man God created him to be.

PRAYER

Father, quiet the turmoil within, and when scary trials come, help me to stand and fight with you by my side. In Jesus' name, Amen.

Be Still to Win

Moses answered the people, "Do not be afraid. Stand firm and you will see the deliverance the LORD will bring you today. The Egyptians you see today you will never see again. The LORD will fight for you; you need only to be still."

EXODUS 14:13–14

The Bible tells us that Moses, speaking on behalf of God and his fellow Israelites, demanded that the Egyptian pharaoh release them from slavery to travel to a land promised to them by God. Pharaoh agreed at first, but as soon as the Israelites left town, he changed his mind and went after them. Now with the pharaoh and his troops behind them and the formidable Red Sea in front of them, the Israelites were literally trapped. Then God told Moses to instruct the people to be still. The Lord had promised to do their fighting for them.

Hold on! That's not how I was taught to fight. I thought we were supposed to go down swinging. As I think back, though, I have to admit that when I try to fight my battles myself, I almost always do—go down, that is.

True to his word, God opened the Red Sea for the Israelites. After they had all gone across to safety, God closed the sea and swallowed up their enemies. He is still keeping his word today, making a way for us where there is no way and swallowing up our enemies behind us. All he asks us to do is be still and trust him.

PRAYER

Father, I praise you for your greatness, and I thank you for fighting for me every day. In Jesus' name, Amen.

Handling Anger

"In your anger do not sin": Do not let the sun go down while
you are still angry, and do not give the devil a foothold.

EPHESIANS 4:26–27

Because our anger is so often undisciplined, we tend to think of it as sin. But the Bible tells us that anger in and of itself is not sin. In fact, anger, like any other emotion, is a normal part of human life. The sinfulness comes when we fail to keep our anger under control. The Bible clearly tells us what we are to do with our anger:

1. "In your anger do not sin." We are to take authority over our anger so that our response does not take us down the path to sinfulness.
2. "Do not let the sun go down while you are still angry." We are to deal with our anger right away. Brooding is nothing more than meditating on our anger, which increases its power. Amends need to be offered and forgiveness extended.
3. "Do not give the devil a foothold." When we handle anger in the wrong way, we give the devil ammunition to use against us and others. Taking care of anger as quickly as possible foils the enemy's plan against us.

We are going to be hurt by others, and we are going to hurt others. It's a part of life. Anger and pain are inevitable; it's what we do with them that counts. We can either defuse anger by making amends and offering forgiveness, or we can open the door and invite the devil in to make things worse. When that happens, everyone loses.

--- PRAYER ---

Father, help me to learn to handle my anger in a way that is pleasing to you. In Jesus' name, Amen.

Smelly Scene

*"Do not be afraid, little flock, for your Father has
been pleased to give you the kingdom."*

LUKE 12:32

I've always wondered about those idyllic drawings and recreations of the scene of Jesus' birth. They seem to be so neat and tidy, with Joseph and Mary standing perfect and serene. I've been in a few barns, and I can tell you they are nothing like that. Mary gave birth in a dirty, smelly stable filled with animals.

I wonder if she didn't say to God, "Really? This is what you've chosen for the birth of the Messiah?" By all accounts Mary was an extraordinary woman. Most likely she endured quietly, thinking instead of the bigger plan and willing herself to be obedient to God by giving birth to the Savior of the world. She may have been given eyes to see that the birth of her most amazing child in such a dark and lowly place was to demonstrate his mission—to bring light to a dark and dying world.

Like Mary, it's best not to question God's ways. We can be sure that he always has a bigger plan in the making, even when things don't make sense to us. We must trust him as Mary did, knowing that he is always planning and arranging things for our good.

PRAYER

Lord God, no matter what I face in this life, no matter what adverse conditions or painful circumstances, I know that I can trust you to make everything work together for my good. In Jesus' name, Amen.

Body Armor

Be strong in the Lord and in his mighty power. Put on the full armor
of God so that you can take your stand against the devil's schemes.

EPHESIANS 6:10−11

I was looking at pictures of our brothers and sisters fighting a war in the Middle East, and I noticed they had one thing in common: even though temperatures can get up to 120 degrees, they all had on full body armor, in addition to helmets, boots, bulletproof vests, goggles, gloves, weapons, and backpacks. They knew they couldn't ask for a time-out in the middle of the battle to prepare. They had to be ready at all times.

The same is true for us as we fight against our enemy, the devil. He waits for just the right moment to take us out. We can't wait until we are under attack to put on our armor. We must be armored up and ready at all times to take a stand against the enemy.

God has given us all we need to deal decisively with the enemy of our souls. When we are ready and listening for God's voice, we will always have the upper hand. Once again, the best defense is a good offense.

PRAYER

Father, I want to learn how to wear my spiritual armor properly. Show me as I put on each piece in preparation for what you've called me to do. In Jesus' name, Amen.

Be Still and Know

"Be still, and know that I am God."

PSALM 46:10

I've noticed that there is always a temptation to be going somewhere, doing something. We fill our calendars, to-do lists, and appointment books to overflowing. A successful day is marked by going to bed exhausted, only to wake to another day just as full as the last. Somehow that doesn't seem right to me. How are we supposed to hear God's voice if we are always racing through life? I think that's what God is talking about when he says, "Be still!"

Why don't we all try being still together, beginning with a prayer? Let's tell God that for the next few minutes, we aren't going anywhere or doing anything. We are just going to be still and wait in his presence. Now, let's clear our minds of all the questions and thoughts about our day. We want to quiet ourselves before him as well. Maybe he'll speak to us this time and maybe he won't, but at the very least, quiet time with him will refresh and uplift us.

From now on, let's meet with God in stillness every day. It might take some getting used to, but once it has become a habit, a healthy one, God is sure to make himself known. Sitting and being still before him may not sound exciting, but every time we are in God's presence, listening for his voice, we are right where he wants us. That's a very exciting place to be.

PRAYER

I'm here, Father, waiting in your presence. It's so peaceful here. In Jesus' name, Amen.

Some Days!

You prepare a table before me in the presence of my enemies.
You anoint my head with oil; my cup overflows.

PSALM 23:5

Some days our cups run over. Everything is in sync! We feel a special closeness to God. Our activities are blessed. We are on a spiritual high. Then there are days when our cups get run over. We feel that God has hidden himself from us. Circumstances seem to be opposing us. We feel as though we are being purposefully attacked. We are on a spiritual low.

On the good days, when our spiritual adrenaline is running high, we praise God and have a strong sense that we are living out our purpose. But what happens on the bad days? Instead of praising God, do we allow ourselves to slip into "poor me" mode, wondering if God is still using us?

How we respond to bad days is extremely important! We can waste time with a pity party, or we can stand firm in faith, believing that God will see us through and teach us something important along the way. Instead of pouting we can reach out to our accountability partners. We can spend more quiet time with God in prayer and Bible reading, searching our hearts.

As we grow in our relationship with God and our recovery, we learn to celebrate the days when our cup runs over and learn from the days when our cups get run over.

PRAYER

Father, I know that today and every day I am safe in your never-failing arms. Help me to use those downtimes productively, ever growing in faith and patience. In Jesus' name, Amen.

Bumpy Ride

God, who said, "Let light shine out of darkness," made his
light shine in our hearts to give us the light of the knowledge
of God's glory displayed in the face of Christ.

2 CORINTHIANS 4:6

I was in Dallas on a stormy overcast day. It was dreary as I looked out the window of the airport terminal at the plane I would soon board for the last leg of my journey home. It occurred to me that it would be a bumpy ride.

Takeoff was a little scary as the plane pitched from side to side and bounced up and down. But as we started up through the clouds, things got brighter. Then we broke through into sunshine so bright that it was almost blinding. We were above the storm.

There are going to be days when the storms are raging around us. That's always a little scary. There will be dark skies, and some days we just know we're in for a bumpy ride. But when we put our trust in God, we can ride above the storms, where the Son is always shining brightly.

Getting to that place above the storm is God's work. He is the pilot of our lives. But he has provided a Forever Family to stand with us until he takes us up and through.

PRAYER

Thank you, Father, for taking me up above the storms where your goodness shines
with more brightness than the sun. And thank you for my Forever Family as well.
In Jesus' name, Amen.

He Gives Rest

"Come to me, all you who are weary and burdened, and I will
give you rest. Take my yoke upon you and learn from me, for
I am gentle and humble in heart, and you will find rest for
your souls. For my yoke is easy and my burden is light."

MATTHEW 11:28–30

I don't know a single person who isn't just worn-out. We are all carrying burdens, loads far too hard to bear. It's so important to know that we don't have to carry those burdens alone.

God's Word says that if we take our burdens to Jesus, he *will* give us rest. He doesn't say that he *can* give us rest or he *might* give us rest. He says that he *will* give us rest. It's a sure thing. All we have to do is show up and unload. How does he do it? How does he lift our burdens off our shoulders and onto his? I don't know. I'm not sure anyone does. What I do know is that I've been there. I've taken my weary self to him—all my hurts, hang-ups, and habits; all my worries about the people I love; all the difficulties that this world can throw at us—and every time, he has comforted me, soothed me, helped me to take a breath, and rest.

Rest is more than an instant in time. It's a process of inner repair and restoration. God can bring rest to our tired backs, but only after we've laid down the load we've been carrying. That's our part—laying it down. Then we can enter into rest.

PRAYER

Father, thank you for letting me unload all my burdens on you, and thank you for sweet rest. In Jesus' name, Amen.

The Pink Elephant

*I know that nothing good lives in me, that is, in my sinful nature. For
I have the desire to do what is good, but I cannot carry it out.*

ROMANS 7:18

Our journey to wholeness begins when we admit that we are powerless over our addictions and compulsive behaviors, that our lives
are unmanageable. But before we can make that admission and take the
first step in recovery, we must deal with denial. It's like the pink elephant
sitting in the middle of the room. No one wants to talk about it or even
acknowledge it in any way. Family and friends often join us in our denial,
not wanting to face the difficult reality. These comments probably sound
familiar:

- "Talking about it only makes it worse."
- "I'm going to pretend this didn't happen."
- "If I tell her that I'm hurt by her words, she might leave me."
- "Come on, I really don't drink that much."
- "Don't worry about me. I'm fine!"
- "My friend drinks more than I do."
- "The only reason I eat is because he makes me so mad!"
- "I wouldn't have to drink if you weren't always nagging me about
  something."
- "I have a tough job. I need a few drinks to relax."

If we allow ourselves to stay in denial, eventually we will lose everyone
and everything we hold dear. Instead, we can be honest with ourselves
and others and begin our journey to wholeness.

PRAYER

*Father, I'm tired of making excuses. Help me face my past and my fears for the
future as I take an honest step toward wholeness. In Jesus' name, Amen.*

A Rigorous Defense

My dear children, I write this to you so that you will not sin.
But if anybody does sin, we have one who speaks to the Father
in our defense—Jesus Christ, the Righteous One.

1 JOHN 2:1

God set the standard impossibly high when he told his children not to sin. After all, we all mess up sometimes. That's why he adds a "but," which serves as a game changer. But ... when we do sin, the Great Judge—God—has appointed the best attorney ever—Jesus Christ—to plead our case before the court of heaven. There is just one witness for our defense, God's Holy Spirit. He testifies that we are God's children and the price for our sin has been paid in full. What a courtroom!

When we sin—and we will even though we try not to—God has already prepared for us to be found "not guilty." It is our enemy who accuses us, fills our hearts with guilt, and tries to break us. He is the one who brings condemnation and judgment down on us—not our gracious, merciful, forgiving God.

We are God's children, and his Holy Spirit resides within us, helping us to recognize sin and identify the enemy's campaigns against us. We have all the tools we need to resist sin, but God knows that we will sometimes allow ourselves to do what we know we should not. When that happens, he has prepared a rigorous defense on our behalf.

PRAYER

Father, thank you for giving me all the tools I need to resist sin—and thank you for loving me enough to provide a defense for me when I fall prey to the enemy and my old nature. In Jesus' name, Amen.

The Dentist

You can't heal a wound by saying it's not there!

JEREMIAH 6:14 TLB

I hate going to the dentist. I mean, I really hate it—and what I hate the most is the lecture. It's the one where the hygienist tells me how I haven't been brushing right and asks if I even bother to floss at all. She reminds me—with a note of condescension—to brush in circles, not back and forth. Then shaking her head as though the entire discussion is hopeless indeed, she tells me that as long as I refuse to follow these guidelines for good oral health, I'll keep getting cavities.

No wonder I put off my last visit until I was in pain—and I mean *bad* pain. Even then, I tried all these things first, hoping to take care of the problem myself:

1. A handful of ibuprofen
2. Herbal remedies
3. Toughing it out
4. Telling myself I'm a man—whoot! whoot!—and I can handle it

Eventually, though, I had to go to the dentist. Had I gone when the tooth first began to bother me, I would have had to endure an uncomfortable morning of drilling, filling, and, yes, the annoying lecture. But because I put it off, I had to endure drilling, a root canal, the annoying lecture, and a huge dental bill.

It never pays to put things off, pretending everything is going to be fine. It just makes matters worse. It's so much better to face up to things and let God help us get them taken care of.

PRAYER

Thank you, Father, for helping me face the difficulties in my life so that you can help me take care of them. In Jesus' name, Amen.

Taking a Hit

May the God of hope fill you with all joy and peace as you trust in him,
so that you may overflow with hope by the power of the Holy Spirit.

ROMANS 15:13

It's funny how we sometimes remember the weirdest things. For example, I remember playing in a high school football game when a huge lineman from the other team appeared out of nowhere and literally took me out! He hit me so hard that I'm surprised I'm not still seeing stars. That incident seems almost funny to me now, but I have other memories that will never be funny. There were times when I was hit so hard right in the heart that I thought I would never heal.

In Celebrate Recovery, however, I've learned that I may never forget the painful hits I've taken in the past, but I can allow God to heal them. I can forgive those who have bowled me over either accidentally or intentionally. I can think about those people and those hits without my blood pressure shooting up.

God doesn't want us to live in fear. He wants us to live confidently, courageously, knowing that he will help us today and tomorrow, just as he helped us overcome our wounds from the past. None of us will ever take a hit worse than the one Jesus took for us on the cross. Jesus knows what it is to feel pain. He overcame his own, and he will help us overcome ours.

PRAYER

Lord, I consider myself blessed to be on your team. I know that even when I'm knocked off my feet, you will be there to pick me up, dust me off, and send me back into the game. In Jesus' name, Amen.

Calming the Storm

*[Jesus] got into the boat and his disciples followed him. Suddenly
a furious storm came up on the lake, so that the waves swept
over the boat. But Jesus was sleeping. The disciples went and
woke him, saying, "Lord, save us! We're going to drown!"
He replied, "You of little faith, why are you so afraid?" Then he got up
and rebuked the winds and the waves, and it was completely calm.*

MATTHEW 8:23–26

One night a bad storm blew through, taking down trees and power
lines all around town. It took us forty minutes to make the drive
to our Celebrate Recovery meeting. Usually it takes just ten minutes.
We were glad to see that the power was on and everything at the church
seemed to be fine.

Shortly after we began our meal, however, we received a call that
there were trees down at our women's recovery home. Two of our men
left immediately to assess the damage. They quickly reported that two
large trees near the house had fallen, but both had fallen away from the
house. Everyone in the house was safe.

As we started our praise and worship, I could not help but think
about how wonderful it is to serve the God who commands the winds,
protects the weak, and calls things that are not as though they are. He is
not only the Creator and Maintainer of the universe, but he is also our
heavenly Father.

We all encounter storms in our lives, some of our own doing and
some the result of others' poor choices. But no matter what, we can trust
Jesus to see us through.

PRAYER

*I praise you, Lord of heaven and earth, who calms the wind and stills the waves. In
Jesus' name, Amen.*

Don't Be Afraid

Ignoring what they said, Jesus told the synagogue
ruler, "Don't be afraid; just believe."

MARK 5:36

We usually hate to admit it, but no matter how big, bad, or important we are, we're all afraid at times. Jairus was an influential man, the leader of the synagogue. But as he watched his young daughter become sicker and sicker, he knew there was nothing he could do to help her. Perhaps for the first time, Jairus must have been truly afraid.

In his anguish, he threw aside his pride and sought out Jesus, falling at the Healer's feet and begging him to come save his little girl. Jesus agreed, but so many others needed his help along the way that by the time they reached his house, Jairus was sure it was too late.

Sure enough, as they approached the house, they were greeted by sounds of mourning and crying. The man's friends ran out to meet him, telling him not to bother Jesus anymore because his daughter was already gone. But Jesus ignored what the others were telling Jairus. Instead, Jesus urged him not to be afraid, but to believe. Then Jesus went into the house, he told the little girl to sit up, and she did!

It's difficult to trust God when we're afraid, when we don't know what to do. God knows that. He didn't condemn Jairus for being afraid, and he won't condemn us either. All he asks is that we choose faith over fear.

PRAYER

Father God, thank you for standing with me when I am most afraid. Like Jairus, I
choose to trust you regardless of what the circumstances say. In Jesus' name, Amen.

A Little Faith

Faith is being sure of what we hope for and certain of what we do not see.

HEBREWS 11:1

Often we take the first step toward recovery because our pain has finally become greater than our fear. We've awakened to the fact that we can't fix it on our own, which has given us the courage to try another way. Now we need faith—just a little is all it takes—to believe that Someone will fill the hole in our hearts.

As we move forward, day by day, in our recovery, we learn that there is Someone waiting to help us, and his name is Jesus Christ. Though we are powerless, he is all-powerful. He knows all about what we've gone through in our past. He recognizes our gifts and potential as well as our weaknesses. He has faced temptation and conquered it. He has felt pain and endured it. He has been abandoned and yet held on to hope. He knows what it is to be human, because he made himself human for our sake.

Along the path to recovery, we will need to have faith in a number of things, such as the steps program that will lead us to wholeness. But we will struggle far less with those things once we have placed our faith in the only One who is faithful. People fail, programs fail, but God never fails. He is worthy of our faith in his goodness and grace, and his timing is always perfect.

PRAYER

Holy Father, thank you for sending your Son, Jesus, to fill the hole in my heart and stand with me as I put my faith in you one day at a time. In Jesus' name, Amen.

Give It Away

I hear about your faith in the Lord Jesus and your love for all the saints.
I pray that you may be active in sharing your faith, so that you will
have a full understanding of every good thing we have in Christ.

PHILEMON VV. 5–6

I think God has a pretty great sense of humor. I can just see him chuck-ling when he put me, an ex-meth addict, together with a friend of mine, an ex-heroin addict, some twenty-five years ago to start our church's first recovery group. The funny thing about that particular pairing was that my friend doesn't do anything fast, and I don't do anything slowly. Maybe God wanted to speed him up and slow me down. All I know is he put two unlikely people together, and yet this ministry became our church's largest local outreach.

In the beginning, it was sometimes just the two of us, but we kept coming back. And that's all God really required of us—faithfulness. He was looking for two people who would commit to coming and giving away what they had been given. And he found that in us.

God is ready to use anyone who is available to do great things, unexpected things, to accomplish his purpose and plan. And he needs people—faithful people, compassionate people, generous people, grate-ful people—to do his bidding.

PRAYER

Father, use me. I want to share what you've given me with others. I want them to know the peace and joy I've found in my relationship with you. In Jesus' name, Amen.

Addressing Fear

They cried to the LORD in their trouble, and he saved them from their distress.

PSALM 107:13

One of the things I struggle with on a daily basis is fear. It might be the fear of disappointing someone, the fear of failure, or the fear of making a costly mistake. I've found that when I give in to fear, it can cripple me and keep me from moving forward in my recovery as well as in my life.

The tricky thing is that we can't trust fear. Think about how fear is like the darkness. When we go into a dark room, we can't see a thing. Even though we might know the room well, once the lights are out, everything seems different. We imagine that things are jumping out to trip us as we shuffle around trying not to run into something and hurt ourselves. In reality, nothing has changed except our perception. The furniture is right where it was; the doors haven't moved. It's the same room it was with the light on. It's just that the darkness distorts things.

Fear does the same thing. It distorts our perceptions, making us lose our sense of reality and focus on "what-ifs." Most of the things we fear aren't real at all; just figments of our imagination. When the truth comes in, it illuminates our minds, just like turning on the light in a dark room. Truth comes from God's Word. So why live in fear when we can open our Bibles and turn on the light?

PRAYER

Lord God, fill me with your truth as I read your Word. I want to live in the light. In Jesus' name, Amen.

Broken Starter

As iron sharpens iron, so one man sharpens another.

PROVERBS 27:17

I needed to go somewhere, but my car wouldn't start. I just sat there for a few minutes, and then I began to consider my options. I could continue to sit behind the wheel, hoping the engine would miraculously turn over, or I could call someone to help me figure out what was wrong. The mechanic I called said the problem appeared to be the starter, and he advised me to have my car towed to his shop. I did what he said and had my car back the next day in working order.

In regard to recovery, we all know how tough it is to get started doing the things we know we need to do—spending quiet time with God, making it to meetings, attending church, supporting and serving others, etc. We can feel overwhelmed and just sit there wondering what to do, as I did when my car wouldn't start. When this happens, we can continue to sit there hoping things will get better on their own, or we can call a sponsor or accountability partner and tell them what's going on. Even more important, we need to follow their instructions carefully. My mechanic told me to have my car towed to his shop. If I hadn't done that, it would still be sitting in my driveway, refusing to start.

No matter what we face in life, we always have options. We can sit there and hope for a miracle or reach out for help.

PRAYER

Father, thank you for placing good people in my life, people committed to helping me when I can't help myself. In Jesus' name, Amen.

Chairman of Celebrate Recovery

My brothers, as believers in our glorious Lord
Jesus Christ, don't show favoritism.

JAMES 2:1

A man displaced by Hurricane Katrina showed up at our open meeting. His outward appearance was foreboding. He wore a black trench coat and a ski cap. He was tattooed, homeless, and tough looking. He didn't speak to anyone. He took a chair from the back row, dragged it to the back wall, and sat down. I thought I'd go talk to him and make sure he was all right and felt welcomed. This is a sample of our conversation. (I use the term loosely.)

Me: "Welcome, I'm Mac."

Man: "So."

Me: "What's your name?"

Man: "Why?"

Me: "No reason in particular." I'm thinking I now need to take a different approach.

Me: "Would you like to sit with me on the front row?"

Man: "You've got to be kidding."

Me: "No."

Man: "All right."

During the meeting, I was thinking about how to get the man to come back. I knew just sitting with me on the front row probably wasn't going to do it. So I asked him if he could come back the following week and help me set up the chairs. He said he would be glad to. He was very faithful to take care of the chairs from that night on and wore a name tag that read: Chairman of Celebrate Recovery.

It's easy to judge people by their outward appearances. But when we reach out to others without bias, we can make an eternal difference in their lives.

---PRAYER---

Father, teach me to reach out to every person you send across my path. In Jesus' name, Amen.

Addressing Anxiety

*He brought them out of darkness, the utter
darkness, and broke away their chains.*

PSALM 107:14

We live in a world absolutely crippled by anxiety. I feel it, and I know my kids do too. It's pervasive in the world around us. We see it even in the faces of strangers in the crowd. Living with anxiety is like being bound by chains.

But worry and anxiety don't help us at all! When we worry, we aren't solving a problem; we are just being bound by it. Like chains, worry and anxiety keep us locked down, unable to move forward. We get stuck. Maybe it's a bill we don't know how we're going to pay. Maybe we worry that we aren't strong enough to stay on the road to recovery. We might even be worrying about those we love.

When we worry, we are telling God, "I've got this one." We *think* we are in control, but we aren't. Worry and anxiety really don't change anything. They just wear us out and keep us tied up. But God will break those chains if we ask him to. Instead of continuing to turn those anxious thoughts over in our minds and worrying about things we can't control, let's leave our anxious thoughts with Jesus and let him break those chains that have us bound.

--- PRAYER ---

*Father, thank you for setting me free from the chains of worry and anxiety. I leave
all my anxious thoughts at your feet. In Jesus' name, Amen.*

Tell Me About Your Day

Be joyful in hope, patient in affliction, faithful in prayer.

ROMANS 12:12

One of the greatest blessings I had when my kids were teenagers was visiting with them at the end of the day. If they'd had a difficult day, I was able to comfort them and be there for them. If they'd had a great day, I was able to share in their delight. I greatly enjoyed our conversations because they were my kids and I loved them deeply.

I remember one of those times in particular. My son was on the water polo team, and they had traveled to an away game where they suffered a painful loss, down by just one goal. I had not been able to attend, but he took me through it play by play, describing how frustrating it was to lose a game his team should have easily won. As I hugged my son good night, it struck me how blessed I was to have shared that moment with him.

In the same way, our heavenly Father desires to hear about our day, both the good and the bad. He never tires of our conversations with him, and he doesn't mind if we go over every detail of the day. He always has time for us. In fact, he tells us to pray continually. He is always listening. Let's make a habit of sharing the events of our day with him.

PRAYER

Father, I am always surprised to realize how much you love me. I will never be worthy of your loving attention, but I will forever be thankful. In Jesus' name, Amen.

Change the Lure

*"I am the gate; whoever enters through me will be saved. They will come
in and go out, and find pasture. The thief comes only to steal and kill and
destroy; I have come that they may have life, and have it to the full."*

JOHN 10:9–10

I love to fish. After a long winter, it's one of the things I look forward to
most. One spring I planned a big trip. I made sure my rods and reels
were oiled and ready with new line, and I had all my lures. I was set for a
great, fun-filled day.

I got to the lake before sunrise. The water was calm, and I just knew
I was going to catch my limit of fish. But after two hours I wasn't having
much luck, so I kept changing lures. I wasn't discouraged. I knew that
if I put the right color or shape on the hook, the fish wouldn't be able to
resist—and I was right! Soon after I put a black and chartreuse split-tail
plastic grub on my line, I got my first catch!

The Bible says that our enemy, the devil, will go to any length to get
us on his line. If we're smart enough to stay away from the lures we used
to take, he'll change it up. God wants us to be wise to our enemy's tactics.
Our heavenly Father is not the source of every bright and shiny thing
that wiggles past us. We must always stop and check with him before
we bite.

PRAYER

*Father, thank you for making me aware that the enemy often changes lures in order
to trap us. This understanding will help to keep me safe. In Jesus' name, Amen.*

Hard Days

"With man this is impossible, but with God all things are possible."

MATTHEW 19:26

There is just no other way to say it—recovery is tough. That is the very first reality we run into as we start working with God to change our lives. There are days when we feel like giving up, throwing in the towel. I've had those days when I woke up expecting things to go wrong. But when change feels impossible, when it feels like we're fighting a losing battle, that's when we need to remember that we are God's children and that with him, all things are possible.

We don't have to give in to our old habits. We don't have to stay stuck. We don't have to give up on broken relationships or shattered dreams. We have hope because we have Jesus in our lives. God is a deal changer. Without him, we're trapped, but with him, anything can happen, even those things we thought were impossible.

On those hard days, we aren't alone. God has promised to stay with us every step of the way. When we have no answers, he has all the answers. When we have no hope, he has more hope than we could ever need. When we think our lives are over, he has plenty more bright tomorrows.

PRAYER

Thank you, Father, for being there for me through all my days, the hard ones especially. I know you are going to see me through. In Jesus' name, Amen.

The Barbershop

Since you are my rock and my fortress, for the sake of your name lead and guide me. Keep me free from the trap that is set for me, for you are my refuge.

PSALM 31:3–4

When I was a teenager, my dad would say, "If you hang out in a barbershop long enough, you're going to get a haircut." He knew my friends were doing things they shouldn't, and the implication was that if I kept hanging out with them, I'd end up doing bad things too. The only thing worse than the saying was the fact that it was true. Of course I gave in to peer pressure. Okay, so it didn't take much pressure for me to give in. But that's me.

We tend to think that peer pressure is something only teenagers face. That would be nice, but it simply isn't true. There are people in each of our lives who aren't thrilled about our desire to seek recovery—people we used to act out with, people who don't like that we've changed because it makes them wonder if they should change, people who used to enable us by keeping our secrets or turning a blind eye to the fact that we have a problem.

When these people turn on the pressure for us to relapse or pretend everything is just fine when we know it isn't, we're going to need a way to stay strong. God is the One—the only One—who can keep us from compromising. He is our strength, our fortitude, our safe place.

PRAYER

Father God, protect me and help me out of the traps that compromise brings. Teach me to love all the people in my life without letting them lead me back into the darkness. In Jesus' name, Amen.

Changing of the Guard

"No weapon forged against you will prevail, and you will refute every tongue that accuses you. This is the heritage of the servants of the LORD, and this is their vindication from me," declares the LORD.

ISAIAH 54:17

While in London we were able to watch the Changing of the Guard at Buckingham Palace. Wow, what pomp and circumstance! The handover ceremony is accompanied by one of the five bands of the Foot Guard, who play traditional military marches, music from films and musicals, and even well-known pop songs. The guards march in a very polished, no-nonsense, dignified sort of way—all with one mission in mind: to protect the queen, to protect the royalty!

While watching all this, I realized that our Protector is with us all the time! There is never a changing of the guard. When we turned our lives over to the care of Jesus Christ, we became sons and daughters of the King of kings, and his Holy Spirit took up permanent residence in our hearts and minds.

The Changing of the Guard is not only beautiful to watch, but it is also a reminder that our God has instituted a better system, one that keeps us safe from the enemy at all times.

PRAYER

Father, thank you for keeping me safe in your watchful care. It's a great honor to be counted as part of your royal family. In Jesus' name, Amen.

Hard Work

All hard work brings a profit, but mere talk leads only to poverty.

PROVERBS 14:23

By the time we come to Celebrate Recovery, most of us realize that our lives are out of whack and we need change. The trouble is that most of us think we can get change now. That's right—instant change! But that's not how recovery works; it's hard work. In fact, sometimes it seems so hard that we feel like throwing up our hands and quitting. Personal inventory? No thanks. Making amends? I think I'll pass. Forgiving those who have hurt us? Not today!

I'm afraid there isn't any "change pill" we can take. The road to freedom from our hurts, hang-ups, and habits comes from Jesus Christ alone. That means his timing. And we have all those principles to work through. I don't mean read through, I mean *work* through. Saying we want change isn't enough. Wishing and hoping, even praying for change isn't enough. Lasting change is a combination of waiting on Jesus and working harder than we've ever worked before.

It takes awhile to break bad habits and establish good ones. It's emotionally exhausting to examine our relationships, take responsibility for what we've done wrong in them, and make them healthy again. It will often be difficult to share with others and deal with issues we would rather sweep under the carpet. It's hard work. But with God's help, we can do it, and when we do, freedom will be ours.

PRAYER

Father, I'm tired of putting all my strength into my recovery. Thank you for giving me your strength and your peace for the work ahead. In Jesus' name, Amen.

The Tenth Step

So, if you think you are standing firm, be careful that you don't fall!

1 CORINTHIANS 10:12

If we are wrong . . . wait, change that . . . *when* we are wrong! No matter how long we've been in a recovery program, we are still going to make mistakes. And when we do, we need to promptly make our amends. We all need to work Step 10 into our lives on a daily basis.

Step 10: We continued to take personal inventory and when we were wrong, promptly admitted it.

I recently received this e-mail from a Celebrate Recovery ministry leader:

I'm pretty disappointed. I understand that you get a lot of e-mails asking you to speak, and it would be difficult to speak at all of them, but I really thought someone would reply back. It wouldn't even have mattered if someone answered for you. It would just be nice to know my e-mail was read. May God continue to bless you and Celebrate Recovery.

Within thirty minutes I e-mailed my amends:

Thank you for your e-mail. I'm so sorry I let you down. We were checking to see if the date was available, and somehow it got lost in the process. I apologize for any inconvenience I caused. Congratulations on your four years. I wish I could have been there. In his steps, Pastor John

I am sharing these notes to show that I'm still working the program every day to the best of my ability. That is how we stay dependent on God's power.

PRAYER

Father, thank you for letting me know when I'm wrong. And thank you for giving me the courage to make amends. In Jesus' name, Amen.

Our Helper

The Lord is my helper; I will not be afraid.
What can mere mortals do to me?

HEBREWS 13:6

I'm a world-class worrier. If there were an NWL—National Worrying League—I'd be an MVP. It's the reason I experienced my first ulcer when I was only nineteen. I remember that the doctor was shocked, asking how a nineteen-year-old managed to get an ulcer.

Worry, fear, and anxiety are three related conditions that attack us all. But some of us just can't seem to hand them over to Jesus and walk away. He has promised to be with us always, helping us, comforting us, and assuring us of his constant care. But we're like children clutching their broken toys, and he can't help us unless we let him.

Sadly, these issues won't fix themselves. We have to be proactive in our journey to recovery. Each time we begin to feel overcome by worry, fear, anxiety, or a combination of the three, we must stop right where we are, pray, and give the situation to God. If there is so much as a tiny hesitation, it helps to remind ourselves that God can handle any and all of our concerns far better than we can handle them on our own. He really does have everything under control.

PRAYER

Father, I give my worry, fear, and anxiety to you. I know that you are in complete control of my situation, and I can trust you to take care of it as you always do. In Jesus' name, Amen.

The Body Is Weak

*"Watch and pray so that you will not fall into temptation.
The spirit is willing, but the body is weak."*

MARK 14:38

Too often in life we begin to think, "I have never been in a better spot than I am right now. If anyone can handle temptation, it is me." We can begin to develop that old God complex that says, "I got this," and start doing things that are likely to lead to unhealthy choices.

There is an old proverb that says, "If you rattle a snake, be prepared to be bitten by it." It is easy to say, "God, why did you let me fall into this temptation?" But if I don't seek him before I jump into the thornbush, isn't it my own poor choice that got me there?

I, unfortunately, have plenty of thornbush scars from poor choices I've made through the years. Day by day, I'm learning how to be more proactive in life instead of reactive to every thornbush that comes along.

I think God in a way is saying, "Help me help you." By seeking him daily we are able not only to heal our old scars but also to keep our hearts from relapsing. This helps me to develop an attitude of gratitude for what I have rather than a poor attitude of wanting what I do not have.

I dare not be complacent. Each day has new challenges and many thornbushes along the path. That's why I must always be seeking after him and trusting him to guide me.

PRAYER

Father God, help me to deal with all the thornbushes on my path today. I will not dwell in the past or in the future, but trust you for today. In Jesus' name, Amen.

Out of Chaos

*In Judah the hand of God was on the people to give them
unity of mind to carry out what the king and his officials
had ordered, following the word of the LORD.*

2 CHRONICLES 30:12

After my son-in-law became adept at cabinetmaking, he began to step into the role of managing the shop. I noticed that things weren't running smoothly. Jobs weren't getting out on time, and the crew too often had to work late to finish up orders. I saw that my son-in-law had decided to do things a little differently from the way we had always done them, so I called him into my office and said, "For things to work smoothly, you need a system that has been proven to work."

"I have a system!" he answered a bit abruptly.

I responded by saying, "Chaos is not a system."

As the silence settled in, I could tell he was getting the point. If he wanted things to run smoothly, some changes would have to be made. Things would have to be done in an orderly manner.

The same principle is true in recovery. If we want our lives to be less stressful, we have to follow an orderly system that has been proven to work. Trying to improvise and make up something new just doesn't work. That's why each of us commits to following a program with a proven track record. It's God's way of keeping our lives running as smoothly as possible while bringing about good results.

PRAYER

Father, I thank you for the Celebrate Recovery program and the people who worked with you to make it part of my successful recovery. In Jesus' name, Amen.

I'm Glad We Met

*Two are better than one, because they have a good return for their
labor: If either of them falls down, one can help the other up.*

ECCLESIASTES 4:9–10

I was celebrating my birthday. It wasn't a landmark year. Not one of the
big birthdays. Just a normal birthday for a normal year. But before this
birthday was over, I had gained an important insight.

On that day, my sweet wife made my favorite breakfast, and my kids
each gave me a card made especially for me. I love how they love me. It
was at work, though, that my insight came. I was checking my e-mails
and noticed that I'd received a short message from a dear friend. "Happy
birthday, my friend," is how it began. Then it said, "I'm glad we met." It
made me think about what the sender had meant in my life. He'd been a
friend and so much more—mentor, teacher, encourager. I was certainly
glad I'd met him. What would this birthday have looked like if it hadn't
been for him?

There are people like this in all our lives—people who have cared
enough to serve us as they would the Lord. These people are the encour-
agers, the lovers, the challengers, the prayers, those who never fail to
believe in us, and those who are always there for us, keeping us focused on
the road of recovery ahead. These are the people we are very glad we met.

— PRAYER —

*Lord, thank you for the people you've placed in my life. I know I didn't meet them
by accident. They were all part of your plan for me. In Jesus' name, Amen.*

The Brightness of Light

*"I have come into the world as a light, so that no one
who believes in me should stay in darkness."*

JOHN 12:46

When I was a teenager, my family and I went to visit some famous caves in Missouri. After several hours inside, my eyes became adjusted to the darkness. The problem came when I went back out into the bright sunlight. My eyes actually hurt. It took a long time for them to adjust to normal sunlight.

Spiritual darkness has the same effect on our spiritual eyes. We can get so used to the life we lived in the darkness that it may actually be painful when we try to live our lives in the light. Pastor Rick Warren said it well: "The truth will set you free, but first it may make you miserable!"

When we first bring our hurts, hang-ups, and habits into the light, it may seem too bright to bear, but once we get adjusted to this new way of living, we will never want to return to the darkness. There is so much to see and do in the light. For one thing, we can see each other, so the light brings us out of isolation and into fellowship. We can't let fear keep us from all God wants to show us.

PRAYER

Father God, my eyes are still weak and in pain from coming out of the darkness and into the light. Help me to get used to living comfortably in the light. In Jesus' name, Amen.

Cleaning Up the Mess

"He himself bore our sins" in his body on the cross, so that we might die to sins and live for righteousness; "by his wounds you have been healed."

I PETER 2:24

My wife and I took two days to make the trip from Colorado to Louisiana. During those two days Hurricane Isaac made landfall. We arrived late at night and felt relieved that we had electricity. We were glad to be sleeping in our own bed after a month away. It wasn't until I went outside the next morning that I noticed the damage from the storm. Everywhere I looked limbs were down, and the yard was a mess. There was a lot of work to do, so much that I felt a little overwhelmed. But I got started by taking care of one limb at a time.

While we are still in darkness, our lives don't look all that bad to us. But when we give our lives to Jesus Christ and his light shines on us, we see the devastation caused by our hurts, hang-ups, and habits much more clearly. As we look around at the broken relationships and dashed hopes, it can feel overwhelming.

There's a lot of work to do, that's for sure. But with God's help, we can start by taking care of one issue at a time and then moving on to the next and the next and the next.

PRAYER

Father, thank you for helping me clean up the debris that litters my life. I know there is a good, blessed life under there somewhere. Help me as I uncover it one issue at a time. In Jesus' name, Amen.

Iron Sharpens Iron

As iron sharpens iron, so one person sharpens another.

PROVERBS 27:17

I was working when I heard someone crying. I went out to check and discovered that it was one of our volunteers. Her husband is an addict, and she's going through some tough times with her daughter as well. She had just gotten off the phone with someone who has been dealing with a lot of the same issues. All at once, she felt joy for the victories she's seen and deep sadness for the battles that still lay ahead.

This volunteer has gone through her own personal hell. Her husband's addiction and her daughter's rebellion have caused her deep grief. But working through the Celebrate Recovery principles has helped her to find victory for herself and learn that she can change only herself—no one else. So that day, when she called the parents of a troubled teen to talk about recovery options, she was able to encourage them. She knew they needed recovery as much as anyone. She sharpened and encouraged them. God used her personal pain to help others.

We all have a story. We've known pain. We've worked through difficult issues. God can use our experiences to sharpen others if we will let him.

PRAYER

Dear Father, thank you for turning my pain into blessing by using it to challenge and encourage others. In Jesus' name, Amen.

Wearing a Mask

Whoever lives by the truth comes into the light, so that it may be seen plainly that what he has done has been done through God.

JOHN 3:21

Pretending that we have all the answers and don't need help from anyone is just another mask we sometimes wear. This mask is particularly harmful because it's yet another mask of denial, and denial keeps us miserable in the present by keeping us handcuffed to our painful past. This is a familiar mask. We've all seen it, and most of us have worn it: "I'm right and everyone else is wrong" or "Others need to learn from me. I have little need to be taught."

I have worn this mask in my life. It's actually difficult to do really, because it allows us to look perfect on the outside while we're screaming in misery on the inside. This is the mask that keeps people at a distance. We wouldn't want them to see the truth reflected in our eyes. At Celebrate Recovery, we learn to surround ourselves with people who will lovingly tell us that we are wearing a mask. We already know, of course, but we try to deny it.

We need to surround ourselves with God's love and daily ask him and our support team to call us out anytime they see us wearing a mask. Our recovery depends on our living honestly and transparently. Deception will always cause us to slip and fall. Besides, masks make us slaves to pretense. Life is so much better without them.

PRAYER

Father, I want to live in honesty and transparency before you and others. In Jesus' name, Amen.

Come Here First

"Come to me, all you who are weary and burdened, and I will give
you rest. Take my yoke upon you and learn from me, for I am gentle
and humble in heart, and you will find rest for your souls."

MATTHEW 11:28–29

I was in a local hardware store that I love to frequent when someone approached the counter looking for a hard-to-find item. The man behind the counter said, "Sure, we have that!"

Then I turned to the man and said, "Yeah, when you can't find it any-where else, come here!"

Without missing a beat, the owner replied, "Why don't you just come here first?!"

I'm not sure why that hadn't occurred to me. I had been shopping at this store for a long time—but only as a last resort.

The same thing is true when we say, "All we can do is pray." Shouldn't taking our problems to God be the first thing we do? And yet many of us waste time trying to do things on our own. We come up short when all the while God has had everything we're looking for—peace, hope, security, love, etc. He has everything we need, so why would we waste time looking anywhere else?

There are no limits to God's resources and no limits to his love for us. He invites us to come freely into his presence and ask him for what we need.

--- PRAYER ---

Forgive me, Father, for wasting my time looking for answers in all the wrong places. I know you are the only Source for those things I need so desperately. In Jesus' name, Amen.

Lie-Down Day

*"Take my yoke upon you and learn from me, for I am gentle
and humble in heart, and you will find rest for your souls."*

MATTHEW 11:29

All I want to do today is lie down . . . but I can't. My kids are arguing, my wife's car has to go to the mechanic, I have urgent e-mails to answer, and the phone won't stop ringing. My to-do list is growing by the minute. This is not a lie-down day!

On days like this—days when our bodies need rest, our souls need rest—where do we turn? In the past we may have turned to something like a drug, a website, a food, a credit card, hoping to find some rest. We might even have found it temporarily. But sooner or later, we have to realize there is just one place to go when we need rest—and that's Jesus.

We don't have to worry about whether he'll be glad to see us; he invites us to come. He knows what we need and how to give it to us. He knows how exhausting it can be just dealing with earthly matters like cars and children and home repairs and money worries and relationships and health problems. And he knows that real rest starts on the inside and moves outward. When we need rest, it only makes sense to go to the One who can help us carry our burdens, strengthen us, and give us the rest we so desperately need.

PRAYER

*Father, for me every day seems like a no-lie-down day. Help me to find the rest I
need and the strength to take care of the business of life. In Jesus' name, Amen.*

The Predictable Pattern of Relapse

If you think you are standing firm, be careful that you don't fall!

1 CORINTHIANS 10:12

If we don't keep our guard up, we can easily fall back into our old self-defeating patterns. This is called *relapse*. Alcoholics start to drink again, overeaters regain the weight they've lost, gamblers return to the casinos, workaholics fill up their schedules again. It's easy to slip back into old hurts, hang-ups, and habits. Regardless of the issue, the pattern is the same:

- Phase 1 is complacency. Relapse begins when we get comfortable. We've confessed our problems, dealt with them, and made real progress. Then we get comfortable and stop praying about it and working at it. Before we know it, we have become complacent.
- Phase 2 is confusion. We begin to rationalize and play mental games with ourselves. We say things like, "Maybe my problem really wasn't all that bad. I could have handled it myself." We forget how bad it used to be. Reality becomes fuzzy and confused.
- Phase 3 is compromise. Temptation is back. We return to the risky situations that got us into trouble in the first place. Compromise may begin with little things, but it won't be long before the ground we've gained is lost.
- Phase 4 is catastrophe. In this phase, we actually give in to the old hurts, hang-ups, or habits. Hate, resentment, and old behaviors return. But we need to understand this: The catastrophe is not the relapse. The relapse began in phase 1 with complacency. The catastrophe is simply the end result, the acting-out phase of the pattern.

PRAYER

Father, keep me from complacency and the patterns that could cause me to slip away from you once again. In Jesus' name, Amen.

Coming Back or Staying Out?

Samson reached toward the two central pillars on which the temple stood.
Bracing himself against them, his right hand on the one and his left hand on
the other, Samson said, "Let me die with the Philistines!" Then he pushed
with all his might, and down came the temple on the rulers and all the
people in it. Thus he killed many more when he died than while he lived.

JUDGES 16:29–30

One day I was studying Hebrews 11, where God's Hall of Famers are listed. One name in particular stuck out, and I wondered why God would place him here along with the great heroes of the faith.

Samson was a relapse expert if there ever was one. Eventually, his relapses caused him to be stripped of his power and suffer grave public humiliation. Then he changed his destiny by proclaiming that enough was enough. Instead of quitting and feeling sorry for himself after a relapse, he asked God to restore his strength one more time so he could take out the enemy. God honored his request and used him in a mighty way. Because Samson didn't let his relapses overwhelm him with guilt, his relationship with God was restored.

Relapse doesn't have to be the end. It can be a new beginning. It can be the point where God really uses us. In recovery, we are reminded that relapse is the end only if we don't get back up. We should never let a relapse keep us from experiencing God's power in our lives.

PRAYER

Father God, thank you for helping me stay away from relapse, but when I fall, help
me to stand up again and proclaim your power one more time. In Jesus' name, Amen.

Our Race

*Since we have such a huge crowd of men of faith watching us from
the grandstands, let us strip off anything that slows us down or
holds us back, and especially those sins that wrap themselves
so tightly around our feet and trip us up; and let us run with
patience the particular race that God has set before us.*

HEBREWS 12:1 TLB

I don't think I've ever seen an athlete prepare for a race by attaching a
parachute to his back. It would only make running his race so much
harder, maybe even impossible, because it would add resistance. Now
maybe that athlete would use a parachute in training, but when the race
is ready to start, he doesn't want anything that will make it more difficult to run.

Our hurts, hang-ups, and habits can work just like that parachute.
They cause resistance that can slow us down, even stop us in our tracks as
we begin our race for healing and wholeness. It would be foolish to hold
onto that junk while we're trying to move forward. Hurts keep us from
being able to reason through obstacles and plan our strategies. Hang-ups
grab at our feet and try to trip us up. And those bad habits, they waste precious seconds on the track and keep us from running effectively.

The race for recovery is difficult enough without carrying the past
with us. The only way to succeed is to unburden ourselves, put on our
track shoes, focus on the finish line, and run for our lives.

PRAYER

*Father, show me how to unburden myself of everything that will slow me down and
hinder my race for recovery. In Jesus' name, Amen.*

The Thief in Our Homes

Do you not know that your bodies are temples of the Holy Spirit, who is in you, whom you have received from God? You are not your own.

1 CORINTHIANS 6:19

God's Word says that our bodies and our minds are God's home, his temple. That's why the thoughts we allow inside are so important. Destructive thoughts damage God's home and steal our joy. Just as we strive each day to make wise choices about the food we put into our bodies, we must make wise choices about what we put into our minds.

Each day, we have the privilege to fill our minds with God's Word and will. When we fill our minds with the world, it's garbage in and garbage out. But when we fill our minds with God's Word, it's blessings in and blessings out.

It is impossible to keep all worldly thoughts from our minds, but we can lessen their influence by doing the following:

- Choose carefully what books, TV programs, and movies we watch.
- Choose wisely who we spend time with.
- Stay away from dangerous sites on the Internet.
- Share our choices with an accountability partner.

On a positive note, we can fill our thoughts—God's temple—with good things by doing the following:

- Start each day with alone time with God.
- Write our favorite Scripture verses on 3 x 5 cards and read them throughout the day.
- Spend time with those who share our desire to put good things into our minds.

PRAYER

Father God, I can see that when I choose you, I am choosing the best for myself and those good choices flow over into the lives of everyone I love, everyone I touch. In Jesus' name, Amen.

Coming Up a Little Short?

The Spirit himself testifies with our spirit that we are God's children. Now if we are children, then we are heirs—heirs of God and co-heirs with Christ, if indeed we share in his sufferings in order that we may also share in his glory.

ROMANS 8:16–17

We all have tough days, when the voice in our heads tells us we aren't measuring up. I've found that reciting the following reminders of how our Father views us can turn my day around:

- God says that I have been rescued from the dominion of darkness (Col. 1:13).
- God says that I am redeemed and forgiven (Col. 1:14).
- God says that I am "holy in his sight" (Col. 1:22).
- God says that I am "free from accusation" (Col. 1:22).
- God says that I am "without blemish" (Col. 1:22).
- God says that I am "perfect in his sight" (Col. 1:28).
- God says that I am "free from sin" (Rom. 6:7).
- God says that I am free from condemnation (Rom. 8:1).
- God says that I am a son/daughter of the King (Rom. 8:16).
- God says that I am an heir of God who created the cosmos (Rom. 8:17).
- God says that I am "white as snow" (Isa. 1:18).
- God says that I have been marked with his Spirit (Eph. 1:13).
- God says that I am a "member of his household" (Eph. 2:19).

This is just the beginning. As we dig into God's Word, we find that it is full of God's proclamations of his great love for us.

PRAYER

Father, thank you for loving me so much more than I can comprehend. In Jesus' name, Amen.

Rejoice in the Lord

Rejoice in the Lord always. I will say it again: Rejoice!

PHILIPPIANS 4:4

Good times and bad times—they are both a fact of life here on earth. That isn't a surprise to anyone, but suggesting that we rejoice in both the good times and the bad times might be. How can we do that? One way is by remembering how good God has been to us in the past, how he has blessed us and stood with us when we were hurting. There are always a multitude of things we can be grateful for. Here are some examples:

- Jesus Christ died on the cross for my sins so that I could be made right with God.
- Jesus Christ rose from the grave, defeating death and granting me life forever with him in heaven.
- I was given another day to live.
- I have people who care about me.
- I have hope in Christ that tomorrow is going to be better.

A good way to keep God's goodness always in the forefront is to start a gratitude list. When we add to the list every day, we begin to see how much God does for us in both the good times and the bad times. We have so many reasons to rejoice!

PRAYER

Father, thank you for seeing me through the bad times and blessing me abundantly through the good times. I owe everything to you. In Jesus' name, Amen.

The Truth and Love

Speaking the truth in love, we will in all things grow
up into him who is the Head, that is, Christ.

EPHESIANS 4:15

We've all been faced with situations where we needed to "speak the truth in love," as the Bible says. But what does that really mean?

Truth is essential in all our meaningful relationships. It is through speaking the truth that we learn to trust one another. If we are lied to, that trust is broken. But for some of us in recovery, sharing truthfully may be difficult because of trust issues from the past. When we have trouble being truthful, we should ask God to help us see if we are transferring old hurts onto another person. We should ask ourselves if our relationships are safe enough for us to share true feelings without the worry of rejection.

Love is also essential to meaningful relationships. It is through love that we learn to accept and care for one another. That is why we must always speak the truth in love. But love by itself can cover up issues, for love without truth is immature. A deeply honest relationship will never develop on the basis of love alone. We should ask if our relationships are safe enough to share our love without the fear of being taken advantage of.

Good relationships rely on a balance of truth and love.

PRAYER

Father, I can see that your relationship with me is based on both truth and love.
Help me to develop my other relationships in the same way. In Jesus' name, Amen.

Crash Up Ahead

Brothers and sisters, whatever is true, whatever is noble, whatever is right, whatever is pure, whatever is lovely, whatever is admirable—if anything is excellent or praiseworthy—think about such things.

PHILIPPIANS 4:8

While I was driving on the interstate, traffic came to a standstill. I wondered what was causing the holdup. Construction? A wreck? Something on the road? For more than twenty miles, I crept along at a snail's pace. When I finally reached the trouble spot, I was surprised to see that only one car was involved in the wreck, and it didn't look very bad. The police, fire, and ambulance were all on the scene, so it must have been worse than it looked. The bottom line, though, was that one car had backed up traffic for miles.

When we ram into a guardrail because we've engaged in a dangerous behavior of some kind, the lives of the people who love us are also affected. The consequences of our actions spill out onto them. If we don't yet care enough about ourselves to make good choices, we should do so for their sake.

Today, I make the choice to think about things that are pure, lovely, admirable, excellent, and praiseworthy. This is a good choice, and good choices also affect those who love us and the lives we touch. When we live in relationship, our choices—both good and bad—are felt a long way down the road.

PRAYER

Father, being in relationship with others is both a serious responsibility and an amazing blessing. Help me to always remember that my personal choices affect everyone around me. In Jesus' name, Amen.

The Tapes

No, dear brothers, I am still not all I should be, but I am
bringing all my energies to bear on this one thing: Forgetting
the past and looking forward to what lies ahead.

PHILIPPIANS 3:13 TLB

Back in the day, I was one of those kids who always had his Walkman on. This was before iPods, even before CDs. We used audiocassette tapes, and I had a nice collection. There were a few I would listen to over and over. In some cases, I listened so many times that I wore them out. At first the label on the front would start getting hard to read. Then the tape itself would start to warp, causing it to slow down and speed up. Eventually, the tape would break, and I'd have to go buy a new copy.

The same thing can happen to the tapes we play in our heads, those recordings from the past that speed up and slow down. If we dwell on them, we will never be able to deal with our bitterness and guilt. They can trap us in our yesterdays.

We will never be free of our hurts, hang-ups, and habits until we face our past recordings and deal with the pain involved with them. That doesn't mean we should ignore them. The answer is to deal with them, give them to God, and get them out of our heads once and for all.

PRAYER

Lord, help me to be rid of the recordings that linger in my head, reminding me of mistakes I've made in my past. Set me free to record the joys of my new life. In Jesus' name, Amen.

Smoke Alarm Warnings

*I will instruct you and teach you in the way you should
go; I will counsel you and watch over you.*

PSALM 32:8

A friend of mine was telling me about a smoke alarm that was beep-ing near his office. It needed a new battery. He went over to ask the people in that area if he could help them change it.

"I hear an occasional beeping in your area," he told them.

Their response was, "Oh yeah, that has been going off for about a week, but we have just tuned it out."

That made me think about how easy it is for some things to slip into our lives. It starts as an annoying beep that can drive us crazy, but the longer we live with it, the more we get used to it. Sometimes those beeps are the Holy Spirit's way of saying, "Something is not right. You need to take care of this problem." If we don't listen to his instruction, we won't be prepared when a dangerous incident occurs.

I know I need to be more attentive to God's voice and instruction. I don't want to become complacent about the warning beeps in my life—the ones God has placed there to alert me when there is danger.

PRAYER

Father, I have learned that it is never your will for us to be taken by surprise. If we are listening, you always send forth a warning. Help me to listen carefully so that I can live in safety. In Jesus' name, Amen.

Declaration of Dependence

Be strong in the Lord and in his mighty power. Put on the full armor
of God, so that you can take your stand against the devil's schemes.
For our struggle is not against flesh and blood, but against the
rulers, against the authorities, against the powers of this dark world
and against the spiritual forces of evil in the heavenly realms.

EPHESIANS 6:10−12

Not long ago, we were in Boston. We had only a day, but we were determined to see some of the sights before we left. Wow, what history! We saw the place where the Declaration of Independence was first read and the decision was made to fight for our country's freedom. We saw where Paul Revere began his famous ride. We saw the *USS Constitution*, aptly named "Old Ironsides."

The United States won the battle for freedom, but there is another battle being waged against our hearts, minds, and souls. The enemy would like us to believe that we can't win; the odds against us are too great. But the truth is that we can't lose. Jesus has already fought the battle for our freedom from sin and won!

Now we must make his victory a reality in our own lives. We do that by signing a Declaration of Dependence—dependence on God, that is. We will then be free to live the lives he intended for us.

PRAYER

Father God, thank you for the many brothers and sisters who stand alongside me as I declare my dependence on you and strive to grasp my freedom in Christ. In Jesus' name, Amen.

Proceed with Caution

Jesus turned and said to Peter, "Get behind me, Satan! You are a stumbling block to me; you do not have in mind the things of God, but the things of men."

MATTHEW 16:23

A while back, I needed to move an extremely heavy piece of furniture. With help from three of my friends, we got the piece onto two dollies and rolled it outside and up the driveway. Everything was going fine until we came to an abrupt stop and the piece almost fell off. We looked around and couldn't find anything out of place—no cracks in the sidewalk, no big obstacles in the way. No one had tripped. Finally we got down on our knees and looked under the dollies. There we found that a small acorn had lodged under one of the tires. That little acorn had stopped four men, two dollies, and a monster piece of furniture in our tracks.

Later, I was thinking that this happens pretty often in recovery. If we ignore small distractions or temptations, they can derail us and destroy what we've worked so hard to accomplish. Our relationships are too too valuable to risk; our hard work, too important to lose. We have to keep our eyes open for anything that can bring our lives to a stop—and that includes pesky little acorns.

PRAYER

Heavenly Father, thank you for showing me those little distractions and temptations before they get in the way of what you're doing in my life. In Jesus' name, Amen.

Toothpaste

*The words of the reckless pierce like swords, but
the tongue of the wise brings healing.*

PROVERBS 12:18

A lmost all of us have been guilty of squeezing the toothpaste tube
too hard. About a week's worth of toothpaste squirts out, and it's
impossible to get any of it back in the tube. The harder we try, the messier
it gets. The same is true when we try to take back hurtful words. Here's
an example.

One Sunday morning during announcements, the pastor told the
congregation that he needed to make a correction to an announcement
in last week's bulletin. It read: "The church will host an evening of fine
dining, super entertainment, and gracious hostility." He assured the
congregation that it should have read: "The church will host an evening
of fine dining, super entertainment, and gracious hospitality." He con-
cluded by saying, "Sorry, folks, we are a loving church, not a hostile one.
We love *hurting* people." Oops!

Words can be downright contrary, can't they? We have to be careful how we use them at all times. Especially when we are angry or hurt,
we need to seek God's wisdom before we start squeezing the toothpaste
tube. We're all going to make errors like the one the unfortunate pastor
made, but just stopping to think before we speak can help us keep our
lives from getting messy.

PRAYER

*Lord God, put a check on my lips. Help me to speak with wisdom and understand-
ing. In Jesus' name, Amen.*

Dirty Hands

Since we are surrounded by such a great cloud of witnesses, let us
throw off everything that hinders and the sin that so easily entangles,
and let us run with perseverance the race marked out for us.

HEBREWS 12:1

During their visit, I took my daughter and her two boys to my brother's fishing tackle store. My brother gave the boys a box of worms to take home. These were real worms, not the plastic variety. The boys played with those worms all week, taking them out of the box, carrying them around on paper plates, putting them back in the box.

Several times a day, the worms would go back in the box, and the boys would say, "Papa, we need cleaning!" You can imagine how dirty those little hands got. Some real scrubbing was needed. After the boys went home, I released the worms into the wild—my backyard. And I can assure all the worm lovers out there, no worms were harmed!

This reminded me, though, that we sometimes like to pick up the dirty things from our past, carry them around, and play with them. Then we come to our heavenly Father and say, "We're through with all that now. We need cleaning." Peace of mind comes when we get rid of the worms and the dirt that comes with them.

PRAYER

Father, thank you for washing away the dirt of my past. Thank you for cleaning
me up and making me suitable to stand in your presence. In Jesus' name, Amen.

The Truth

Jesus said, "If you hold to my teaching, you are really my disciples. Then you will know the truth, and the truth will set you free."

JOHN 8:31–32

Reserving time daily to read the Bible is one of the most important disciplines we learn in recovery. It's so essential because it is the primary source for the truth. And the truth is what sets us free from the past and from the painful hurts, hang-ups, and habits that haunt us in the present. Here's a list of some of the things we learn from the Bible about ourselves as followers of Christ:

- We learn that we are not in control of anything, but Jesus is in control of everything. This truth sets us free from thinking that we have to have it all together. Our job is to trust God—who does have it all together.
- We learn that we have all sinned, we've all made mistakes, and only Jesus is perfect. This truth frees us from thinking we have to be perfect. We can admit we've blown it.
- We learn that because Jesus is perfect and because he died on the cross, we can trust him to be our Savior. The greatest freedom is being free from our sins. This truth frees us from the delusion that we can change ourselves. Only God can do that.

The Word of God, the Bible, is filled with truth! It contains the truth about God, the truth about ourselves, and the truth about what God expects of us here on earth. Reading his Word every day can make us new people.

PRAYER

Father, thank you for your Word. I go to it because I want to know the truth, and I'm never disappointed. In Jesus' name, Amen.

His Presence Is Peace

*Do not be anxious about anything, but in everything, by prayer
and petition, with thanksgiving, present your requests to God.
And the peace of God, which transcends all understanding,
will guard your hearts and your minds in Christ Jesus.*

PHILIPPIANS 4:6–7

I have been doing a lot of studying in the book of Philippians, specifically the fourth chapter. I was struck by what it really means to have peace in *all* circumstances. Isn't that contrary to what the world tells us?

Many of us grew up believing the only way we can have joy and peace in our hearts is if everything in our lives is going right. If everything was going our way in all circumstances, we thought we really had something to be happy about. So we ran from our problems, hid from them, ignored them. And that brought us just what we didn't want—more conflict at home or at work.

I now know that true peace is not the absence of conflict but rather the presence of Jesus Christ. I am learning to take all my problems to him rather than pushing them under the carpet and trying to forget about them. True peace is the presence of righteousness in the midst of the conflict. When we keep our eyes on Jesus, he will guide us along the mountaintops and through the valleys.

PRAYER

Father, thank you for meeting me and giving me peace in the midst of my problems and conflicts. In Jesus' name, Amen.

Dish the Dirt

Do not let any unwholesome talk come out of your mouths,
but only what is helpful for building others up according
to their needs, that it may benefit those who listen.

EPHESIANS 4:29

According to the dictionary, gossip is "a report, often malicious, about another person's behavior." It's a big relationship killer and should be avoided at all costs. I was reminded of this when someone said to me, "Did you hear about—?"

My immediate response was, "Do I need to hear this?"

The person speaking was a little taken aback by my response, but it did take the conversation in a different direction. The point is that gossip is harmful, and just about the only way to catch yourself before you get caught up in it is to prepare a response ahead of time.

Does that mean we go around with our heads in the sand, unwilling to acknowledge that someone has a problem? Of course not. But the Bible is clear about what to do when we become aware of another person's unwise behavior. In Matthew 5, we are told to go to that person and address it directly. What should we do if another person has a problem with us? The same thing. We go and work it out. Our first thought should always be to restore the relationship by speaking words of truth and encouragement.

PRAYER

Lord God, I know there is something compelling about hearing of someone else's failures. Maybe it makes us feel better about ourselves in comparison. But I see the damage gossip can cause. Help me do what is pleasing in your sight. In Jesus' name, Amen.

The Way Out

No temptation has overtaken you except what is common to mankind. And God is faithful; he will not let you be tempted beyond what you can bear. But when you are tempted, he will also provide a way out so that you can endure it.

1 CORINTHIANS 10:13

I've been going to the same barber every three weeks for close to a year now. Every time I go, I get the same cut. I like the guy, but right now I'm not happy with him because a few minutes ago, he took a hunk out of the sideburn portion of my beard—the one I've been growing for months, and it was just now starting to look right.

When I first saw that missing hunk, about half an inch, my mind went crazy. *All that time and effort for nothing. What was that guy thinking? He must not have been paying attention. Now I'll have to shave, give up on my beard.* Once I calmed down, though, I reminded myself that hair grows back, and the truth is that no one looks at me as closely as I look at myself.

Some people fall out of recovery that way. One little thing goes wrong, and they're ready to abandon the whole project. They think, *Well . . . I blew it. I might as well go back to my old habits.* That's as crazy as me giving up on my beard because it has one flaw. The human mind will always want to give up, to find a way out of the hard work of recovery, but we can't give it what it wants!

--- PRAYER ---

Father, thank you for helping me to move forward when I slip rather than letting it ruin everything I've worked for. In Jesus' name, Amen.

We May Fail

The LORD himself goes before you and will be with you; he will never
leave you nor forsake you. Do not be afraid; do not be discouraged.

DEUTERONOMY 31:8

We may fail—let me change that—we *will* fail! That's a fact. But the good news is that God will never fail us! We are imperfect. If we think we aren't, we can ask our loved ones and accountability partners or sponsors. God, on the other hand, is perfect—completely and unfailingly perfect! God has promised never to fail us, but what does that mean, exactly?

Does it mean he will never let us struggle? Does it mean he will never let us have losses? Does it mean he will never let us get into financial trouble? Does it mean he won't let us suffer the consequences of our actions and behaviors? It does not! We will have struggles, losses, problems, consequences, but he will always be with us—no matter what we face.

When we make poor choices, we have to face the consequences. When others make poor choices that affect us, we may have to face the hurt. But God will always be there to pick us up, dust us off, and put us back on our feet again. And we can help ourselves by seeking his will before we make a potentially risky choice and by setting appropriate boundaries for those we know are not always safe to be around.

PRAYER

Father, I believe your words of promise that you will always be there for me. Show
me how to live wisely. In Jesus' name, Amen.

The Eleventh Step

Let the word of Christ dwell in you richly.

COLOSSIANS 3:16

We have taken ten steps now on our road to recovery. We are living out the decision we made in Step 3. We are growing in our understanding of God, improving our conscious contact with him, and conducting honest inventories on a regular basis.

> *Step 11: We sought through prayer and meditation to improve our conscious contact with God, praying only for knowledge of his will for us and power to carry that out.*

As our relationship with God deepens, it's important for us to reserve time apart with him every day. During this time, we learn to focus on him through prayer and meditation. When I say *prayer*, I simply mean talking to God. For me, meditation is just getting quiet so we can hear what God is saying. I don't get into some yoga-type position or murmur, "Om, om, om." I simply focus on and think about God, a certain verse of Scripture, or maybe even just one or two words. This morning I spent ten or fifteen minutes just focusing on one word: *gratitude*.

Talking to God and listening for his voice is the best way to silence those old familiar friends of past dysfunction. They want to interrupt my quiet time with God because they don't want me to hear him say that I have great worth, that I bring him joy. I know that my talks with God strengthen me to meet the challenges of each day.

PRAYER

Dear Father, thank you for always being there for me, always listening, loving, teaching, strengthening, and encouraging. In Jesus' name, Amen.

Distractions

*Do not be anxious about anything, but in everything, by prayer
and petition, with thanksgiving, present your requests to God.
And the peace of God, which transcends all understanding,
will guard your hearts and your minds in Christ Jesus.*

PHILIPPIANS 4:6–7

The used snowplow I bought for our driveway needed some work before it would be 100 percent usable. That was on my mind as I sat down with my wife for our daily devotional time together. My mind kept drifting, and then I came to these words in the devotional I was reading from: "Each time you *plow* your way through the massive distractions to communicate with me, you achieve victory." Isn't that great? God used the very words I was reading to get my attention back to where it needed to be.

This happens during prayer time as well. In fact, a friend told me that every time he starts praying, his mind drifts to something else. I told him I know exactly what he's talking about. Sometimes I'll be in prayer and my mind will drift to a cabinet I'm making or some other project.

I'm sure we all have trouble staying focused at times. From now on when it happens to me, I'm going to stop and say, "Sorry about that, Father. I'm back, and I really want to stay focused. Please help me." I believe God knows that we struggle with this, and just like he used the words of that devotional to speak to me, he will find a way to help us get back on track when we ask him.

───────── PRAYER ─────────

*Father, thank you for helping me stay focused on you during our time together.
I don't want distractions to keep me from receiving all you have for me. In Jesus'
name, Amen.*

Serving Others

*If serving the LORD seems undesirable to you, then choose for yourselves
this day whom you will serve, whether the gods your forefathers served
beyond the River, or the gods of the Amorites, in whose land you are
living. But as for me and my household, we will serve the LORD.*

JOSHUA 24:15

I've noticed that some days, I'm all gung ho to serve the Lord. But there
are other days when I don't feel nearly as determined. We all have
these dull, unenthusiastic days, and sometimes we're just in a bad mood.
That's why God challenges us each and every day to *choose* whom we
will serve. It's more than a once-in-a-lifetime choice, more than a yearly
choice, more than a daily choice. There are times when we have to renew
our decision moment by moment.

All our choices are this way, really. We *choose* to stay in love with our
spouses, we *choose* to continue to attend meetings, we *choose* to open up to
our friends, we *choose* to be honest about our situations, we *choose* to put
others first. So why would it be different with our decision to serve God?

The good thing is that all those mental gymnastics don't mean
a thing. They are just feelings, and for the most part, feelings can't be
trusted. So we shouldn't put ourselves down on those days when we're
less than gung ho. We just choose to go on, knowing that God sees our
hearts and knows our true motivations.

----- PRAYER -----

*Father, forgive me for those low days when I struggle with commitment. I choose to
choose you each and every day. In Jesus' name, Amen.*

Welcoming Change

Create in me a pure heart, O God, and renew a steadfast spirit within me.

PSALM 51:10

One of the most frustrating things we can experience in our recovery is when someone close to us is hurting and needs to make changes, but they just won't accept help. I have learned the hard way that if I push the needed changes on them, it just doesn't work.

Change is possible in our lives, but only if and when we come to a place where we are ready to accept it. That time usually comes when our pain becomes greater than our fear. Even when we have been in recovery for a while, we can still struggle with change. And yet change is necessary if we are to find wholeness. It is also a constant, for we live in a changing world.

Often our reluctance to accept change is just fear of the unknown. Even an unhappy, tumultuous known can sometimes trump an unknown. "If I admit my problem, will I lose my family?" we might ask. "If I walk away from these friends, will I find others?" We aren't sure what change will look like, so we hold back, and until we are ready to move forward, recovery comes to a standstill.

Accepting change is an exercise in trusting God. It's never easy, and it always carries with it an element of uncertainty. But change is also the only way to find lasting peace and happiness. Our journey to recovery won't succeed without it.

PRAYER

Father, help me to invite change into my life, no matter how unsettled that might make me feel. Let me see it as a demonstration of my trust in you. In Jesus' name, Amen.

Don't Break the Shell

*Consider it pure joy, my brothers, whenever you face trials of
many kinds, because you know that the testing of your faith
develops perseverance. Perseverance must finish its work so that
you may be mature and complete, not lacking anything.*

JAMES 1:2–4

One nine-year-old grandson's teacher brought duck eggs to class so the children could incubate them and see them hatch. On the big day, the eggs started to move around a little, and small holes appeared where the ducklings were trying to break out. Of course the children wanted to help the ducklings break free, but the teacher told them that the struggle would actually make the ducklings stronger and better able to survive. The teacher and her students stood by and patiently watched as each duckling broke free.

This lesson is true in life as well. We've all had times when we cried out to God, angry that he hadn't intervened and spared us some painful episode in our lives. But God knows that it's through our struggles that we are strengthened for the battle ahead. Sometimes he does rescue us immediately, but other times he stands by, patiently watching as we push past obstacles in our paths.

Just as that wise teacher knew what was best for the ducklings, God knows what is best for us. It might not be what seems obvious at first, but it is always what we need. And he is always standing by, talking us through to freedom.

PRAYER

Thank you, Lord, for seeing what I need in my life and taking care of me even when I don't understand what you're doing. I trust you. In Jesus' name, Amen.

Wise People

Walk with the wise and become wise, for a companion of fools suffers harm.

PROVERBS 13:20

One of the keys to successful recovery is accountability. We all need people in our lives to pray for us, encourage us, be there for us, and tell us when we are misbehaving. For that, we need individuals who are wise and have the following traits:

W—Walk the road to recovery with us. We need people in our lives who are honest enough to admit that they have their own problems and brokenness, and who have experienced the healing power of Jesus Christ themselves.

I—Integrity. We need people who are the same at church as they are at home, people whose walk matches their talk.

S—Similar struggles. Of course, we can learn from people who don't identify with our recovery issue, but we also need those people in our lives who know what we're going through because they've been there themselves.

E—Encouraging attitude. We should find people who will encourage us, celebrate our victories, and urge us to enjoy the steady growth rather than look for the big, easy change.

Our journey will be smoother and our success greater if we surround ourselves with people who are WISE!

PRAYER

Thank you, Father, for putting wise people in my life. I know that they understand what I need to stay on the path to recovery. In Jesus' name, Amen.

What Are You Feeding Yourself?

Let us examine our ways and test them, and let us return to the LORD.

LAMENTATIONS 3:40

A few years ago, my doctor told me I needed to drastically reduce the sodium in my diet. He said I would also have to change my diet to include more fruits and vegetables, less bread, and fewer sweets. In short, I would have to eat less of the things I enjoyed and more of the things I don't. This was not happy news, but my doctor shared this with me: our bodies crave what we feed them.

Apparently, the more healthy foods we feed our bodies, the more our bodies want them. Just as my body craved sweets because that's what I was feeding it, my body would crave fruit and vegetables if that's what I taught it to expect. I tried it, and it worked. My body began craving what I was feeding it.

I couldn't help but see that our minds also crave what we feed them. If we are filling our minds with lies, that's what they will crave. If we are filling our minds with the world's values, that's what they will crave. And that's exactly why our bodies and minds become addicted to and crave even those things that are harmful and destructive—because they've become used to them.

Understanding makes a big difference in our ability to change. Once we know why we feel a draw toward our old habits and addictions, we can start to put them behind us and choose something better.

PRAYER

Lord, I want to crave only what you have approved for my life. Help me as I make a transition to a better way. In Jesus' name, Amen.

Trust the Alarm

*Blow the trumpet in Zion; sound the alarm on my holy hill. Let all
who live in the land tremble, for the day of the LORD is coming.*

JOEL 2:1

My wife and I were sleeping quietly, enjoying a vacation night in our camper, when the propane gas alarm went off. It's one of the loudest, most annoying alarms imaginable. We both jumped out of bed. My first thought was to turn the alarm off since I couldn't smell gas. In my groggy state of mind, I felt sure it was a false alarm, and I was tempted to get back in bed and go back to sleep. But sane reasoning prevailed. After an hour-long investigation, I was able to confirm a false alarm.

Alarms are designed to keep us safe. We undo their usefulness when we fail to respond to them. When we turn our lives over to Jesus Christ, the Holy Spirit of God takes up residence within us. He is there to comfort and fill our hearts with God's love. But he is also there to warn us when we are in danger. Like an alarm sounding, God's Spirit tells us to stop; slow down; turn around; get out of harm's way. He is watching out for our good.

When we feel the prodding of the Holy Spirit inside us, telling us that something is wrong, it might be tempting to tell ourselves that we're just nervous or overreacting. But it's never a good idea to disarm what God has placed in our lives to keep us safe.

PRAYER

Father, thank you for giving me your Holy Spirit to impart comfort, wisdom, and understanding to alert me to danger. In Jesus' name, Amen.

Alarms

Be sure you know the condition of your flocks,
give careful attention to your herds.

PROVERBS 27:23

My car makes a bell sound when something is wrong. For example, if I'm running low on gas or the door is open while the car is on, I'll hear a binging sound. Today, it started binging, but I couldn't identify what was wrong. I was parked, the car was off, plenty of gas—so? Then I realized the key was in the ignition. My car was warning me not to get out of the car and leave the key inside.

Most of us will agree that warnings are important. That's especially true in recovery. The warnings won't be alarms or bells or flashing lights. There won't be binging sounds. But when we hear them, we'll know that we are in danger of either relapsing or taking on another hurt, hang-up, or habit that will end up slowing down our progress and keeping us from being free.

Some warning signs are simple—like feeling tired, unappreciated, entitled, easily offended. Sometimes they come in the form of an uneasy feeling, usually when we're with someone we shouldn't be with or in a place that isn't safe for us. At other times the warning urges us to do something, to take action.

These warnings won't do us any good if we ignore them. But when we pay attention, we could prevent ourselves from getting sidetracked and missing out on the good things God brings to our lives.

PRAYER

Father, thank you for the warnings you place before me. I know they are for my good. In Jesus' name, Amen.

What Did You Get?

*In him we have redemption through his blood, the forgiveness
of sins, in accordance with the riches of God's grace.*

EPHESIANS 1:7

What did you get?" Those are the words we generally hear from one another the day after Christmas. We enjoy sharing the surprises and wonderful gifts we received. As a kid, I could hardly wait to find my friends and tell them what I got.

Earlier today I was thinking about what incredible gifts I have already been given. I have rich relationships and a wonderful family. Most of all, I am loved by the King of kings, my Savior, Jesus Christ. I am thankful that the Lord not only likes me but truly loves me. I'm not sure why, because I'm one messed-up guy. It reminds me of a quote from the movie *A Bug's Life*: "You're weird, but I like you."

I'm so grateful that the Lord loves me despite all my flaws. He has given me a gift I don't deserve. That gift is the Father saying, "No matter what you have done, I will wipe it away." It doesn't matter how many earthly possessions we receive. What matters is that we have been given the gift of life and mercy and grace from our heavenly Father. Let's stop for a moment and let that sink in.

PRAYER

Thank you, Lord, for the gift of your love. I don't deserve it, but I receive it with a grateful heart. In Jesus' name, Amen.

Don't Minimize . . . Delete!

Since we are surrounded by such a great cloud of witnesses, let us
throw off everything that hinders and the sin that so easily entangles,
and let us run with perseverance the race marked out for us.

HEBREWS 12:1

The other day I was working on my computer. I had three projects in the works, so I would minimize one project's document and move to the second. Then I'd minimize that one and move to the third. Icons at the bottom of the screen let me know that my documents were close at hand.

Two of the projects were work related, and the third was a fun project. I was trying to stay focused on the important tasks, but that fun project kept whispering to me, "You don't need to work on those other two. Open me. You know you want to. Come on! Have some fun!" Finally, the fun project became so distracting that I had to delete it from the screen.

I'm pretty sure that's what the writer of Hebrews meant when he said to get rid of those things that so easily entangle us. Most of the time, it's not enough to just minimize the bad habits that got us into recovery. They will always be sitting down there in the corner of our minds, whispering to us. The only way to stay focused on the work God has called us to do is to delete those bad habits once and for all.

PRAYER

Heavenly Father, thank you for helping me clear the screen of distractions that keeps me from the work you've given me to do. Help me to focus as I do on what is pleasing in your eyes. In Jesus' name, Amen.

Daddy Date

My soul thirsts for God, for the living God.
When can I go and meet with God?

PSALM 42:2

What is the best gift we can give our children? No matter what they might say if we asked them, the answer is time. That's how we show them they are important, by showing that we're not too busy to pay attention to them. I'm not suggesting that we allow them to be rude, butting into conversations or making unreasonable demands. What I mean is that we demonstrate to our children that they are precious to us by spending time with them and being interested in what they are interested in.

In our family, we have "daddy dates." This is special one-on-one time when I am focused just on that child. It's time when we can talk without distractions, and we spend time doing things that are fun for both of us. Sometimes we go shopping; other times we just sit and talk. We may read a comic book together or go to a ball game. The point isn't what we do but that we do it together.

Our heavenly Father longs to have daddy dates with us as well. He tells us in his Word, the Bible, that when we draw close to him, he will draw close to us. He invites us to come into his presence anytime. He loves it when we just sit and talk, especially when we are willing to set aside all the distractions and focus just on Him.

PRAYER

Father God, thank you for allowing me to spend time with you whenever I want. Thanks for listening when I need to talk and using me to accomplish your purposes. In Jesus' name, Amen.

Real Love

If I speak in the tongues of men and of angels, but do not have love,
I am only a resounding gong or a clanging cymbal. If I have the gift
of prophecy and can fathom all mysteries and all knowledge, and if
I have a faith that can move mountains, but do not have love, I am
nothing. If I give all I possess to the poor and give over my body to
hardship that I may boast, but do not have love, I gain nothing.

1 CORINTHIANS 13:1–3

What does the word *love* really mean?

L stands for *large*. Real love, the kind God gives, is big enough to cover everyone, not just the people we love and cherish and enjoy being around. It includes the unlovable and even those who don't deserve the love we offer them.

O stands for *open*. We need to keep our hearts and eyes open to see the opportunities God puts in our paths each day— opportunities to love someone who is hurting, someone who needs to experience real love, someone who might not find love anywhere else.

V stands for *value*. We must love and value others as we do ourselves! Do we choose to love based on the world's approval or God's? If we love only as the world loves, we do not know real love at all.

E stands for *extra mile*. Our love for others is shown by our willingness to go the extra mile for them. Love always does more than is expected and doesn't keep a record of it. It's never about what that person will do for you next.

PRAYER

Father, thank you for loving me with a true and lasting love. In Jesus' name, Amen.

Follow the Sign

There is a way that seems right to a man, but in the end it leads to death.

PROVERBS 14:12

During our downtime at a retreat, several of us decided to take a bike ride. After riding a couple of miles of trails, we decided to head back to the hotel. We came to a sign that told us to go in a certain direction. After a short discussion, we agreed that the sign must have been turned wrong. We were convinced that it was pointing in the wrong direction. We just knew we were right, but it turned out we were wrong. We ended up going an extra mile out of our way before we arrived back at the sign. This time we followed its direction.

So what did I learn?

1. God gave us a road map in the Bible. We should follow the signs in it.
2. Just because everyone decides to go a certain way doesn't make it the right way.
3. Go back and check the road map.
4. Sometimes one voice of reason saying, "Let's follow the map," can keep the whole group from going the wrong way. Be that voice!
5. Don't be afraid to speak up, but always do it in love.

PRAYER

Lord, give me the courage to speak up when I should and always do what I know is right. Thank you for keeping me going in the right direction. In Jesus' name, Amen.

Groans

*In the same way, the Spirit helps us in our weakness. We
do not know what we ought to pray for, but the Spirit
himself intercedes for us through wordless groans.*

ROMANS 8:26

I spent some time with friends who had experienced a family tragedy. Their grief was palpable, and they were shaken to the core. As
we drove to their house, my wife and I talked about what to say and do
once we got there. We knew our words would be empty. We knew they
probably wouldn't be able to put their pain into words or tell us what they
needed. In light of that, we decided to just sit with them and be there.

I couldn't help remembering all the times I've been in pain and how
hard it was to pray. I couldn't even put the words together. I certainly
wasn't able to tell God what I needed from him because I didn't know
myself. But God is so good! His Holy Spirit translates even our sighs and
groans and tears into prayers and pleas.

In this life, there is no way to avoid pain and tragedy. It strikes us all
from time to time. When that happens, we can take comfort in the fact
that God understands even what we can't put into words, and he is there
for us always. He promises that when we invite him into our lives, we
will never again face painful times alone. He will be with us every step
of the way.

--- PRAYER ---

*Father, my life is in your hands. Thank you for being there whenever I need you,
ready to comfort me with your presence. In Jesus' name, Amen.*

Slips and Falls

Be on your guard; stand firm in the faith; be men of courage; be strong.

1 CORINTHIANS 16:13

Every once in a while, I'll be walking along, minding my own business. Then all of a sudden, I trip, slip, and *bam!* I'm on the ground and not sure what happened. It is easy to become so consumed with the actual "fall" that we don't ask ourselves what caused it in the first place. I have found that learning why I fell can be quite valuable. If I can understand how I ended up where I am, then I have a better chance of preventing a future fall. There is an old saying, "Do not look where you fell, but where you slipped."

Sometimes slips can actually prevent a fall by causing us to pay attention to where we are and what's going on around us. When I use the word *slips* in this instance, I'm not referring to relapse. Relapse is the actual fall. Taking a drink, looking at Internet porn, getting into another unhealthy relationship, etc.—these actions are the actual fall.

So let's pay more attention to the slips, and if we do end up falling, we should not be discouraged. Instead, we should get back on our feet and move forward. And most of all, we shouldn't try to do it alone. We should confess the fall to God and our accountability team. They will help restore us.

PRAYER

Father God, thank you for granting me pardon when I fall and for putting people in my life to help me get up and try again. In Jesus' name, Amen.

The Price of Freedom

*It is for freedom that Christ has set us free. Stand firm, then, and
do not let yourselves be burdened again by a yoke of slavery.*

GALATIANS 5:1

I've been remembering this morning that our country's freedom is not, and never was, free. I've buried some friends who were soldiers, even during our latest war in the Middle East. But it was Vietnam that affected me the most. My dad was called to serve, and he was gone for more than a year.

My mom had a little tape recorder, and we would sit around and record messages to send him. We hoped that hearing our voices would be comforting. I also remember that we checked the mail every day to see if we had received a recording from him. When we did get one, we'd run into the house, call everyone together, and listen. Just hearing his voice made us feel better. It gave us hope that he would come home soon. And thanks to God, he finally did.

The freedom of worship we enjoy in our country was purchased by the lives of those brave warriors—both men and women—who didn't come home, those who paid the ultimate price. We should give thanks every day for those who bought our freedom and for Jesus Christ who paid the ultimate price for our eternal freedom. His death and resurrection bring us hope that one day we will be with our heavenly Father forever.

PRAYER

*Heavenly Father, thank you for the freedoms you have given us through your Son,
Jesus, and those who have given their lives so that we might be free to worship you.
In Jesus' name, Amen.*

Turn to Him

*Is anyone among you in trouble? Let them pray. Is
anyone happy? Let them sing songs of praise.*

JAMES 5:13

I admit it: I tend to go to God more quickly during the hard times of
life. When things are going badly, I don't hesitate to run to him for
help. I've done that over and over. I have no trouble praying when the
chips are down. I can also tell you that God has never let me down—not
once, not ever. Of course he shows up to help me in his own way and his
own timing, but he has never left me hanging.

Here's the strange part—at least I think it's strange—when the
trouble passes, my prayers slow down. And when things are great, I tend
to lean on my own power and understanding. Then it's back to crises,
and I'm back on my knees. I'm pretty sure this happens to a lot of us. We
tend to think that it's easier to turn to God when we know we need him.
We hesitate to bother him with our daily trials.

God makes it clear in his Word that he wants us to turn to him in all
our circumstances, thanking him for the good and running to him when
times are bad. Or we could say that what God wants is for us to make him
the center of our lives. That way he is always with us, no matter what's
going on in our lives.

PRAYER

*Lord God, thank you for hearing me when I pray and being with me through all the
times of my life. In Jesus' name, Amen.*

Heightened Awareness

*The heavens tell the glory of God, and the skies
announce what his hands have made.*

PSALM 19:1 NCV

I was walking out to my car and there it was—a sky filled with starlight and all the brilliant colors of the universe. I just stood there and took it all in. What an amazingly creative God we serve. I realize how easy it is to get wrapped up in life and overlook his beauty all around us. It's so important to slow down and experience his greatness for a few moments each day.

We should ask ourselves, *What are those things that take our breath away?* For me it is watching my grandkids play, seeing my family pray and laugh together, and listening to my Celebrate Recovery brothers and sisters share their latest victories.

I continue to be amazed by my changed heart that has the ability to see even adversity as a gift, to love and appreciate all that the Lord's given me, to see the value in the smallest things in my life, and especially to cherish the moment when I see a turning point in the life of a friend that will lead to healing and freedom.

God's presence in our lives gives us heightened awareness of his greatness. Let's take a deep breath and drink it in.

PRAYER

Almighty God, your greatness is beyond my ability to comprehend. Thank you for being a big God in my life. More than I could ever need. In Jesus' name, Amen.

Don't Miss the Treasure

The kingdom of heaven is like treasure hidden in a field.
When a man found it, he hid it again, and then in his joy
went and sold all he had and bought that field.

MATTHEW 13:44

While vacationing on the Florida coast, I went out for a walk on the beach very early in the morning. I wanted to see the sunrise, and I also wanted to see what treasures (shells) I could find. I was surprised to see someone coming toward me from the other direction. I could hardly believe there were two of us walking the beach at that hour.

All of a sudden I began to worry that the other person would find treasures that were meant for me, so I started looking for the big shells way ahead of where I was walking. Nothing. Feeling a little sheepish, I slowed almost to a stop, and there at my feet was the biggest, most beautiful shell I'd seen since we arrived.

That precious shell made me wonder how many other treasures I had missed because I was trying to look too far ahead. God wants to bless us while we are enjoying the sand, the surf, and the sunrise of each day. He doesn't want us to be so preoccupied with claiming our blessings that we miss out on the beauty he has placed at our feet.

PRAYER

Lord God, thank you for the beauty all around me. Help me not to retreat to the past or run ahead to the future, but walk in the treasure-filled steps you have for me today. In Jesus' name, Amen.

Loving Others

*Dear friends, let us love one another, for love comes from God.
Everyone who loves has been born of God and knows God.*

1 JOHN 4:7

I have a favorite restaurant where I often meet people for lunch. I'm probably there three or four times a week, and I always order the same thing. As good as the food is, there's something about the restaurant that I like almost as much—they know me. They know what I'm going to order, where I want to sit, and what I'll want to drink. In fact, if I decide to order something else, they get a little shaken up. I love this feeling. I love feeling like I'm known, like I'm welcome.

At Celebrate Recovery, we can honor God by making others feel known and welcome. We can remember their names and offer a hello, maybe even a hug. We can let them know we're glad they came and hope they'll come back. These small gestures could make the difference between someone staying bound by addiction and someone finding freedom and wholeness.

Celebrate Recovery is a family, a big family with open arms. It's spread out and maybe a little crazy, but we love it when people come in and get involved. Most of all, this is a place where people can come to find a relationship with God and receive all the benefits that come with knowing him. Let's show God's love to everyone who comes through the doors.

--- PRAYER ---

Thank you, Lord, for using us to reach people with a message of hope and let them know that they can be whole again. In Jesus' name, Amen.

Refocusing My Mind

Whatever you have learned or received or heard from me, or seen in
me—put it into practice. And the God of peace will be with you.

PHILIPPIANS 4:9

One night when I thought everyone was sound asleep, I got up. My wife had the same idea at the same time. We ran into each other in a completely dark room, and we both yelled. What a surprise for both of us!

In my recovery, there are times when I would be walking through my day, expecting certain things to happen in a certain way and—*bam!* I was blindsided by something completely unexpected, like a temptation or conflict. But I've learned that the only way I can manage such times positively is by refocusing my mind on positive truths.

In recovery, I learned that if I don't want to act in negative ways, I must not think and meditate on negative things. What I think will, to a great extent, determine how I feel. And how I feel will almost always determine how I respond to life's unexpected encounters in the dark.

Today if I find myself entering the "dark zone" because something hasn't gone my way or something unhealthy has crossed my path, I can make a good choice. I can choose to refocus my mind on God's truths and respond in a way that's pleasing to him.

--- PRAYER ---

Father, you are so faithful. You always help me to find my way, even in the dark-
ness. In Jesus' name, Amen.

Driving on the Wrong Side

"Do not be afraid, you who are highly esteemed," he said. "Peace!
Be strong now; be strong." When he spoke to me, I was strengthened
and said, "Speak, my lord, since you have given me strength."

DANIEL 10:19

On a recent trip to England, I found out firsthand what it's like to drive on the other side of the road. The first time I slipped behind the wheel on the passenger's side of the car, everything in me was shouting, *Don't do it! This is just wrong!* But the more I drove, the easier it became. It may never feel comfortable, but practice is making me a stronger wrong-side-of-the-road driver.

This experience reminded me that in recovery there are things I don't always feel comfortable doing—going to meetings, attending church, serving others, facing painful issues. Fortunately, I had a good sponsor who told me early on that when my head starts telling me it's not comfortable, I need to get my rear end in gear and get going! My head will eventually catch up. He assured me that doing things outside my comfort zone would make me a stronger person.

Listening to God's Holy Spirit and the people he puts in our lives—like sponsors, accountability partners, and mentors—keeps us on the right side of the road.

PRAYER

Father God, thank you for helping me step out of my comfort zone and learn new things. In Jesus' name, Amen.

Praying for Our Enemies

"I tell you, love your enemies and pray for those who persecute you."
MATTHEW 5:44

There is one person in my life who has the ability to make my blood boil. When I think about that person, who has done so much harm to my family, I tense up and grind my teeth. What might seem strange is that even though I've forgiven this person, I still have such an extreme reaction.

Somehow I don't think I'm the only one who feels this way about someone in their life. Many of us struggle to forgive those who have hurt us deeply, whether through abuse, cheating, lying, or even ignoring us. Forgiveness is so important to recovery, so how can we be sure we have truly forgiven these people?

One way we can realize true forgiveness for others is to pray for them. We might be tempted to pray for bad things to overtake them wherever they go, but I mean praying in these ways:

- We can pray that God will go to work in their lives.
- We can pray that God will get their attention before it's too late and change them.
- We can pray that God will bless them.
- We can pray that God will do for them what he has done for us.

I'll be honest, I don't enjoy praying for a person who has hurt me and my family. But I know that when I pray, I release that person's control over me. True forgiveness frees us both.

PRAYER

Father, I pray for that person who has hurt me. I pray that you will reach out and draw that person to you. Your love knows no bounds. You can change anyone. In Jesus' name, Amen.

Why Does God Comfort Us?

*Praise be to the God and Father of our Lord Jesus Christ, the
Father of compassion and the God of all comfort, who comforts
us in all our troubles, so that we can comfort those in any trouble
with the comfort we ourselves have received from God.*

2 CORINTHIANS 1:3–4

Why does God comfort us? That seems like a silly question. He comforts us in our time of trouble because he is our loving heavenly Father. In fact, he loves us so much that he sent his Son, Jesus, to the cross to die for our sins so that we might be with him forever.

There's another reason why God comforts us, however. This reason is borne out in the Scriptures as well. God comforts us in our troubles, hurts, hang-ups, and habits so that we can comfort others in their troubles, hurts, hang-ups, and habits.

This verse in 2 Corinthians 1 best describes what we do at Celebrate Recovery. In fact, it is the job description of every member of this program and others as well. We heal best when we help others to heal. We stay positive when we help others to stay positive. It's the power of giving and receiving, or in this case, receiving and giving. Each time we help someone else, we learn a crucial lesson again, reinforcing our own recovery. What a mighty God we serve!

PRAYER

Dear Father, thank you for the privilege of reaching out to others as they face the struggles I've faced. Thank you for helping me so that I can help you help others. In Jesus' name, Amen.

Facing the Son

All of us who have had that veil removed can see and reflect the glory
of the Lord. And the Lord—who is the Spirit—makes us more
and more like him as we are changed into his glorious image.

2 CORINTHIANS 3:18 NLT

My wife and I were on the road one morning right before sunrise. We passed a field with thousands of sunflowers. They were a beautiful sight! Unusual, too, because we noticed they were all facing the same way—east. Then we understood. Those sunflowers were waiting for the sun to come up. As the first rays spread across the horizon and washed over their faces, the flowers came to life.

When we got home, I did some research and learned that sunflowers follow the path of the sun throughout the day. By evening, they are all facing west. Then during the night they turn to the center before resetting east to face the sunrise again.

Isn't this a beautiful message to all of us God-followers? We should wake in the morning ready to soak up God's love, his light, and his glory. Then we should reflect it to others throughout the day. At day's end, bathed in peace, we rest. There's a lovely simplicity to living like the sunflowers and keeping our faces to the Son, our Lord Jesus.

PRAYER

Father God, I can hardly contain myself when I realize that you've placed your
message of love in every part of your creation. In Jesus' name, Amen.

Time to Trust

Trust in the LORD with all your heart and lean
not on your own understanding.

PROVERBS 3:5

I keep hearing people say, "I have trust issues." It's like a new catch-phrase for "Back off a little; I've been hurt." But the truth is, we trust complete strangers every day. We trust other drivers to stop at the light when it turns red. We trust the person at the coffee shop to give us decaf—as ordered. We trust the person who fixes our lunch at the diner. We trust the new hygienist at the dental office to get our teeth clean. We do a lot of trusting, and yet we have a hard time trusting God.

God is no stranger. He created us and has been watching over us all these years—even when we didn't know he was there. He knows us, but we don't know him. If we want to get rid of our trust issues, we need to spend time with God, getting to know him. No, it isn't really like trusting the barista who comes into our lives for just a moment. God comes to stay. And we aren't trusting the hygienist with our lives, only our teeth. Trusting God will take some time and effort, but it's time well spent. As we begin to comprehend his faithfulness and purity, we trust him all the more.

Trusting God becomes easier with each prayer, each passage of Scripture we read. As we get to know him, trusting him becomes the easiest thing of all.

PRAYER

Father, I trust you more and more every day. Thank you for dismissing my past trust issues by replacing them with your complete faithfulness. In Jesus' name, Amen.

Answer Yes

"Simply let your 'Yes' be 'Yes,' and your 'No,' 'No';
anything beyond this comes from the evil one."

MATTHEW 5:37

Remember in grade school when you were passed a note that read, "Do you like me? Check yes or no!" Life is full of questions. How about "Would you like fries with that, sir?" or "Do you want to go ahead and have that tooth filled today?"

Some of life's questions are big. How we answer them can actually steer our lives down the right path or a completely disastrous one. Consider these life-changing questions:

- Will you believe and receive me as your God and stop playing god in your own life?
- Will you finally believe that you matter to me?
- Will you trust me to help you through *anything* and *everything*?
- Will you turn your life over to me?
- Will you do the necessary work to examine your life so that together we can remove your character defects and replace them with truth?
- Will you trust me to heal your heart so you can forgive those who have wronged you so terribly?
- Will you trust me for the courage to make amends to those you have hurt?
- Will you fully receive my grace in your life?
- Will you spread the Good News to others and serve others daily?

When we are ready to answer "yes" to these questions, God can and will renew, replant, restore, and rebuild our lives into a path of hopefulness, selflessness, service, growth, and truth.

PRAYER

Father, I want all my answers to be yes. Thank you for renewing my life. In Jesus' name, Amen.

Facing Our Fears

"Have I not commanded you? Be strong and courageous.
Do not be terrified; do not be discouraged, for the LORD
your God will be with you wherever you go."

JOSHUA 1:9

A while back, a woman in our recovery group told me that she had faced one of her fears. "It wasn't a very big one," she added. I urged her to tell me more, and she did.

"I'm afraid of bugs. I can't even bear to touch one," she told me. "But the other day there were some crickets in my house. I tried to shoo them out, which didn't work. I thought about squashing them, but I couldn't bring myself to do it. Finally, I couldn't think of any other way to get them out except to catch them and carry them outside. That was so hard, but I did it. I could feel them moving in my closed hand, and I almost lost it, but I held on until I was outside. Afterward, I felt good about facing my fear, even if it was just a small one."

"There's no such thing as a small fear," I told her. "All our fears are big. Anytime we overcome one of them, we come away better prepared for the next hurdle in our lives. We know for a fact that victory is possible. I can't wait to see what you're going to tackle next!"

In a way, we grow by going from fear to fear. With each victory, we gain courage and confidence until we become fearless, able to do without hesitation all God asks of us.

PRAYER

Father, I want to be fearless, but I'm still pretty fearful. Help me as I strive to conquer one fear at a time. In Jesus' name, Amen.

What Is Important

*Teach me to do your will, for you are my God; may
your good Spirit lead me on level ground.*

PSALM 143:10

I have a lot to do today. It isn't the busiest day I've ever had, but I've crammed a lot into the next few hours. I've got meetings, Celebrate Recovery tonight, work, family obligations, and errands to run. It isn't going to be easy to get it all done. In fact, it will be impossible. Something is going to have to wait.

My to-do list for today can be broken down into three parts. There are the things that *need* to get done, the things that *should* get done, and the things that *would be nice* to get done. For example, my kids want me to go play laser tag during lunch. Spending time with my kids is a high priority, so that floats to the top of the list. Spending time with God in prayer and the Word—also a high priority. Getting the backup external hard drive for my computer falls into the *would be nice* category.

There will always be things that need to be done and people who would like our time. Establishing priorities can take some of the stress out of making the right choices. High priority should be those things that last (usually things involving relationships). We can't put the low priority items off forever, but we can plug them in around the things that really matter.

───────────── PRAYER ─────────────

My Father, you are the most important Person in my life and the highest priority for my day. Thank you for giving meaning to everything I do. In Jesus' name, Amen.

The Twelfth Step

Brothers, if someone is caught in a sin, you who are spiritual should restore him gently. But watch yourself, or you also may be tempted.

GALATIANS 6:1

Modern technology is something else! Take, for example, an old, beat-up soft drink can: dirty, dented, with holes in it. A few years ago, it would have been thrown into the garbage and deemed useless, of no value. But these days, it can be recycled, melted down, purified, and made into a new can, shiny and clean, something that can be used again.

Step 12: Having had a spiritual experience as the result of these steps, we try to carry this message to others and to practice these principles in all our affairs.

Our pain can be recycled as well! When we allow God's purifying fire to work on our hurts, hang-ups, and habits, they can be melted down and used again in a positive way. Recycling our pain in this way—in God's way—can help others see that the recovery principles will work for them just as they've worked for us. It can serve to encourage others that they too will come through the darkness into Christ's glorious freedom and light.

At Celebrate Recovery, we know that pain has value, as do the people who experience it. Our pain has meaning because it has been transformed by God's hand. We have purpose because he has turned our lives around.

──────── PRAYER ────────

Dear Jesus, thank you for redeeming my pain. Thank you for transforming it for your glory and for the sake of those who need to know that recovery is possible. In Jesus' name, Amen.

You'll Love This

In his heart a man plans his course, but the LORD determines his steps.

When we have experienced something great, it's just natural that we want others to share that experience as well. This can happen in recovery. We want others, especially those close to us, to find their way to freedom just as we have. We want to push and prod and assure them by saying, "You'll love this. Really, you will! This is definitely going to work for you just as it did for me." Unfortunately, this righteous desire can cause us to stand in the way of what God is doing in their lives.

I've worked with lots of hurting people through the years. I wanted every one of them to recover, but I've learned that I can't make that happen. I've learned to say, "I can't want this for you more than you want it for yourself, my friend."

If we are doing all the work in someone's recovery and they are relying too much on us, we are doing them an injustice. Each person must fight their own battle for wholeness in unison with the Lord. We are there to complement and encourage, to stand beside them, to pray, and to add to what the Lord is already doing in their lives.

PRAYER

Heavenly Father, show me how to share with others, encourage others, and help them find their way without being in the way! In Jesus' name, Amen.

Fan the Coals

*For this reason I remind you to fan into flame the gift of God, which
is in you through the laying on of my hands. For God did not give us a
spirit of timidity, but a spirit of power, of love and of self-discipline.*

2 TIMOTHY 1:6–7

I woke up early and went into the den to put some logs on the fire. Some
mornings, there are embers left from the night before, but this morning the fire seemed cold. It looked like I would have to start over. I began
to clear out some ashes and quickly uncovered a little pocket of red-hot
coals. The fire wasn't out after all; it was just a little cold. I fanned the
coals, added some kindling, and before I knew it, I was adding logs to the
growing flames.

Sometimes this happens to Christians. It seems that their fires have
gone out, but it's more likely they've just grown a little cold. If we look, we
will probably find a little pocket of hot coals that we can fan into a lively
fire. We might do that by taking them to lunch, writing them a letter, or
scheduling some time to hang out and have some fun. We can also offer
to talk about a passage of Scripture or pray about something together.

At one time or another, we all need someone to help us get those
flames going again. Whether we are fanning someone else's coals or
someone else is fanning ours, it's a service of great importance to God.

PRAYER

*Father, make me sensitive to those around me who need to be encouraged. And thank
you for those you send when I need someone to fan my coals. In Jesus' name, Amen.*

A Mother's Love

This is what the LORD says: "I will extend peace to her like a river, and the wealth of nations like a flooding stream; you will nurse and be carried on her arm and dandled on her knees. As a mother comforts her child, so will I comfort you."

ISAIAH 66:12–13

My beautiful daughter and her husband have been blessed with the most amazing set of twins that I have ever seen! (I admit this grandpa might not be completely objective.) Over the last two years, it has been one of my greatest joys to watch my daughter love her babies more and more with each passing day!

She continues to gladly sacrifice her sleep, home-cooked meals, and outside interests for her little ones. She simply says, "They are 100 percent dependent on someone taking care of them and watching over them. In the blink of an eye, they will be heading off to preschool."

Her type of love for them models God's love for you and me. God desires us to be completely dependent on him, following his will for us on a daily basis for the rest of our earthly lives. I understand that many of us may not have received that kind of love and care from our own mothers and fathers. But please understand that was not God's will. God promises he will give us the kind of comfort a godly mother gives her child. Just think of what he has sacrificed for us. That is truly unconditional love!

PRAYER

Father, thank you for loving me in the same way you designed a mother to love her children. Your ways are always good. In Jesus' name, Amen.

Fellowship

Every day they continued to meet together in the temple courts. They broke bread in their homes and ate together with glad and sincere hearts, praising God and enjoying the favor of all the people. And the Lord added to their number daily those who were being saved.

ACTS 2:46–47

One of the keys to recovery is fellowship. While there is no substitute for an active prayer life and good Bible study habits, there have been times in my life when I survived because of fellowship. Spending time with spiritually minded people gave me the strength and encouragement I desperately needed.

Because of that, we love to ask people from our church and recovery groups to share Sunday dinner with us. Our whole family looks forward to it. It would never happen if we waited until everything at our house was just right. It's sharing your life with someone that matters, not a perfect house or well-manicured lawn.

In the book of Acts, the Bible tells us that early Christians met primarily in each other's homes. They shared a meal with each other, got to know each other, strengthened and encouraged each other. Hospitality blesses on both sides—the one who is invited and the one who does the inviting. It's always a good time when we open our hearts and our homes to others. The fellowship we offer may be just what someone needs to keep walking toward successful recovery.

PRAYER

Lord God, thank you for the people who opened their arms to me during my recovery. Show me how I can do the same for someone else. In Jesus' name, Amen.

Alone Time

*Jesus went with his disciples to a place called Gethsemane, and
he said to them, "Sit here while I go over there and pray."*

MATTHEW 26:36

Just before Jesus was arrested and crucified, he needed to spend some
time alone praying to his Father. He took Peter, James, and John with
him and asked them to stay back a little and keep watch for him. Once
alone, he fell on his face before his heavenly Father and poured out his
heart to him about what he would be facing.

Jesus knew the importance of quiet time with his Father. He knew
where his strength would come from, the strength he needed to carry
out the mission God had given him. The gospels record that this was a
regular practice for Jesus. He would go alone to the Garden to pray, or to
the mountains to pray. He sometimes sent his disciples on ahead, while
he refreshed himself through communion with his Father.

When we have given our hearts and lives to God, he becomes our
heavenly Father as well, and just like Jesus, we have access to him whenever and wherever we ask for it. That quiet time is essential if we are to
stay on the road to recovery and carry out the mission God has for our
lives. My private sanctuary is my backyard. I love breathing the fresh air
and feeling the warmth of the sun on my back as I pray and listen to my
loving Father! I look forward to my alone time with him.

PRAYER

*Thank you, Father, for the times we are alone together. Thank you for the strength
and refreshment that time brings. In Jesus' name, Amen.*

Filling the Holes

The heart of the discerning acquires knowledge,
for the ears of the wise seek it out.

PROVERBS 18:15

The towel hook in our bathroom used to be about one inch above eye level. As long as a towel was hanging on the hook, it was visible. But take away the towel, and it became a hazard. Twice in one week I ran into it, and both times my wife said, "Why don't you move it up three inches where you won't have to worry about it?"

That sounded like a reasonable solution, but I kept thinking that moving the hook meant I would have to patch the holes, and that was more than I felt like taking on. Until a week later, when I ran into the hook again and this time, I hit it hard. I looked at my wife with blood streaming down my face, and she didn't have to say a word. As soon as the bleeding stopped, I got my screw gun, putty, and paint, moved the hook up three inches, and patched the holes.

In recovery, we can talk ourselves out of changing things because we're concerned about all the holes we will have to fill. That seems like more work than we feel like taking on until … one day the pain becomes so great that we no longer care how many holes we have to fill. We have to have relief! We surrender! Filling those holes is worth every moment we spend doing it. And soon we don't even remember where those holes were or why we put off filling them.

PRAYER

Father, thank you for motivating me to finish the job my recovery started so that my joy will be complete. In Jesus' name, Amen.

God's Triple Power Surge

*God did not give us a spirit that makes us afraid but
a spirit of power and love and self-control.*

2 TIMOTHY 1:7 NCV

It's a shame, but many Christians have no power in their lives because they aren't plugged into the Power Source. When we're plugged into God's power, he supplies us with all we need: power, love, and self-control. This is God's triple power surge—the three things we need in order to be healthy, happy, and whole.

We need power to break habits we can't break on our own. We need power to do what we know is right but can't seem to do on our own. We need power to break free from the past and let those memories go. We need power to get on with the kind of life God wants us to live. We need a power much greater than ourselves—we need the power that only God can supply.

We need the love of others and the ability to love them back. We need to let go of the fear of getting hurt and develop the ability to establish deep, meaningful, loving, authentic relationships rather than superficial, hurtful, selfish ones. Love like that comes only from God.

We also need self-control, but we can't have self-control until Christ is in control of us. When Christ is in control, we understand, perhaps for the first time, what it means to get it all together. When we're not trying to pull ourselves up by our own bootstraps, we find that Christ will stand us on our feet.

We can have access to God's triple surge of power, love, and self-control if we stay connected to the Power Source.

PRAYER

Thank you, Lord, for your power in my life. In Jesus' name, Amen.

First Class

*Our citizenship is in heaven. And we eagerly await a Savior
from there, the Lord Jesus Christ, who, by the power that enables
him to bring everything under his control, will transform our
lowly bodies so that they will be like his glorious body.*

PHILIPPIANS 3:20–21

Not long ago my wife and I were boarding a plane to Colorado on Christmas Day. We handed our tickets to the attendant, but when she scanned them, the machine kept indicating there was an error. We were starting to get nervous, wondering if we had lost our seats. How would we explain that to our grandkids who were eagerly awaiting our arrival?

Just then another attendant asked to see our tickets. Without looking up, she said, "Oh, the Owens. I have new tickets for them." Then without explanation, she handed us first-class tickets and wished us a Merry Christmas! As we settled into our roomy seats, I thought about our heavenly Father and the joy he must receive when I finally surrender my control, pride, anger, selfishness, and all the other tickets I'm carrying, allowing him to give me new tickets stamped "First-Class Citizen of Heaven!"

Jesus has paid for our first-class tickets. He's standing at the counter, ready to exchange them for our messed-up tickets that won't go through the scanner. Let's claim our new tickets and find our seats.

— PRAYER —

Thank you, Father, for your daily, abundant provision for us. We think so small when you think so big. Thank you for your constant goodness. In Jesus' name, Amen.

The Puzzle

All have sinned and fall short of the glory of God.

ROMANS 3:23

One Sunday afternoon a father was trying to take a nap, but his little boy kept bugging him, saying, "Daddy, I'm bored." So, trying to occupy him with a game, the dad found a picture of the world in the newspaper. He cut it into pieces and said, "Son, see if you can put this puzzle back together." The dad lay back down to finish his nap, thinking the map would keep his son busy for at least an hour or so. But in about fifteen minutes the little guy woke him up: "Daddy, it's all put together."

"You're kidding," the dad marveled. He knew his son didn't know all that much geography, so he asked, "How did you do it?"

"It was easy. There was a picture of a person on the back of the map, so when I got my person put together, the world looked just fine."

When we first enter recovery, our lives are like that puzzle, aren't they? In pieces, scattered randomly. We don't even know where to begin the process of recovery. But God does, and he puts us back together, placing each piece where it belongs. We shouldn't worry about what our world looks like now. As our lives take shape the world around us will take shape as well.

—————————— PRAYER ——————————

Father, my life was not a pretty picture. I was badly broken and scattered. Thank you for putting me and my world back together. In Jesus' name, Amen.

Your Story

*"I know the plans I have for you," declares the LORD, "plans to prosper
you and not to harm you, plans to give you hope and a future."*

JEREMIAH 29:11

One night two of our grandsons were riding in the car with us and one said, "Papa, tell us a Bible story." So I thought I would tell them about some biblical moms. First I told them about Moses' mom and how she protected little Moses from being killed by the evil king. Then I told them about Hannah and how she made a promise to God. She said, "If you give me a son, I will commit him to your service for all his life." Then I said, "God gave her a son, and he became a mighty servant, prophet, and preacher." In the lull that followed, one of the boys asked what the mighty servant's name was, and the other boy shouted out, "Papa!"

Needless to say, my being confused for the great prophet Samuel made for a good laugh, but I had to thank my heavenly Father once again that my grandsons will never know the man I used to be. They love me so much that it wasn't a stretch for them to think that God would write a story about me! And you know what? He did! No, it isn't Samuel's story, but it is a story about grace, forgiveness, love, mercy, goodness, redemption, and rescue. It is a story of surrender and recovery and healing.

God has a story about each of us. It's a story that was written long before the foundations of the earth. It unfolds as God's grace brightens each new morning.

PRAYER

Thank you, Father, for writing the story of your love and grace in my life. In Jesus' name, Amen.

God Likes You

He rescued me because he delighted in me.

PSALM 18:19

In Celebrate Recovery we learn how much God loves us even though we are messed-up people. It's not that he loves our messes. It's that he loves who he created us to be and who we will be again once he puts us back together. But first we have to admit our brokenness.

In Psalm 18, the great King David cried out to God for help. His situation was dire. He was being pursued by powerful enemies who wanted nothing less than to take his life. David was a clever man, no doubt about it, but he admitted that this time, his foes were too strong for him. Without God's help, he was certain he would perish. Not only that, but he also was confident that God would rescue him because, as he wrote in verse 19, "God delights in me."

God feels no different about us than he felt about King David. God delights in us as well. The trouble is that we don't know it. We admit we need God's help. We ask for it. But then we wonder if he will act to save us. Soon the enemy tells us that we're worthless, and we lose our faith as well. Don't listen to the enemy's lies but instead walk as David did, in the confident persuasion that God delights in us.

PRAYER

Father, thank you for loving and delighting in me. Though I don't understand it, I receive it with all my heart. In Jesus' name, Amen.

God's Plan

*Since my youth, God, you have taught me, and to this day I
declare your marvelous deeds. Even when I am old and gray,
do not forsake me, my God, till I declare your power to the next
generation, your mighty acts to all who are to come.*

PSALM 71:17–18

I was at my dad's house making a few repairs. He's getting older and
doesn't get around as well as he once did. As I was working, he came
over and started offering advice and asking questions. At first I felt myself
getting a little frustrated with him, but then I began to think about how
this man loved me through all my years of addiction. My heart immediately softened.

It didn't take long for me to realize that the repairs weren't the reason
I was there. This precious man who meant so much to me was feeling
lonely. So after I got him back to his chair, I sat down beside him, and we
talked. We remembered old times when I was growing up. There were
tears in his old eyes and in mine as well.

After a while he looked at me and said, "You know I might be old, but
God still has a plan for me. There's someone I'm supposed to help today.
I don't know what the future holds, but I know who holds the future."
He was right. That someone was me. My dad was still teaching me by
reminding me that relationships matter most. The love we share with
others is the only thing we can take with us to heaven.

—— PRAYER ——

*Lord God, I thank you for the special people you have placed in my life and the love
and encouragement they have given me. In Jesus' name, Amen.*

Don't Say That!

My dear brothers, take note of this: Everyone should be quick to listen, slow to speak and slow to become angry, for man's anger does not bring about the righteous life that God desires.

JAMES 1:19–20

My wife and I boarded the plane and settled into our seats for the long flight home. But when the flight attendant asked that we turn off all our electronic devices, my wife realized that she didn't have her phone. She rushed to the front of the plane and pleaded with the attendant to call the gate agent. But there was no answer, and she was told that nothing more could be done. The flight attendant gave my wife a phone number to call when we landed in Dallas. Dejected, she came back to her seat.

I was trying to be supportive, but I couldn't help thinking about all the trouble this careless little incident would cause and who might, right now, be accessing all our personal information. I wanted to scold her, *Don't you know you're always supposed to check for your items before you get on the plane? I can't believe you let this happen.*

Here's the first miracle—I didn't say any of that. Instead, I told her I was sorry this happened, that I knew she didn't mean to leave her phone. And then I assured her that it would all work out. The second miracle followed closely. About fifteen minutes into the flight, the attendant came back waving my wife's phone. The pilot had retrieved it through his window from the gate agent. Enough said!

PRAYER

Father, thank you for helping me hold my tongue when I feel like lashing out at others. I know that angry words don't glorify you. In Jesus' name, Amen.

God's Rainy Days

The temptations in your life are no different from what others
experience. And God is faithful. He will not allow the temptation
to be more than you can stand. When you are tempted, he
will show you a way out so that you can endure.

1 CORINTHIANS 10:13 NLT

I once heard someone say, "All sunshine makes a desert." It takes rain to turn a desert into an oasis. I know that's been true in my life. I'm not saying I look forward to rainy days, but I've learned that it's during those times that I grow the most. We should embrace those days when struggles, trials, and even temptations come our way. It's the only way that our dry, arid hearts can begin to grow and blossom and flourish.

God doesn't bring us troubles. There are plenty of those in this world already. But God does use those troubles to teach us, strengthen us, and bless us. When they come our way, we can take those troubles to our heavenly Father and trade them in for blessings. Over the course of time, we become like a well-watered oasis, flourishing despite the intense sunlight.

God is a loving Father who wants only what is best for us. He has promised to walk with us through any trouble we encounter and bring us wisdom and understanding along the way.

PRAYER

Father, thank you for walking with me through the inevitable troubles of life. I
know that you are bringing me showers of blessings. In Jesus' name, Amen.

Can We Help?

*We are God's workmanship, created in Christ Jesus to do good
works, which God prepared in advance for us to do.*

EPHESIANS 2:10

I bought a shelf for our daughter that had three dreaded words stamped
on the outside of the box: "Some assembly required." Our two grandsons were upstairs, so I thought this might be a good time to put it
together. But I had no sooner taken it out of the box than I heard two
little pairs of feet coming down the stairs. Of course they were all ready
to help me out.

Honestly, my first thought was, *How come their dad can't keep them
busy while I put this together?* But what came out of my mouth was, "You
bet, let's look at the instructions." It took twice as long as it should have
because they had to handle every piece, put pieces where they didn't go,
and, of course, temporarily lose a couple of pieces. In the end, the shelf
was assembled and I heard them exclaim as they went back upstairs, "We
helped Papa build a shelf for you, Mama!"

Much like building a shelf, God sends us people who want to jump
right in to recovery, but they soon find they're in over their heads. God
allows us to guide them through his instruction manual, the Bible, helping them piece it together one step at a time. This rarely goes smoothly,
but, in the end, we get through it somehow, and that's really the point
after all.

───────────── PRAYER ─────────────

*Father, thank you for those you sent to help me put my life back together. In Jesus'
name, Amen.*

Forgiveness and Reconciliation

"If you forgive men when they sin against you, your heavenly Father will also forgive you. But if you do not forgive men their sins, your Father will not forgive your sins."

MATTHEW 6:14–15

We've all heard of the great patriarch Abraham, right? Well, it happens that he had a son—Isaac—who had been promised to him by God and who was born in Abraham's old age. Isaac and his wife, Rebecca, had two sons, twins. The older—by a matter of minutes—was Esau, and the younger was Jacob.

The customs adhered to at that time gave the birthright, the inheritance, to the older son. So Esau was the big winner. In fact, he was also his father's favorite because of his hunting prowess. However, Jacob tricked Esau into handing over his birthright. Then he deceived Isaac into placing his blessing on himself, the younger son.

As is so often the case with inheritances, this treachery split the brothers apart. Fearing retaliation, Jacob went on the run. Years later, Jacob decided to return home, his entire family and fortune in tow. He labeled his flocks and herds as gifts and sent them on ahead to appease his brother. But to Jacob's surprise, Esau greeted him enthusiastically and welcomed him home. Esau didn't care about revenge. He wanted his brother back.

Forgiveness is the key to reconciliation. The forgiveness Jesus gives brings us reconciliation with our heavenly Father. If our relationships aren't what they should be, we might need to give or receive forgiveness.

PRAYER

Father, thank you for the stories of forgiveness you've placed in the Bible as examples to us. In Jesus' name, Amen.

Can I Get a Little Help?

Two are better than one, because they have a good return for
their work: If one falls down, his friend can help him up. But
pity the man who falls and has no one to help him up!

ECCLESIASTES 4:9—10

I was working by myself one day, pulling electrical wire through some pipe. I should have waited until I could find someone to help me, but I didn't. It seemed like an easy task that I could take care of without bothering someone else.

Well . . . I was very wrong. The electrical supply company had cut one of the wires thirty feet short, but without someone watching at the other end, I had no way to know that, no one to tell me to stop. I realized I had to pull the short wire out, but then I pulled out the wrong wire. My easy job had now become pretty complicated, and I was getting frustrated. It took all day to do what would have taken only a couple of hours if I had asked for help.

This happens all the time in recovery. Instead of asking for help, we say, "I got this." That's when the trouble starts. This is just one more reminder to me that in Celebrate Recovery, when we say, "No one walks alone," we mean it. It is vital to have somebody on this road to recovery with me, someone who is able to see what I can't see.

PRAYER

Father, thank you for the people you've placed in my life to help me on my journey
to recovery. In Jesus' name, Amen.

Going to Any Length?

*Blessed is the one who perseveres under trial because, having
stood the test, that person will receive the crown of life that
the Lord has promised to those who love him.*

JAMES 1:12

My wife and I were driving down the interstate when we saw a limousine pulled off on the shoulder with its hood up. The limo was surrounded by men dressed in tuxes, which led us to believe the group was headed to an important function. As we pulled over to offer assistance, we noticed that the men were loading up in the back of an old pickup, whose driver had also stopped to help. Riding in style was plan A, but plan B was to get to their destination anyway they could.

In recovery, there are many days when things don't go as planned. That shouldn't be a shock to anyone. But just like the men piling into the old pickup, we can't let anything get in the way of us getting to our destination. Healing and wholeness are too important to miss.

There will always be inconveniences, breakdowns, and storms that mess with our plans. We must be committed to doing whatever we have to do to stay on track and become the men and women God created us to be.

PRAYER

Father, thank you for helping me stay in the race, no matter what inconveniences or difficulties come my way. Help me to remember that my recovery is too important to miss. In Jesus' name, Amen.

Two Natures

Put to death, therefore, whatever belongs to your earthly nature: sexual immorality, impurity, lust, evil desires and greed, which is idolatry.

COLOSSIANS 3:5

When I turned my life over to Jesus Christ, I was told that a big part of the process was for me to start putting to death my old, earthly human nature. All I could think about was what a tall order that would be. I wondered how I would ever get through it. The answer came in an early morning Bible study I was attending with several other men.

One of the men, who doesn't speak up much, said, "If we're going to put to death our old, earthly nature, we have to stop feeding it." It took me a few minutes to digest this, but then I got it: we stop feeding the old nature and start feeding the new nature. In both my words and actions, I refrain from contact with sexual immorality, impurity, lust, evil desires, and greed. Instead, I use my words and actions to feed my new nature, consisting of compassion, kindness, humility, gentleness, patience, love, and all that leads to godliness.

Mixing the two never works because the evil, dead nature always contaminates the new, living nature. Take my word for it: we all have to choose and then support that choice with our words and actions.

PRAYER

Father, I could never live a life of godliness without your Holy Spirit living in and through me. I surrender myself to you. Do your good work in me. In Jesus' name, Amen.

Good Morning

*Everything exposed by the light becomes visible, for it is light
that makes everything visible. This is why it is said: "Wake up, O
sleeper, rise from the dead, and Christ will shine on you." Be very
careful, then, how you live—not as unwise but as wise, making
the most of every opportunity, because the days are evil.*

EPHESIANS 5:13–16

While visiting our daughter and her family, my wife and I would
hear little footsteps on the stairway every morning right at
6:00 a.m. Our sweet four-year-old grandson was looking for Mamie
and Papa. We began to anticipate these visits by lying there in the dark,
waiting for him to round the corner and exclaim, "Good morning!"

One morning we got more than we were expecting. Instead of coming into our room as he usually did, he flipped on the light, and the room
went from total darkness to bright light in an instant. What a shock! But
how could we fault the little guy, who just wanted to see his Mamie and
Papa?

When the light of God's presence came into my life for the first time,
my whole system went into shock. It took me some time to adjust, but I
knew full well that God can't pull us out of darkness gradually. It has to
be an instant transformation. Even though in some ways it's painful, I
won't fault my heavenly Father. I know that he loves me. He wants me to
be free from the past and illuminated and inspired by the future.

PRAYER

*Father, thank you for waking me up with the brightness of your presence. I would
be no one and nowhere without your love. In Jesus' name, Amen.*

Air Masks

Follow my example, as I follow the example of Christ.

1 CORINTHIANS 11:1

When I fly, I almost always ignore the preflight "in case of emergency" instructions. But the one that always gets my attention is about the air masks that will descend if the plane loses cabin pressure. The attendant instructs that we should secure our own mask before securing our children's masks. This really goes against my grain. It feels wrong to tend to myself before seeing to the safety of my little ones. But if it came to it, I would do as instructed because I've come to see the reasoning behind it: unless I tend to myself first, I could lose consciousness and we would all be doomed.

This is a well-known concept in recovery as well. We are constantly hearing that serving others is one of the greatest priorities. It keeps us humble, positive, and connected. But before we can serve others, we have to secure our personal recovery by making the working of our program the greatest priority of all. It might seem tempting to hide behind serving others so that we don't have to face some of the painful issues that come up. It might be easier to serve others than to do the really hard work involved in our own recovery. But unless we are going to meetings, reading our Bibles, taking personal inventories, making amends, and forgiving, what we try to do for others will fall far short of success.

I'm going to heed the instructions on the airplane and in my recovery so that everything I do will make a difference.

PRAYER

Lord God, help me to help others by helping myself. Thank you for showing me what must be done first. In Jesus' name, Amen.

Back in the Coop

We know that anyone born of God does not continue to sin; the One who was born of God keeps them safe, and the evil one cannot harm them.

1 JOHN 5:18

One morning we were awakened at 3:00 a.m. by a life-and-death battle on our front porch. One of our chickens had ventured out from the coop and encountered a raccoon. So what if she had found her weight in tasty bugs under our front porch light? That didn't matter now—her life was at stake. Because I'm an egg lover, I went out and rescued that foolish chicken. She was missing a few feathers and looked pretty rough, but at least she was alive and back in the coop.

Sometimes I convince myself that I don't need the help and protection found in my Celebrate Recovery family, and I try to go it alone. Every time, I end up in a fight that doesn't go well for me. All the things I find attractive about being on my own turn out to be nothing compared to my safety. At those times, all I can think about is getting back to my family and God's protection.

God has given us our "forever family" for a reason. We're safer when we stay in the coop with the other chickens. It might look like we're missing out on something fun or interesting, but the truth is, leaving those who care about us and venturing out on our own is risky business—and not at all worth it.

PRAYER

Father, thank you for the protection you've given me through my forever family. May I always appreciate where you've placed me and the people you've placed me with. In Jesus' name, Amen.

All Things

I can do everything through him who gives me strength.

PHILIPPIANS 4:13

This is the best remedy I know for those times when we feel stuck, discouraged, like change might never come. Try applying this scriptural answer to your greatest concerns:

- I feel like I'm always going to fail.
I can do everything through him who gives me strength.
- I don't think I will ever get better.
I can do everything through him who gives me strength.
- I know other people have found victory through Celebrate Recovery, but I don't think it will happen for me.
I can do everything through him who gives me strength.
- It feels like this is too hard.
I can do everything through him who gives me strength.
- What if I try and try but I fail?
I can do everything through him who gives me strength.

When things feel impossible, when you feel like you can't do it, remember, "I can do everything through him who gives me strength."

It doesn't matter if we've been in recovery for years or we just started. It doesn't matter if we have lots of sobriety or if we're still trying to figure out what that even means. We are going to have tough times when we feel like we can't do it. And that's a good place to be, because when we realize that we can't do it, we allow God to have the room to move in our lives. On our own, we don't have enough power. But . . . we can do all things through him who gives us strength.

PRAYER

Father, I can do everything you ask of me because of the strength you place within me. In Jesus' name, Amen.

Guilty or Not Guilty

*Whoever keeps the whole law and yet stumbles at
just one point is guilty of breaking all of it.*

JAMES 2:10

In an early morning Bible study, we were reading James 2:10. This verse tells us that those who break one part of the law are guilty of breaking the whole law. I sadly admit it—I am a lawbreaker. We all are. It wasn't long before someone asked the obvious question: if we are lawbreakers, how is it that God calls us his holy children? The answer is filled with intensity and emotion. God can call us his children because of what Jesus did on Calvary's cross more than two thousand years ago.

With fierce intentionality, Jesus allowed himself to be nailed to the cross, and our sins were nailed there with him. Our sins cannot be counted against us ever again. On those days when I fall short and disappoint everyone, including myself, I know my Father is looking back at what Jesus did—and I relax knowing that everything has been set right. I have been found "not guilty."

Those of us who have chosen to surrender our lives to God are children of the Most High King. How wonderful it is to know that our sins have been taken care of, the penalty paid, and our place in our Father's family ensured.

PRAYER

Heavenly Father, thank you for providing a way where there was no way, for rescuing me and making me your child. In Jesus' name, Amen.

We Are Better Together

As iron sharpens iron, so one person sharpens another.

PROVERBS 27:17

I knew I was right. I just knew it. I had been arguing with a close friend of mine, and I knew it in my bones that he was wrong and I was right. I couldn't understand why he wouldn't just admit it. Then I got on the phone with my sponsor.

After explaining how I was right and how it was my friend's obligation to apologize for being so wrong, I paused to let my sponsor respond. I was sure he would back me up, maybe even call my friend and explain to him how right I was. Instead, he asked me this piercing question: "Do you want to be right, or do you want to be well?"

He went on to tell me that I was so concerned with being right that I hadn't heard my friend at all. I might be right, but I was also wrong. I wasn't thinking of my friend. I just wanted to win. This was not a big issue—it was silly. It was time to let it go before it hurt our relationship. So I did.

God is pleased when we make ourselves accountable to him through a close friend, sponsor, or accountability partner. They can help us see things we can't see for ourselves. They can look into our lives and speak the truth in love. And we can do the same for them.

PRAYER

Father God, thank you for the people you've placed in my life to help me find my way. I know how important they are. In Jesus' name, Amen.

Help Is on the Way

*"I tell you, whatever you ask for in prayer, believe that
you have received it, and it will be yours."*

MARK 11:24

I was praying over some prayer requests when I saw this one: "Dear Lord: Give me the patience to wait on your timing . . . and also please hurry up!" It was actually comforting to me to learn that I'm not the only one who sometimes thinks like this. I constantly have to remind myself that God is not working on my timetable.

One of the most difficult lessons I've had to put into practice in recovery is "one day at a time." It seems simple enough, but it's tough. I recently received an answer to a prayer I've been praying for more than two years. I came close to giving up a number of times. Since the prayer hadn't been answered on my timetable, I figured the answer was no.

Looking back, I can see that had God answered in the way I wanted him to, things probably would not have gone as well. God worked things out better than I expected. What a surprise! Right? I know that God always answers my prayers, but I've learned that his answers can be *yes, no, later,* or even *greater.* His timing is always perfect. My timing can never be compared to his.

PRAYER

Father, thank you for looking past my impatience and doing your good work in my life. Thank you for always answering my prayers. In Jesus' name, Amen.

Breathe Deep

He is the God who made the world and everything in it. Since he is
Lord of heaven and earth, he doesn't live in man-made temples, and
human hands can't serve his needs—for he has no needs. He himself
gives life and breath to everything, and he satisfies every need.

ACTS 17:24–25 NLT

There is so much pain, noise, and confusion in our earthly lives that we can find it difficult just to breathe. We face control issues, power struggles, political battles, dishonesty, family disagreements, arguments, crying, pain, grief, pride, abuse, stubbornness, withdrawing, addictions, bruises, disappointments, perfectionism, fear, anxiety, worry, corporate ladders, overwhelming responsibilities, taxes, debt, backbiting, despair, cheating, mistrust, betrayal, stress, relapse, lying, moral failure—the list is never-ending.

Fortunately, God's Word says that he himself gives breath to everything and satisfies every need. When I feel totally overwhelmed by life, I often read Psalm 23 aloud:

The LORD is my shepherd, I lack nothing. He makes me lie down in green pastures, he leads me beside quiet waters, he refreshes my soul. He guides me along the right paths for his name's sake. Even though I walk through the darkest valley, I will fear no evil, for you are with me; your rod and your staff, they comfort me. You prepare a table before me in the presence of my enemies. You anoint my head with oil; my cup overflows. Surely your goodness and love will follow me all the days of my life, and I will dwell in the house of the LORD forever.

When our souls are restless, we must take time to rest in the lap of our King Jesus. No matter what noise we are battling, we can always find quietness in his presence.

PRAYER

Heavenly Father, I come to you ready to give you everything I have, everything I am.
Thank you for helping me find quietness in the midst of the noise. In Jesus' name, Amen.

Holiday Stress

"Come to me, all you who are weary and burdened, and I will give you rest."

MATTHEW 11:28

The holidays are stressful. I know if I let my guard down, I'll end up dealing with that stress in an unhealthy way, making poor choices, reacting badly, and sometimes even isolating myself from those most equipped to help me.

I have heard many people in recovery say, "I hate the holidays! I am just ready for this to be over." But what if we changed our attitudes and said, "Lord, the holidays can be tough and stressful, especially dealing with family, but I want to use this time of year for your glory"? Could this simple change in perspective mean a more peaceful and joyous season?

Early on, when we first see the decorations in the stores, we can ask God to help us use the season to grow in the fruit of the Spirit—love, joy, peace, patience, kindness, goodness, faithfulness, gentleness, and self-control. In this way, our seasonal challenges become training exercises. It's a great plan with one condition: We must not try to do this alone. We have to be intentional about staying connected with accountability partners, making our meetings, saturating ourselves with positive relationships, spending quality time with God, serving others, and maintaining our established boundaries with dysfunctional family members.

Instead of dreading the holidays, let's change our language to: "The holidays are tough, but the Lord is teaching me so much! I can feel myself growing every day."

--- PRAYER ---

Father, I would be nothing without your Holy Spirit living and moving within me. I want to see fruit growing in my life during this holiday season. In Jesus' name, Amen.

Go Ahead, Open Your Gift

Encourage one another daily, as long as it is called Today.

HEBREWS 3:13

At Christmastime I'm like a child. I buy a gift for my wife and then I can't wait to give it to her. As soon as I get it wrapped and under the tree, I'm asking her if she wants to go ahead and open it. It drives her crazy! But she smiles and says, "Come on, honey. It's just a few more days until Christmas." I love to give her gifts and watch her open them. But I know too that the greatest gifts are those that we give all year long. They are unwrapped, unplanned, don't cost a dime, and they can change a life for the better.

I'm talking about gifts like a word of encouragement during a difficult time, a hug when we really need it, a helping hand from a neighbor, a smile to warm the day of a stranger, a commitment to pray for someone else's need. Gifts like these are a form of service to others. They benefit both the giver and the receiver, and they are especially valuable for those of us who are journeying toward recovery. Taking the focus off of ourselves and putting it on others helps us to grow spiritually and emotionally. And it could mean a second wind for someone who is struggling, ready to give up and fall back into old habits. Best of all, these gifts don't have to wait to be opened. They bless us every day of the year.

PRAYER

Thank you, Father, for the simple gifts that bring gladness to our hearts. In Jesus' name, Amen.

The Special Guest

To him who is able to do immeasurably more than all we ask of imagine,
according to his power that is at work within us, to him be glory in the church
and in Christ Jesus throughout all generations, for ever and ever! Amen.

EPHESIANS 3:20–21

I saw this post on the National Celebrate Recovery Training Page: "We have a special night planned tonight at CR, and I am excited for you to meet our special guests. They have never been to CR, and they are intrigued enough to come and see what all the fuss is all about. They have been watching us from afar and have decided that they want to see if this is something they might want to be a part of."

Who is the special guest? It's the person who is going to visit for the first time—the one who has finally gotten up enough courage to attend a meeting and see if we are who we claim to be. That person will be looking to see if this really is an environment that focuses on God's love and grace. Will they feel accepted? Will they find hope and peace? What they discover might lead them to wholeness and recovery, or it could send them away even more discouraged and disillusioned.

Being ambassadors for Christ has never been an easy task. We want to honor and represent him in the best way we can, by showing others what he has brought to our lives. Let's open our arms and receive all the special guests he sends our way.

--- PRAYER ---

Father, you have done so much for me. Show me how to reach out to others with the
same love and grace that was bestowed on me. In Jesus' name, Amen.

Hard Heads

When we were controlled by the sinful nature, the sinful passions aroused by the law were at work in our bodies, so that we bore fruit for death.

ROMANS 7:5

As difficult as it is to believe, I've come to realize that I'm a hard-headed guy. For instance, I asked a friend to help me hook up a trailer to my truck. He guided me back and started lowering the jack onto the trailer ball. "It won't go on," he told me. "Oh yeah it will," I responded. "We just need a bigger hammer." I grabbed a hammer and beat on the jack, crawled underneath to take a look, crawled back out, beat on it some more—and then it came to me! I had pulled a bigger trailer the day before and had replaced the ball that fit this trailer with a larger one. No matter how hard I tried to force it, it wasn't going to work.

It's natural to want to do things our own way and to think we can force things to come out the way we want. But when we've worn ourselves out hammering and beating away, it's time to listen to God saying, "That doesn't fit in your life. I have something that will fit much better."

In recovery, I am learning that forcing things to happen is something I did in my former life. Turning my life over to God's care and control is the absolute best thing I've ever done.

--- PRAYER ---

Thank you, Father, for taking control of my life and showing me a better way. In Jesus' name, Amen.

Doing It Right

Being confident of this, that he who began a good work in you
will carry it on to completion until the day of Christ Jesus.

PHILIPPIANS 1:6

As a legalistic Pharisee, Saul said of himself that he was from the right family, the right church, and the right side of the tracks. He noted that he had attended the right schools and had all the right teachers. He was so convinced that he was legally faultless that he felt he had the right to put to death those he felt were wrong! As far as the world was concerned, he certainly did do it all right.

However, when Saul became a Christian, things changed, beginning with his name. We know him as the great apostle Paul, who wrote nearly two-thirds of the New Testament.

After his conversion, Paul said that he had a terrible dilemma. Although he knew the right thing to do, he always ended up doing the wrong thing. He realized that he needed God's grace more than the vilest sinner.

It doesn't matter what side of the tracks we come from, where we studied, or how closely we follow rules set down by men. If we aren't changed by the power of God through the Lord Jesus and washed clean by his shed blood, we are nothing—less than nothing. It is only in relationship with our Creator that we find the grace to do things right.

PRAYER

Holy Father, thank you for showing me through the life of the apostle Paul that there is nothing in me good enough to merit your love. Your grace and forgiveness have brought me into relationship with you. In Jesus' name, Amen.

What Did They Say?

"Do not fear, for I am with you; do not be dismayed, for I am your God. I will strengthen you and help you; I will uphold you with my righteous right hand."

ISAIAH 41:10

All we have to do is close our eyes and remember for a moment what it was like to be out there struggling, desperately wondering if there was any hope for a better life, any future without addiction. There are still so many people out there, people just like we were once, people who could find hope and a future through Celebrate Recovery.

Those of us who have already entered into recovery and seen how God has helped us through Celebrate Recovery now have an opportunity to give back. We can do this by welcoming those who come to us wondering if this is a place where they can receive God's grace and love—or if it's all just more hype.

This is part of a letter from a newcomer who found refuge in CR: "I was a newcomer. I was filled with fear, trying to convince myself that I didn't need anyone. But I took a chance and signed up for a step study, and it was the start of something awesome and beautiful for me. Jesus became real to me through the study. I felt God's unconditional acceptance and grace from the members of the group. This CR family was the first 'safe' family I've ever had."

The newcomers are depending on us to keep our hearts open for them and show them what God's love can do.

PRAYER

Father, thank you for bringing me to a place where I can receive the help I need. Thank you for welcoming arms to draw me in and help me heal. In Jesus' name, Amen.

Witnesses in the Grandstands

Since we are receiving a kingdom which cannot be shaken, let us have grace,
by which we may serve God acceptably with reverence and godly fear.

HEBREWS 12:28 NKJV

My wife and I were traveling through a beautiful, hilly Kansas countryside. Atop one hill, I could see a cemetery in the distance with tombstones shining brilliantly white in the early afternoon sun. The scene brought to my mind many of God's precious saints.

In fact, that was not far from the purpose for our trip. My father and my wife's mother, great warriors for God, were both at the end of their lives. My dad was a loud, triumphant warrior who loved being on the front lines giving hope to the hopeless. My wife's mom was gentle and soft-spoken but no less passionate about touching the lives of those who seemed to have been forgotten.

A short time later, as I prepared to officiate the service for my mother-in-law, I turned in my Bible to Hebrews. There in the margin of the eleventh chapter, I wrote her name. Clearly it belonged there alongside all the other heroes of faith God had himself memorialized. Through the years, I've added many names in that margin, heroes of faith God has sent to help pave the way for me, heroes who never gave up on what God was doing in my life and the lives of so many others. Let us take time to celebrate these heroes of the faith and bid them not "good-bye" but "see you soon."

PRAYER

Father, thank you for the faithful servants you have placed in my path, those who have made all the difference in my life. In Jesus' name, Amen.

Taking Action

I urge you, brothers, in view of God's mercy, to offer your bodies as living sacrifices, holy and pleasing to God—this is your spiritual act of worship.

ROMANS 12:1

Even after we admit that our lives are out of control, we can still get stuck in a cycle of failure that keeps us bound by guilt, anger, fear, and depression. How do we get past those old, familiar, negative barriers that keep us from freedom and wholeness? We do that by taking action. Making a choice requires action.

The trouble is that most of us don't like making decisions. We would rather just follow the crowd because that's easier than stepping out and doing what we know is right. We procrastinate about making commitments that will allow change to occur, clinging instead to our hurts, hang-ups, and habits. We forget that failing to choose is in itself a choice.

All we really need is the willingness to make a decision. God will help us with the rest. Why should we continue to struggle when the road to relief, wholeness, freedom, and a new life is just one choice away? That's where all true recovery begins, with action. And that action can open up a whole new way of living.

PRAYER

Father, I'm tired of fighting to stay alive, wondering if there is any hope for me. I am taking action right now, asking for your help and asking for the strength to pursue recovery. In Jesus' name, Amen.

Celebrate Recovery Revised Edition Participant's Guides

John Baker

Recovery is not an overnight phenomenon, but more like a journey. The purpose of Celebrate Recovery is to allow us to become free from life's hurts, hang-ups, and habits. By working through the eight principles of recovery based on the Beatitudes, we will begin to see the true peace and serenity that we have been seeking.

The four participant's guides in the Celebrate Recovery program are:

- Guide 1: Stepping Out of Denial into God's Grace
- Guide 2: Taking an Honest and Spiritual Inventory
- Guide 3: Getting Right with God, Yourself, and Others
- Guide4: Growing in Christ While Helping Others

The participant guides are essential to the person in recovery to take part in because it makes everything personal.

Available in stores and online!

ZONDERVAN®
.com

Celebrate Recovery Bible

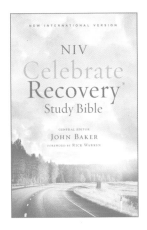

The *Celebrate Recovery Bible* offers everyone hope, encouragement, and the empowerment to rise above their hurts, hang-ups, and habits. This life-changing Bible is based on the proven and successful Celebrate Recovery program developed by John Baker and Rick Warren.

With features based on eight principles Jesus voiced in his Sermon on the Mount, this insightful Bible is for anyone struggling with the circumstances of their lives and the habits they are trying to control.

- Articles explain eight recovery principles and the accompanying Christ-centered twelve steps
- 112 lessons unpack eight recovery principles in practical terms
- Recovery stories offer encouragement and hope
- Over 50 full-page biblical character studies illustrate recovery principles
- 30 days of devotional readings
- Side-column reference system keyed to the eight recovery principles and topical index
- Complete text of the New International Version

Available in stores and online!

Celebrate Recovery Journal

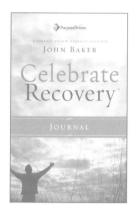

This journal is specially designed to complement the Celebrate Recovery program. The content guides you through the recovery process in a step-by-step fashion. Includes tips on how to benefit from journaling, specific Scriptures pulled from the Celebrate Recovery program, a section to help facilitate a 90-day review of your journaling progress, and a prayer request area to document God's answer to prayer.

Available in stores and online!